Studies in Literature

Second Series

Studies in Literature

Second Series

By

Sir Arthur Quiller-Couch, M.A.

Fellow of Jesus College
King Edward VII Professor of English Literature
in the University of Cambridge

GREENWOOD PRESS, PUBLISHERS
WESTPORT, CONNECTICUT

Originally published in 1922
by G. P. Putnam's Sons, Cambridge, England

First Greenwood Reprinting 1970

Library of Congress Catalogue Card Number 76-100198

SBN 8371-3905-8

Printed in United States of America

PREFACE TO THE AMERICAN EDITION

IN prefacing a previous volume of *Studies in Literature* I allowed that the word "Studies" might well seem an exorbitant one for the familiar discourses bound within its cover, and gave half a promise to justify the title more thoroughly next time. That half-promise I am not keeping: and I want my American readers to forgive me, as I think they will when they know the reason why.

The experience of any teacher at Oxford or Cambridge in 1914 was as sorrowful as it was proud. He had packed in June and left a town teeming with balls, concerts, garden parties, river parties, all the happy riot that celebrates the close of an academic year: God's plenty—God's best plenty, of youth! He returned in October, to an empty university, to courts in which his was the only footfall, his the only litten window—to the short days, the long nights, the College

> more dreary cold
> Than a forsaken bird's-nest filled with snow.

Then, by and, by it was borne in upon us that the generation which had flown with such a rush of wing, in two weeks of August, would never come back, or a few stragglers only. I remember sitting in King's College Chapel on the third All Souls' Day of the War, while the Vice-Chancellor recited the names of the sons of Cambridge who had fallen during the year, and the bare recital took more than forty minutes. Is it any wonder that, sitting by the Combination Room fire, after four years, we told one another that when the War ended there would be few young men for us to teach; and that, after teaching these, we could only spend the remainder of our days in studies which, at some later time, a recovered world might haply find serviceable? Well, anyhow, so it was: and under that conviction, in 1918, I gave my half-promise.

But then the miracle happened. The young men came pouring back from War, and overflowed us in such numbers that we could scarcely lodge them save by resort to medieval devices. They were not—woe is me!—the young men we had "loved and lost awhile." But they were eager, and multitudinous; and neither the capacity of our lecture-rooms nor the frame of a college staircase had been prepared for any such invasion. If the hungry generations were not to tread us down—unless the hungry sheep were to look up and be not fed—we had to snatch the disused crook from the corner and employ it for all it was worth. And *that* is why these lectures—all spoken before a Cambridge audience (with the exception of the first, which inaugurated a "Byron Lectureship" at Nottingham University College) have missed to make good my half-promise.

ARTHUR QUILLER-COUCH.

Cambridge, April, 1922

CONTENTS

STUDIES IN LITERATURE

BYRON

I

IT were dangerous, perhaps, for a visitor to let himself overflow and expansively praise the people of Nottingham for endowing, in their University College, an annual lecture under the great name of Byron. It may be that some pride of county association, of property in him; some sense that he who was in many ways a man of the world—who, more than Odysseus of old "saw many cities of men and was acquainted with their spirit"—does yet peculiarly belong to you by race and birth and those early influences of which no man ever rids himself—has at least as much to do with it as your discernment that the greatness of Byron needs proclaiming and specially needs it just now. But, however it came about, I congratulate you: and however much I wish you had chosen someone to do it better, I am proud to make an essay here upon an act of justice that, in England at any rate, badly needs the doing.

More than thirty-five years ago Matthew Arnold made bold to prophesy thus:

These two, Wordsworth and Byron, stand, it seems to me, first and pre-eminent . . . , a glorious pair, among the English poets of this [nineteenth] century. Keats had probably, indeed, a more consummate poetic gift than either of them; but he died having produced too little and

3

being as yet too immature to rival them. I for my part can never even think of equalling with them any other of their contemporaries;—either Coleridge, poet and philosopher wrecked in a mist of opium; or Shelley, beautiful and ineffectual angel, beating in the void his luminous wings in vain. Wordsworth and Byron stand out by themselves. When the year 1900 is turned, and our nation comes to recount her poetic glories in the century which has then just ended, the first names with her will be these.

The passage is notorious for a clever wayward injustice it does to Shelley. (The only void in which Shelley ever beat his luminous wings in vain was a void in Mr. Arnold's understanding.) But will it last in equal disrepute for its prophecy concerning Byron? The year 1900 has been turned, and eighteen years have been added, and today (let us be frank about it) that prophecy has come nowhere near fulfilment. Indeed promise of defeat followed close on its utterance, when Swinburne—who of all men then alive to be listened to —Swinburne, professed hater of despotism, who of all men might have been counted on to lift a louder trumpet and resound the rally—Swinburne, who had written in praise of Byron words so noble that they might well seem to melt into a pledge to escort a fellow-spirit through darkness and detraction up to glory—

Tarry, dear cousin Suffolk!
My soul shall thine keep company to heaven;
Tarry, sweet soul, for mine, then fly abreast!

—when Swinburne so promptly wheeled back on past praise and joined with the revilers to revile—so persuasively too! But that the absurdity was possible may teach us two things: the first, that in these days a claim for Byron really needs pressing among his countrymen;

the second that one who presses it must first lay his account with their present neglect, and—what is more —recognise it for an *obstinate* neglect, born not of idleness or indifference but of positive reluctance to allow the claim. Indeed the other day a teacher in an ancient University advertised a course of lectures on the "Romantic Revolt" in English Poetry and left Byron out!

This reluctance begins and ends at home. On the continent of Europe, through which his poetry first ran as a flame, it has endured and burnt constantly. When he died, on the 19th of April 1824, at Missolonghi, the Greek Provisional Government in the midst of the Easter festival, closed all shops and public offices, and proclaimed, with salute of guns, a general mourning for twenty-one days. Today I take down from the shelf a volume (dated 1905) by Dr. George Brandes—it is Volume 4 of a series treating of *Main Currents in Nineteenth Century Literature* and treats particularly of *Naturalism in England*, and this is what I find. Dr. Brandes, viewing the movement by *his* sense of proportion, assigns 33 of his pages to Wordsworth, 17 to Coleridge, 12 to Southey, 25 to Scott, 19 to Keats, 17 to Landor, 43 to Shelley, and no less than 116 to Byron! It is obvious that between this foreign critic and our domestic lecturer we must strike a balance somewhere, somehow. And Byron belongs to *us!*

> There may be cities who refuse,
>   To their own child·the honours due,
> And look ungently on the Muse;
>   But ever shall those cities rue
> The dry, unyielding, niggard breast,
> Offering no nourishment, no rest,
>   To that young head which soon shall rise
> Disdainfully, in might and glory, to the skies.

II

Easy talk about reaction will not carry us very far. The first two cantos of *Childe Harold* appeared on March 10, 1812, and, as everyone knows, Byron flashed into sudden, dazzling fame. Edition crowded on edition. Before its appearance Tom Moore gratified his lordship by expressing a fear that it was too good for its age. To this the late Professor Nichol somewhat tartly (but in my opinion very justly) retorted that this is precisely what it was not.

Its success was due to the reverse being the truth. It was just on the level of its age. Its flowing verse, defaced by rhymical faults perceptible only to finer ears, its prevailing sentiment, occasional boldness relieved by pleasing platitudes, its half affected rakishness, here and there elevated by a rush as of morning air, and its frequent richness—not yet, as afterwards, splendour—of description, were all appreciated by the fashionable London of the Regency; while the comparatively mild satire, not keen enough to scarify, only gave a more piquant flavour to the whole.

For three full heady years Byron—a spoilt child from the cradle—knew the idolatry of this society and inhaled its incense. His name (I can conceive no more illustrious triumph, in England, for art over the popular imagination) figured in the shop-windows over new styles in collars and neck-ties. The young shopman behind the counter read his poems, and on Sundays walked Hampstead Heath as a full-blooded Giaour arming an Odalisque—and after all, when we consider, this was a deal better than playing the "Abstract Buck" on the model of the Prince Regent. Byron in fine and in the language of the day was the "rage": and he fed it lavishly: all too carelessly as an artist, and with seeming carelessness as a dandy who chose to be a genius; yet all the while with an irritable care which vanity taught vanity to conceal. These three marvellously successful years were his worst, whether we take him as artist or as man; years in which he poured out *The Giaour, The Bride of Abydos, The Corsair, Lara.* There was no resisting them. "*Lara,*" says he, "I wrote while undressing after coming home from balls and masquerades, in the year of revelry, 1814." Now in 1814 a class in England—Byron's class—was celebrating the apparent end of the Napoleonic struggle. It had profiteered pretty successfully through that struggle; it was emerging in a triumphant political position; and its exultation shaped itself in the form of the improved Brighton Pavilion and the sort of behaviour that went on inside it. (The Brighton Pavilion, you may remember, was adapted to resemble the Kremlin at Moscow.) Our rulers, long denied Continental travel, were hungry for foreign parts, where Byron had been; for foreign titillations, which *Childe Harold* had enjoyed and reported. "Sentimentalists," says George Meredith, "are a perfectly natural growth of a fat soil," and sentiment is an even readier coinage than hypocrisy for the tribute that vice pays to virtue. What sentimentalist of the Regency could command his duct of tears over such a passage as

> He who hath bent him o'er the dead,
> Ere the first day of Death is fled,
> The first dark day of Nothingness,
> The last of Danger and Distress,
> (Before Decay's effacing fingers
> Have swept the lines where Beauty lingers,) . . .

or refuse a thrill to the question

Know ye the land where the cypress and myrtle
Are emblems of deeds that are done in their clime?
Where the rage of the vulture, the love of the turtle,
Now melt into sorrow, now madden to crime?

When writing like that enjoys a rage—a patently excessive rage—we ought not to grieve that reaction comes, nor to grieve that it comes swiftly: but we may deplore (I think) when it descends upon the poet at the hands of those who taught him to be overweening, and afterwards found sanctuary for their sins of taste in the violence they contributed to his punishment. As Macaulay noted, the age set about smashing its idol in characteristic British fashion, assailing not the poetry he had written up to 1816, and not at all (of course) themselves for its having entranced them; but assailing the man for having been wicked in a wicked age; and this although his wickedness was half a parade of perverse vanity, and although, as a fact, he was so innocent of the charge upon which they seized as to be helpless before it, in a bewilderment at what it all meant.

We know no spectacle [says Macaulay] so ridiculous as the British public in one of its periodical fits of morality. In general, elopements, divorces, and family quarrels, pass with little notice. . . . But once in six or seven years our virtue becomes outrageous. We cannot suffer the laws of religion and decency to be violated. We must make a stand against vice. We must teach libertines that the English people appreciate the importance of domestic ties. Accordingly some unfortunate man, in no respect more depraved than hundreds whose offences have been treated with leniency, is singled out as an expiatory sacrifice. If he has children, they are taken from him. If he has a profession, he is ruined. He is cut by the higher orders and hissed by the lower. He is, in truth, a sort of whipping-boy, by whose vicarious agonies all the other transgressors of the same class are, it is supposed, sufficiently chastised. . . . At length our anger is satiated. Our victim is ruined and heart-broken. And our virtue goes quietly to sleep for seven years more.

III

So it happened with Byron. But a hundred years is a long while: and I cannot agree with Mr. Coleridge, Byron's latest and best editor, when he wistfully opines that "perhaps, even yet, the time has not come for a definite and positive appreciation of his genius. The tide of feeling and opinion must ebb and flow many times before his rank and station among the poets of all time will be finally determined." Surely, in 1918, we can hold our minds aloof from the passions of 1818 (amid which the fourth and last canto of *Childe Harold* appeared) and judge Byron's claim dispassionately, even as we can judge the claim of Burns, another poet whose private life, if you will, came short of edifying. Is Byron's poetry great poetry? Is it genuine poetry? Does it ring true? Is it *sincere?* Yes, there we have— for all poetry, greater or less—the critical word— *sincerity*. Though poetry speak with the tongues of men and of angels, and have not *sincerity*, it is become as sounding brass or a tinkling cymbal.

We shall apply that crucial test later. For the moment we must deal with some awkward preliminaries, since—to speak bluntly—a great deal of Byron's writing before 1816 forces on us the question, Whether it be poetry at all? Well, if we would do our critical duty, and be clear about Byron, let us have it out even with *that* question, though it involve our making some damaging, almost desperate, admissions.

To begin with, no ear trained upon the exquisite lyric of Shelley, with its jet and fall, its modulated runs, pauses, linked lapses—all natural as movement of water is natural—can miss to detect Byron's lyrical gift as cheap, almost null. Take a chorus from *Heaven and Earth* and set it beside a chorus from *Prometheus Unbound*, and it reads like a schoolboy's exercise—

Oh son of Noah! mercy on thy kind!
What! wilt thou leave us all—all—*all* behind?

But let us take a lyrical stanza or two—

The Assyrian came down like a wolf on the fold,
And his cohorts were gleaming in purple and gold;
And the sheen of their spears was like stars on the sea,—

which, with the rest of *Hebrew Melodies* reads to me, I confess, like turgid school-exercise work: or

Oh! what is more brave than the dark Suliote,
In his snowy camese and his shaggy capote?
To the wolf and the vulture he leaves his wild flock,
And descends to the plain like a stream from the rock,

. . . .

Then the Pirates of Parga that live by the waves,
And teach the pale Franks what it is to be slaves—.

I protest that my tongue stammers against continuing. Now remember that readers of the Regency admired that by the thousand, and then set it beside these long neglected stanzas by Shelley—

Pause not! The time is past! Every voice cries, Away!
Tempt not with one last tear thy friend's ungentle mood:

Thy lover's eye, so glazed and cold, dares not entreat thy
    stay:
Duty and dereliction guide thee back to solitude.

Away, away! to thy sad and silent home;
    Pour bitter tears on its desolated hearth;
Watch the dim shades as like ghosts they go and come,
And complicate strange webs of melancholy mirth. . . .

Thou in the grave shalt rest—yet till the phantoms flee
    Which that house and heath and garden made dear to
    thee erewhile,
Thy remembrance, and repentance, and deep musings are
    not free
From the music of two voices and the light of one sweet
    smile.

Surely, after that, the thumped-out rhythm of even
the best lyric of Byron's is hard to pass: and we have
had Tennyson, too, and Swinburne to educate us:
Swinburne, for example:

    And Pan by noon and Bacchus by night,
        Fleeter of foot than the fleet-foot kid,
    Follows with dancing and fills with delight
        The Mænad and the Bassarid;
    And soft as lips that laugh and hide
    The laughing leaves of the trees divide,
    And screen from seeing and leave in sight,
        The god pursuing, the maiden hid.

I am hardy—and hardier, being one who deplores the
almost complete tyranny of the lyric in these days—to
claim that it has at any rate trained the Englishman's
lyrical ear: and so must own that the foreigners—
especially the German, who makes no account of this
defect in Byron, himself lacking the instruction, even

the vocal apparatus, to detect it—can bring little or nothing to help Byron against his countryman's damaging criticism.

For a second point: Byron, who wrote much in blank verse, had, to the end, small sense of it. Of the slide of cæsura by which Milton's organic line almost draws tears by its very perfection, he had no sense at all; as none for the handling by which Shakespeare at the last tamed it, not only to "perform at point" anything from a shearers' feast to the broken outcry of royal Lear, but set it humming to the soul in all undersounds and oversounds. By a perversity Byron chose to admire the line of Pope, which, admirable in itself, of all lines least suited our poet's genius: while his own careless fluidity precluded that neatness which the Popian line most demands. In plain words, Byron did not take enough trouble—a source of failure in many walks of life. When the good Sir Walter Scott, reviewing *Cain*, wrote that in this "very grand and tremendous drama," Lord Byron "has certainly matched Milton on his own ground," the mountain brought forth a little mouse predestined for Matthew Arnold to play with, in Matthew Arnold's pretty feline way. But the mischief goes down beyond carelessness: the carelessness being but symptomatic. Too often Byron's blank verse has no nerve of life. *There* resides the malady of such lines as:

> Souls who dare look the Omnipotent tyrant in
> His everlasting face, and tell him that
> His evil is not good

(at which Arnold scoffed) or:

> Unless you keep company
> With him (and you seem scarce used to such high
> Society) you can't tell how he approaches.

These defects—and not a few others, from clumsiness
of dramatic touch down to sheer bad grammar, *vulgarly*
bad grammar—stare at us out of Byron's page. But
poetry can have all these faults and remain poetry—
remain even high poetry—so it be fervent, imaginative,
and (above all) sincere.

IV

What, then, of Byron's sincerity? You will know
M. Scherer's dictum: "This beautiful and blighted
being is at bottom a coxcomb. He posed all his life
long." I shall presently try to show that four words in
that judgment convert the whole to a falsehood. But
again let the devil's advocate have his way for a while
with Byron the man. I shall in this audience presume a
knowledge at least of the main facts of his life. You
know that he was well born, if it be well born to come
of a line of strong men, arrogant under title of nobility,
eminently unlike their poorer neighbours, and able—
though too often in sinister ways—to assert this un-
likeness for superiority, warranting a claim to be a law
to themselves. You know the story of the fifth—the
"wicked"—Lord Byron; how he killed his kinsman and
neighbour Chaworth by some sinister sword-play in
a darkened room in Piccadilly, and thereafter (having
escaped by verdict of his peers) lived out a mad and
morose life—by report a haunted one—at Newstead,
shooting at bottles for distraction, and absolutely
ignoring the brat at Aberdeen who, in default of direct
issue, was to succeed him.

You know that the father of this brat was Captain
John Byron, a spendthrift and heartless rake; that the
mother was a vulgar, doting, illiterate Scotch heiress,

who, having been wickedly abandoned to bring the child up, did, to spoil him, all that pretentiousness in penury, all that fondness combined with ungovernable temper, could possibly achieve. You know, moreover, that the child was born with a club foot, and was of a vanity so sensitive that the deformity (a slight one) tortured his life—and this though, as all contemporaries testify, he grew to a young man of winning, of surpassing, personal beauty, with a face as it were a vase nobly cut in ivory or alabaster and lit from within: "the only man I ever contemplated," testified Charles Mathews, "to whom I felt disposed to apply the word beautiful." Byron left among his papers a note of the feeling of horror and humiliation that came over him as a child when his mother, in one of her gusts of passion, taunted him with being "*a lame brat!*" and if you turn to the opening lines of *The Deformed Transformed*, his last, unfinished drama, you will read that taunt still seared on his memory, as, pursuing, you will find the whole poem vibrant to its torture. Yes, Byron was abnormally, even insanely, sensitive; and, as sensitiveness promotes vanity, Byron was inordinately vain; and, as vanity leads to posturing, and posturing to pretence, and pretence to downright lying, we may, if we will, damn Byron on all these counts. There is, unhappily, evidence that even of the last he was not guiltless.

Thus far, then, the devil's advocate has his way. Yet, in Portia's words:

Tarry a little; there is something **else.**

V

Suppose a man, noble of nature, at bottom fiercely proud and courageous, but spoilt in childhood and so sensitive to the world's opinion that, the world flattering him for an idol, he returns the compliment by making the world his god. Suppose that world to be the Mayfair of the Prince Regent's day—a tawdry society of war-profiteers swollen upon the miseries of a bowed and ruined populace—a society to my mind even more hateful, because falser, in its smug godliness than in its vices. It has flattered this man to the skies, and he repays it with *Thou art my God: in Thee do I put my trust.*

Now suppose this man, so sensitive, of a sudden exposed to a false charge of which he cannot even learn the particulars. Suppose him to look around in dismay —for the calumny, whatever it is, has leapt up within his own doors, from the very breast of his wife, and escaped into the street. Still he is confident. The world, in which he has trusted, will rally to him, will not fail him.

But lo! it has as suddenly crumbled, fallen away. He is alone, deserted, naked as Lear. The pavement of popularity has broken up and become a hissing. Its stones are burning marl to his feet. He, like Lear, must go out a wanderer.

Now such a reversal of fortune—to use the Aristotelian phrase—if it befall a weak man, a fribble, a coxcomb, such as Byron seems to M. Scherer, merely ends him. He awakes from illusion, he has lost the breath of his being; nothing remains but to turn his face to the wall. Such a stroke descended on Byron. It cut sheer down through tissue and nerve of one of the most sensitive men ever born. And he screamed—as how should he not, being such a man? But I say to you that the surgery cut down to a man, to a great man, to a great poet—and saved his soul. It cut down through affected or practised falsities, to the truth which lay in the kernel of the man. And I say to you that, in this matter of truth, while it is well for us that we demand exactitude of statement, strict correspondence of report with fact, as one test of an English gentleman, it were better if we demanded a higher allegiance—allegiance to the truth within him. You may never in your life have said a word false to fact, and yet all your life by timidity and paltering with essential truth have been playing false before men. In our hearts we all know it; that orthodoxy is, with many, a lie of the soul. Of that lie, having proved it a lie and by bitter experience, Byron became (because among men of his age he saw it, for what it was, most definitely) the deadliest denouncer.

VI

I shall return to this. For the moment I ask you to take April 25, 1816, the day on which Byron sailed from England for ever, and to set that for a mark dividing all that he wrote before from all that he wrote afterwards: and I promise you that with this simple book-marker between what to discard and what to retain, you will never again doubt that he was a great poet.

Still using April 1816 for book-marker, divide the first two cantos of *Childe Harold* from the remainder, begun in early May of that year. Who can fail to perceive the sudden deepening of the voice to sincerity, the as sudden lift to music and imagination? Who can fail to feel that out of mere Vanity Fair we have passed at one stride into a region of moral earnestness, into acquaintance with a grand manner, into a presence? The very exordium gives the convincing

shock—the exordium in which he proclaimed—as
Shelley also proclaimed—that he, the poet, has power
actually to embody his thoughts, give them life and
yield them over "nurselings of immortality."

He, who grown agèd in this world of woe,
In deeds, not years, piercing the depths of life,
So that no wonder waits him—nor below
Can Love or Sorrow, Fame, Ambition, Strife,
Cut to his heart again with the keen knife
Of silent, sharp endurance—he can tell
Why Thought seeks refuge in lone caves, yet rife
With airy images and shapes which dwell
Still unimpaired, though old, in the Soul's haunted cell.
'Tis to create, and in creating live
A being more intense, that we endow
With form our fancy, gaining as we give
The life we image, even as I do now—
What am I? Nothing: but not so art thou,
Soul of my thought! with whom I traverse earth,
Invisible but gazing, as I glow
Mixed with thy spirit, blended with thy birth,
And feeling still with thee in my crushed feelings' dearth.

We pass a few stanzas, and come to the account of
Brussels and the night-alarm before Waterloo. Who
can read it and find not (in Sidney's phrase) his heart
moved more than with a trumpet? Still we pass, to
dwell at its close, dwell upon the exquisite stanza to
young Howard—Byron's kinsman—who fell in the
swoop of Vivian's cavalry upon the dying final attack
of the French guard:

There have been tears and breaking hearts for thee,
And mine were nothing, had I such to give;
But when I stood beneath the fresh green tree,

Which living waves where thou didst cease to live,
And saw around me the wide field revive
With fruits and fertile promise, and the Spring
Come forth her work of gladness to contrive,
With all her reckless birds upon the wing,
I turned from all she brought to those she could not bring.

If any man deny that for poetry—deny to that last line, with its dragging monosyllables, the informing touch of high poesy—let us not argue with him. Let us content ourselves with telling him.

VII

I repeat that if we take April 25, 1816, the date on which he sailed from England, and place it in our Byron for a book-marker, we shall find ourselves, by that simple act, made ready to face his disparagers. "The one great thing," says Lacordaire, "is to have a life of one's own"; and from that date Byron, who had hitherto lived in the opinion of others and fed on it and written much shoddy to please it, found himself—and found a great poet. Let there be no nonsense about his rising upon any stepping-stone of his dead self to higher things. Byron's self underwent no kind of dissolution: it came through its ordeal very much alive; defiantly the same soul as ever, with head bloody but unbowed and with heart more arrogant than ever. Through torment and bitterness he had attained to "know the heavenly powers"; to know them—if I may conjecture his own addition—a devilish sight too well. Henceforward he stands opposed to them: but he stands up. You may smile at any man—small bi-forked creature that he is—standing up, questioning, arraigning, denouncing the higher powers; but you must acknowledge the right of the challenge. If God created man in his image, man has a right (shall we not even say, a duty?) to erect himself to the fullest inch of that image, and ask questions. Does it not, at any rate, argue a certain nobility of mind (if exorbitant) in one betrayed by his fellow-creatures, that he walks straight up and has it out with the Creator himself?

That is what—in *Manfred*, in *Cain*, in *Heaven and Earth*, in *The Vision of Judgment*, in *The Deformed Transformed*—substantially in every line he wrote after that Spring of 1816, informs his purpose. He hates Castlereagh, and all jackals; Brougham, and all sham opponents of tyranny. He disdains its stupidity in George III, its fungoid growth in George IV, the heartless and brilliant *expertise* of Wellington in saving the world for the benefit of a class. He sees War for what it is, or at any rate for what he believes it to be—a piratical hazard of the powerful, cruelly employing the unreasoning but agonising mass of mankind as dupes and victims. And, proud rebel that he is, he carries the question (Shelley, too, carried it) up past your George the Third, Wellington, Castlereagh, to hand it, with Lucifer's own politeness, to the Almighty in session. "Your pardon, Sire,—but, with such agents, *is* the judge of the Earth, just now, doing right?"

At any rate, to take hold upon Genesis and shake it, as Byron and Shelley did in an age (with difficulty conceivable by us) when even to venture a doubt that the Universe came into being in six days of twenty-four hours by the clock was to evoke every curse of the orthodox, is an act of intellectual courage, and remains that in despite of Goethe and his dictum that "the moment Byron begins to reflect, he is a child." It may be simple: but it is, or was, a thought; and to utter and maintain it, against the England of Byron's day, required a mind very high above childishness: nay, a mind that had some measure of the Titanic: for, be the thought itself simple, the challenge is the grand challenge of Prometheus.

Many have noted that in all good portraits of Byron his head has a poise, his face a *lurid* look, as of one who dwelt in a region above his fellows, in a high atmosphere where tempests are more frequent, more terrific —but more frequent also and closer, clearer, more rarefied, are the vistas of Heaven. It is the face of Lucifer, star of the morning—of Lucifer, the accuser with the beautiful curled lip—equally the accuser whether at Heaven's gate claiming George III for hell, or prompting Cain to demand of God himself, concerning Adam's transgression:

> What had *I* done in this?—I was unborn:
> I sought not to be born; nor love the state
> To which that birth has brought me. Why did he
> Yield to the Serpent and the woman? or
> Yielding—why suffer?
>   What was there in this?
> The tree was planted, and why not for him?
> If not, why place him near it, where it grew
> The fairest in the centre? They have but
> One answer to all questions. "'Twas *his* will,
> And *he* is good." How know I that? Because
> He is all-powerful, must all-good, too, follow?

But (to leave theology alone and deal only with Byron's attitude towards *earthly* despots) I will ask you to consider this one point upon which some thought will be usefully expended, whether you apply it to the Europe of today, again staggering—blinded, almost broken—out of a stupendous war upon human liberty, or prefer to narrow it backwards down and upon an academic theme, "The Romantic Revival in English Poetry." If, and while, you so narrow it, I yet beg you to reflect that, of its pioneers, Coleridge tottered through opium to Highgate; Wordsworth, after a few glorious years, settled to live comfortably beside the cataracts of the Lake Country that had haunted him like a passion—and ended with Ecclesiastical Sonnets and Sonnets in Defence of Capital Punishment; Southey, the Pantisocrat, turned renegade and kept in long domesticity *his* home fires burning with duplicate proofs of articles betraying his old faith. But, of the ensuing rank of rebels, the great ones—Shelley, Keats, Landor, Byron—for various reasons found England no place for them, departed into exile, and in exile died. Let us weigh their names today against those of Frere, Castlereagh, Gifford, Lockhart, ask which were—after all and on the whole—in the right, and beware how *we* persecute for opinion.

We have only to read a list of the poems poured forth in those first months of passionate exile and we stand amazed before an energy which seems almost maniacal. We examine them, and are amazed yet more by their poetical strength. *Chillon*, the *Stanzas to Augusta*, *The Dream*, the awful poem on *Darkness* with its most awful conclusion—but suffer me while I read it:

And War, which for a moment was no more,
Did glut himself again:—a meal was bought
With blood, and each sate sullenly apart
Gorging himself in gloom: no Love was left;
All earth was but one thought—and that was **Death,**
Immediate and inglorious; and the pang
Of famine fed upon all entrails—men
Died, and their bones were tombless as their **flesh;**

The meagre by the meagre were devoured,
Even dogs assailed their masters, all save one,
And he was faithful to a corse, and kept
The birds and beasts and famished men at bay,
Till hunger clung them, or the dropping dead
Lured their lank jaws; himself sought out no food,
But with a piteous and perpetual moan,
And a quick desolate cry, licking the hand
Which answered not with a caress—he died.
The crowd was famished by degrees; but two
Of an enormous city did survive,
And they were enemies: they met beside
The dying embers of an altar-place
Where had been heaped a mass of holy things
For an unholy usage; they raked up,
And shivering scraped with their cold skeleton hands
The feeble ashes, and their feeble breath
Blew for a little life, and made a flame
Which was a mockery; then they lifted up
Their eyes as it grew lighter, and beheld
Each other's aspects—saw, and shrieked, and died—
Even of their mutual hideousness they died,
Unknowing who he was upon whose brow
Famine had written Fiend.   The World was void,
The populous and the powerful was a lump,
Seasonless, herbless, treeless, manless, lifeless—
A lump of death—a chaos of hard clay.
The rivers, lakes, and ocean all stood still,
And nothing stirred within their silent depths;
Ships sailorless lay rotting on the sea,
And their masts fell down piecemeal: as they dropped
They slept on the abyss without a surge—
The waves were dead; the tides were in their grave,
The Moon, their mistress, had expired before;
The winds were withered in the stagnant air,
And the clouds perished; Darkness had no need
Of aid from them—She was the Universe.

Such things as that—with *Manfred, Mazeppa, Beppo, The Lament of Tasso, The Prophecy of Dante*—come not of determination of words to the pen, but are creations, heaved out from the volcanic breast of this man.

VIII

It happened—as such things do happen—that this soul, turned inward upon itself and, having found itself, preoccupied with expressing itself—that Byron, alone, or having only the Alps and Shelley, most etherial of men, for his spiritual companions—blundered, in *Manfred* and *Cain*, over the edge of that actual and fatal ground on which all the serpents of scandal were hissing lies about him—and about Shelley, with *The Revolt of Islam* and some utterly false deductions for all their excuse. "The time Byron and Shelley spent together" —I quote here from Dr. George Brandes—

profitable and enjoyable as it was, would have been happier but for the behaviour of some of their fellow-countrymen whose curiosity led them to dog the footsteps and spy the actions of the two poets. English tourists had the incredible impertinence to force their way into Byron's house. When a stop was put to this, they stood with telescopes on the shore or on the road; they looked over the garden-wall; and hotel-waiters were bribed, as the Venetian gondoliers afterwards were, to communicate all that went on.

Hired spies never fail with a story: it is the goods they are paid to deliver. Rumours, all false, spiced and garnished up to meet the market of scandal, were duly indited in the letters of these tourists and posted to England—"gossip" by degrees making the poets out to be incarnate devils.

It consequently hardly surprises us to read that, one day at Madame de Staël's, when Byron was announced, a pious old English lady, Mrs. Hervey, the novel-writer, fainted when she heard his name.

But Byron, aware of the hubbub, kept unaware of the particular lie and now too scornful to enquire, writes on and on. His task is to arraign the wickedness before which men fawn—spiritual wickedness in high places.

And so—as it might seem by felicitous chance, out of an experiment in *Beppo*—but truly by destiny—all his fortunes with his insurgent wrath against them, his knowledge of men and cities, his fatal sensual half-knowledge of women, with that noble damning core of true intuition ever torturing our Lucifer wide-eyed for the best thing missed, for salvation lost—all his facility of wit, his perfectness in the note of conversation among well-bred men and women; his own very considerable grasp of politics; his sense of Europe; his sense of the hypocrisy underlying all received government, all received religion; his sense of seas and mountains and vast natural forces amid which man may be viewed at will as a controlling engineer or a derisory ape; —all these (I say) in the end miraculously met together, found the measure and stanza exactly suitable to them and to Byron's genius, and combined in *Don Juan*.

I believe *Don Juan* will some day be recognised for one of the world's few greatest epics. I am sure that it is, after *Paradise Lost*, our second English Epic. *Don Juan* has this, at any rate, in common with the *Iliad* itself: it belongs with heart and soul to its age—a remarkable age, too, in human history—and it paints that age with such lively intensity, with such a sweep of power, that no generation to come will ever be able

to dispute the picture. Still less will anyone dispute the
play of life in the story, with its multitudinous variety
of movement. It undulates like an ocean sweeping the
reader along upon its waves, carrying him from shores
familiar to shores romantic, from mart to mart of traffic,
passion, intrigue, to shipwreck him but—as Odysseus
was shipwrecked long ago—to leave him stretched, with
the brine on his nakedness, on sands in the bland sunlight, caressed by soft winds, gazing up faint and half
awake into the eyes of young love, innocent and startled.
But I pass over the famous passage of Juan's first meeting with Haidée, to read you another—yet more characteristic perhaps—describing her father's—the pirate
Lambro's—unexpected return and intrusion on their
festal love-making.

> He saw his white walls shining in the sun,
>   His garden trees all shadowy and green;
> He heard his rivulet's light bubbling run,
>   The distant dog-bark; and perceived between
> The umbrage of the wood, so cool and dun,
>   The moving figures, and the sparkling sheen
> Of arms (in the East all arm)—and various dyes
> Of coloured garbs, as bright as butterflies.
>   .   .   .   .
>
> And still more nearly to the place advancing,
>   Descending rather quickly the declivity,
> Through the waved branches, o'er the greensward glancing,
>   'Midst other indications of festivity,
> Seeing a troop of his domestics dancing
>   Like Dervises, who turn as on a pivot, he
> Perceived it was the Pyrrhic dance so martial,
> To which the Levantines are very partial.
>
> And further on a group of Grecian girls,
>   The first and tallest her white kerchief waving,

Were strung together like a row of pearls,
    Linked hand in hand, and dancing; each too having
Down her white neck long floating auburn curls—
    (The least of which would set ten poets raving);
Their leader sang—and bounded to her song
    With choral step and voice the virgin throng.

And here, assembled cross-legg'd round their trays,
    Small social parties just begun to dine;
Pilaus and meats of all sorts met the gaze,
    And flasks of Samian and of Chian wine,
And sherbet cooling in the porous vase;
    Above them their dessert grew on its vine;—
The orange and pomegranate nodding o'er,
Dropped in their laps, scarce plucked, their mellow store.

A band of children, round a snow-white ram,
    There wreathe his venerable horns with flowers;
While peaceful as if still an unweaned lamb,
    The patriarch of the flock all gently cowers
His sober head, majestically tame,
    Or eats from out the palm, or playful lowers
His brow, as if in act to butt, and then,
Yielding to their small hands, draws back again.

·   ·   ·   ·   ·   ·   ·

Here was no lack of innocent diversion
    For the imagination or the senses,
Song, dance, wine, music, stories from the Persian,
    All pretty pastimes in which no offence is;
But Lambro saw all these things with aversion,
    Perceiving in his absence such expenses,
Dreading that climax of all human ills
The inflammation of his weekly bills.

·   ·   ·   ·   ·   ·   ·

Perhaps you think, in stumbling on this feast,
    He flew into a passion, and in fact

There was no mighty reason to be pleased;
  Perhaps you prophesy some sudden act,
The whip, the rack, or dungeon at the least,
  To teach his people to be more exact,
And that, proceeding at a very high rate,
He showed the royal *penchants* of a pirate.

You're wrong.—He was the mildest mannered **man**
  That ever scuttled ship or cut a throat;
With such true breeding of a gentleman,
  You never could divine his real thought;
No courtier could, and scarcely woman can
  Gird more deceit within a petticoat;
Pity he loved adventurous life's variety,
He was so great a loss to good society!

For a second specimen of the poem's quality I choose
Juan's encounter with the highwayman in Canto XI:

Don Juan had got out on Shooter's Hill;
  Sunset the time, the place the same declivity
Which looks along that vale of Good and Ill
  Where London streets ferment in full activity,
While everything around was calm and still,
  Except the creak of wheels, which on their pivot he
Heard,—and that bee-like, bubbling, busy hum
Of cities, that boil over with their scum:—

I say, Don Juan, wrapt in contemplation,
  Walked on behind his carriage, o'er the summit,
And lost in wonder of so great a nation,
  Gave way to 't, since he could not overcome it.
"And here," he cried, "is Freedom's chosen station;
  Here peals the People's voice nor can entomb it
Racks—prisons—inquisitions; Resurrection
Awaits it, each new meeting or election.

"Here are chaste wives, pure lives; here people pay
  But what they please; and if that things be dear,

'Tis only that they love to throw away
  Their cash, to show how much they have a-year.
Here laws are all inviolate—none lay
  Traps for the traveller—every highway's clear—
Here"—he was interrupted by a knife,
With—"Damn your eyes! your money or your life!"'—

These free-born sounds proceeded from four pads
  In ambush laid, who had perceived him loiter
Behind his carriage; and, like handy lads,
  Had seized the lucky hour to reconnoitre,
In which the heedless gentleman who gads
  Upon the road, unless he prove a fighter
May find himself within that isle of riches
Exposed to lose his life as well as breeches.

Juan, who did not understand a word
  Of English, save their shibboleth, "God damn!"
And even that he had so rarely heard,
  He sometimes thought 'twas only their "Salām,"
Or "God be with you!"—and 'tis not absurd
  To think so,—for half English as I am
(To my misfortune), never can I say
I heard them wish "God with you," save that way;—

Juan yet quickly understood their gesture,
  And being somewhat choleric and sudden,
Drew forth a pocket pistol from his vesture,
  And fired it into one assailant's pudding—
Who fell, as rolls an ox o'er in his pasture,
  And roared out, as he writhed his native mud in,
Unto his nearest follower or henchman,
"Oh Jack! I'm floored by that ere bloody Frenchman!"

Those who approach *Don Juan* with preconceived notions of what an Epic should be, may deny it the title if they will. *I* call it an Epic: but, Epic or not (as we consent or refuse to be slaves to definition), it is **a**

tremendous poem. If I hesitated at all to commend it
to the young, I should hesitate not in prudery—for
youth, the natural time of temptation, is the time to
meet it and be trained to overcome it. I should hesitate
rather because the poem appeals less to the young than
to intelligent and mature men and women who (as
Nichol puts it) "have grown weary of mere sentiment,
and yet retain enough of sympathetic feeling to desire
at times to recall it." The poem, in short, addresses
middle age, as Montaigne's Essays address middle age.
If we are wise we shall come to them both at last.

Anyhow (to quote Nichol again) "in writing *Don
Juan*, Byron attempted something that had never been
done before, and his genius so chimed with his enterprise
that it need never be done again." Like many another
epical undertaking—the *Faerie Queene* for example—
it survives as a broken pillar on the author's grave.
Byron himself, even in the act of writing it, scarcely
suspected that this was his grand charge against the
forts of hypocrisy and despotism. He dreamed of
action: and the circumstances of his death have clouded
in the biographies the glory of the greater performance.
He had written:

And I will war, at least in words (and—should
　My chance so happen—deeds), with all who war
With Thought;—and of Thought's foes by far most rude
　Tyrants and sycophants have been and are.
I know not who may conquer: if I could
　Have such a prescience, it should be no bar
To this my plain, sworn downright detestation
Of every despotism in every nation.

The war against the forts of folly, the enemies of
Thought, is—alas! must be—unending. But, for

Byron's temporal victory, seek in *Don Juan*. *Don Juan* was his Heights of Abraham: and falling, he passes into a splendour of memory.

You know the end: how he died as a man should, although not actually on the field of battle as he had anticipated in the lines entitled *On this Day I Complete my Thirty-Sixth Year:*

> The Sword, the Banner, and the Field,
>   Glory and Greece around me see!
> The Spartan, borne upon his shield,
>   Was not more free.
>
> Awake! (not Greece—she *is* awake!)
>   Awake, my spirit! Think through *whom*
> Thy life-blood tracks its parent lake,
>   And then strike home!
>
> Tread those reviving passions down,
>   Unworthy manhood!—unto thee
> Indifferent should the smile or frown
>   Of Beauty be.
>
> If thou regret'st thy youth, *why live?*
>   The land of honourable death
> Is here:—up to the Field, and give
>   Away thy breath!
>
> Seek out—less often sought than found—
>   A soldier's grave, for thee the best;
> Then look around, and choose thy ground,
>   And take thy Rest.

He died at Missolonghi, on the 19th of April, 1824, of a fever caught from the marshes there in the heat of organising the grand struggle by which Greece won her liberty. "Byron is dead." Tennyson has told us how, when the news reached England, he, a young man, went about all day speechless, or only saying to himself "Byron is dead," "Byron is dead!" Let Swinburne, in token of our pardon for later offences, be allowed to recover an earlier word and speak it for the last:

His work was done at Missolonghi; all of his work for which the fates could spare him time. A little space was allowed him to show at least a heroic purpose, and attest a high design: then with all things unfinished before him and behind, he fell asleep after many troubles and triumphs. Few can ever have gone wearier to the grave; none with less fear. He had done enough to earn his rest. Forgetful now and set free for ever from all faults and foes he passed through the doorway of no ignoble death, out of reach of time, out of sight of love, out of hearing of hatred, beyond the blame of England and the praise of Greece. In the full strength of his spirit and body his destiny overtook him and made an end of all his labours. He had seen and borne and achieved more than most men on record. He was a great man, good at many things, and now he had attained his rest.

SHELLEY (I)

I

SHELLEY perished in 1822, at the age of thirty, by the foundering of a small yacht in the Gulf of Spezzia. He and a friend, Edward Williams, had planned her to their liking—"a perfect plaything for the summer," and there had been great stir and animation at Casa Magni, the seaside villa which the Shelleys and the Williamses rented together, when at length the toy craft hove in sight, rounding the point of Porto Venere.

During a week or two her owners played with her and proved her, as they thought. The time was midsummer, and the weather glorious. On June 19th they put more boldly to sea, made a prosperous run, and dropped anchor in the port of Leghorn, where Shelley was eager to greet Leigh Hunt and his family, just arrived in Italy. On July 8th the little boat put out on her return voyage. The wind was fair, but the glass portended a change. She was last observed off Via Reggio about ten miles out. Then the cloud of a summer squall hid her from view.

The two bodies came ashore some ten days later. Shelley's was easily identified: in the coat-pockets were two thin volumes, the one of Sophocles, the other of Keats: and (as all the world knows) three friends—

Byron, Trelawny, Hunt, all voluntary exiles from England—built a pyre on the beach by Via Reggio and burnt what was mortal of Shelley. As all the world knows also, the ashes rest at Rome shadowed by the monument of Caius Cestius and hard by the tomb of Keats with its inscription, "*Here lies one whose name was writ in water.*"

So Shelley had died as rashly as he had lived. He who had been used in his youth to wile away hours in making paper boats and watching them float till they foundered, cast his life away in a not dissimilar toy.[1]

---

[1] The *Ariel* foundered: she did not capsize. But I make nothing of the theory that she was deliberately run down by the crew of a local felucca in the belief that "Milord Inglese" [Byron] was on board, and with intent to possess themselves of his gold. This yarn rests on nothing better than a report, at fourth hand, of a death-bed confession made forty years later, by an old fisherman (name not given) to a priest (name not given), confided by him to "an Italian noble residing in the vicinity" (name not given), who made it known to some-one (name not given) who told some-one else, who made it public in *The Times* over the initials V. E. in a letter addressed "Rome," and dated "December 28, 1876"! Trelawny, who had heard the story from his daughter a few weeks before, in a letter also written from Rome, backed it as solving "that which for half a century has been a mystery to me and others." But Trelawny in 1875 was a very old man: he had never in his life been a trustworthy witness to fact: and his own first-hand narrative of the circumstances of Shelley's last voyage, and of the burning on the beach abounds in violent self-contradictions. In this world it is foolish to multiply villainy *præter necessitatem*, and foolisher to eke it out with folly. The little craft may (though I don't believe it) have been run down accidentally, being out of control, and the crew of the felucca may very well have picked up a spar or two and decided to say no more about it. But even predatory Genoese would scarcely choose a particularly vicious gale from which they were running for shelter as the moment to run down an open boat (she was undecked and ballasted with pig-iron) which would sink in a few seconds, for the sake of a bag of gold, which, however supposititious, would disappear with her. She was dredged up some weeks later, when it was found that her starboard quarter had been stove. This may have happened through collision with another boat: more likely, by the fall and pounding of a mast. The little

In this way the divine spirit of Shelley was quenched for us, of its rashness. At thirty, all is over with it: and three figures—fellow-exiles from that England in which he had been heir to a title and comfortable estates—stand upon the shore in the smoke of his funeral pyre.

II

If I contrast that end with Wordsworth's, who, by twenty-two years Shelley's senior, outlived him by twenty-eight and died quietly in his bed by Rydal Water, in 1850—who died poet laureate, to bequeath to Tennyson (as Tennyson put it):

> This laurel greener from the brows
> Of him that utter'd nothing base—

do not consider me as, even for one moment, inciting you to any disparagement of Wordsworth. No man in this age can disparage Wordsworth but at extreme danger to his soul: and the world—let us thankfully acknowledge—has been long and honestly in process of doing fair justice to him and to Shelley, atoning for the sins of those critics, their contemporaries, who treated both with indiscriminate abuse *so long as they wrote effectively*. But the difference is, if you will reckon it, that Wordsworth was granted just half a century more of life than Shelley: or (to put it yet more sharply) if we subtract the first twenty years of life and set them aside as a time of preparation, Shelley had ten years,

---

craft was ticklish—a freak, built under protest: and of each of her crew of three a sailorman might well say

> Vetabo . . . in isdem
> Sit trabibus fragilemve mecum
> Solvat phaselon.

as against Wordsworth's fifty, in which to move the
hearts of men.

This computation may seem to you idle enough; and
the idler, perhaps, when I add that, in point of fact,
Wordsworth's grand period of harvest was as brief as
Shelley's, if not briefer, and that after 1814 (say) the
mass of his writing exhibits him as a spent man. Still
it is worth our noting that when death violently and
prematurely snatched Keats, Shelley, Byron, none of
these was a spent man. On the contrary, in each of
these it quenched a plenitude of power and killed a
wealth of promise on which we can but sadly speculate.
And again it is worth our noting perhaps that while
Wordsworth outlived detraction long enough to look
back to see it in true perspective, for what it was worth,
and to forgive, if he had the nobility to forgive, in the
wisdom of age all such

> old, unhappy, far-off things,
> And battles long ago;

the curses and clamours followed Keats, Shelley, Byron
to the end of their days, and rang in their ears—rang
them down—as they went under and at once

> outsoared the shadow of our night;
> Envy and calumny and hate and pain.

This is worth your noting, I say. But I would dwell
today, and quite dispassionately, upon two historical
points which a little reflection will make clear.

III

In the first place you are sometimes asked—by
examiners and persons of that kind—to account for the

dearth of English poetry between the death of Byron and the publication of Tennyson's first volume. You might as intelligently be asked to give reasons for the dearth of dramatic performances in Campania in the generation after 62 A.D. when Herculaneum and Pompeii were overwhelmed in fire and ashes. Let us pass 1827, the year of *Poems by Two Brothers;* and come to 1830 the year of *Poems, Chiefly Lyrical.* In that year, if the gods had spared them, Keats would have been but thirty-five, Shelley thirty-eight, and Byron but forty-two; three poets of unchallengeable genius at an age when genius finds mastery and flies upon surest wing to its mark. Bethink you what would have remained of Shakespeare, or of Milton, had either been killed at thirty; conceive what a gap would have been left in our literature: and allow that a nation cannot slay its prophets and have them. Our nation preferred, at the close of a long war, to trust the counsels of a Sidmouth, a Castlereagh, and Eldon: and I leave you, my audience, to draw the comparison between those days and these, with the moral. At any rate let us not humbug ourselves with plausible explanations why England lacked poets (let us say) in 1825 or thereabouts. She lacked them simply because she had killed them: lacked for poetry as simply and surely as a nation will lack for milk in a couple of years if she kill off her heifer calves today.

In other words, if we could refer what is called The Romantic Movement to a Registrar-General of Births, Deaths and Marriages, he would probably report something to this effect—The pioneers of that movement, whether by dint of abjuring their early enthusiasm for the French Revolution or by gentler process of forgetting it, attained to a fair end of ripeness. Coleridge, notoriously careless of his health, reached sixty-two, Southey sixty-nine, and Wordsworth eighty. The lives of the men they encouraged, inspired—and survived— had no actuarial value worth discussing.

Further, if under guidance of your own natural feeling you put yourselves back and try to think what the young men of that date would be thinking about the untimely deaths of Keats, Shelley and Byron as compared with the almost fierce longevity of some of their seniors (Landor died at eighty-nine), you will understand what passions burned in them. It was in 1845, five years before Wordsworth's death, that Browning printed *The Lost Leader:*

> Just for a handful of silver he left us,
> > Just for a riband to stick in his coat . . .
> Shakespeare was of us, Milton was for us,
> > Burns, Shelley, were with us—they watch from their
> > > graves!
> He alone breaks from the van and the freemen,
> > —He alone sinks to the rear and the slaves!

Ten years later we get in verses slight enough (to my thinking) and as poetry valueless:

> Ah, did you once see Shelley plain,
> > And did he stop and speak to you
> And did you speak to him again?
> > How strange it seems and new!

Yet the slight thing is valuable historically, and I desire to impress on you—in a generation out of which all that redeems the lines may be rapidly fading—how much meaning, of my own recollection, must have charged them when they were written. For I am old enough to have lived and talked with men to whose youth Shelley

and the younger Carlyle purveyed the main spiritual
sustenance. Carlyle lived, as Wordsworth had lived,
to become a soul's tragedy: but Shelley—drowned, like
Lycidas, in his prime—had died before time could soil
him or his flight be dulled by any sad afterthought.

I have been turning over some manuscript poems left
by a young man of that time. His name was Luke
Daniel, and his trade carpentry.

He had, though by many years his junior, been a
friend of Ebenezer Elliott, the "Corn-Law Rhymer,"
from whom may be he learned that passion for Shelley
which in turn he passed on with his friendship to another
junior, my own father, in whose notebooks I find the
poems. It is highly improbable that they will ever see
print: and if I ask you to listen to a verse or two, it is
only to show how Shelley's revolutionary spirit, Shelley's
dream of beauty, lived on and together inhabited the
heart of a country-born worker in London in the middle
of the last century.

I turn over many pages filled with the old Chartist
spirit, calling witness to the sufferings of the poor,
denouncing the selfishness of the rich: of poems that
begin with

> The lords of food and raiment
> Are wrangling o'er the spoil . . .

and the like, all reminiscent of Shelley's

> Men of England, wherefore plough
> For the lords who lay ye low?

and I come on this, headed by two lines of Shelley's:

> The owl delights in midnight,
> The lark in early dawn,

But I delight in nothing now,
    Since my true love is gone.

Had he but left me like the flower
    Has left the matron thorn,
Like her the burden of the fruit
    I had in silence borne.

As she devoutly trusteth
    The promises of Spring,
To come again and bless her limbs
    With his sweet covering:

So had I trusted my true love
    Through all the storms that rave
About this bleak and bitter world:
    —But he is in his grave.

I turn another page and my eyes light upon this sonnet
(licentious in form) upon a performance of *Romeo and
Juliet* seen long ago at the Haymarket:

All that is true of love is everlasting:
    It fades not with the fading bloom of youth,
Nor sickens, like an appetite with fasting,
    Into a gnawing weakness.   It is Truth
Submitting to denial and disguise,
    Yet ever contradicting Falsehood's tongue
With the mute glance of her accusing eyes,
    And ever proving to the thoughtless throng
The hollowness of all their sophistries.
    Ay! among us, beneath a northern sky
She holds low converse on her balcony
    With her own heart, 'neath the same stars that met,
Ages ago, the dark Italian eye
    Of old Verona's darling Juliet.

I have seen sonnets very far worse than that in print: nay have recommended many worse ones for publication. Indeed, should this present lecture attain, in time, to print, I shall count on those lines written long ago by a quite forgotten man, to redeem one page of the volume. I quote them and the others, however, less for their own sake than for my present purpose. You perceive in a moment, of course, that these and the other lines I read to you, whatever their defects, are steeped in Shelley.[1] I would have you feel as I have often felt at night in some London thoroughfare—say the long length of Oxford Street or the Tottenham Court Road when the furniture shops have closed their shutters upon *their* glimpses of Paradise on Earth—a sense of the multitudes that, thanks to Shelley, have trodden those ways with a glimpse of the true Eden in their souls. And I want you especially to summon this sense whenever you hear Shelley dismissed as ineffectual. His time was short. His genius did not operate immediately, as Byron's did, or as Tennyson's did, or even as Browning's did when the match reached the magazine. For certain his genius in operation must be given more time than Wordsworth's, patient as that is, before we recognise it for what it was meant in the end to be—a "healing power": for while Wordsworth reconciles the mind with Nature by withdrawing it from fret of politics back to the countryside and primitive rural needs— "I will lift up mine eyes unto the hills, from whence cometh my help"—Shelley will arraign politics and

---

[1] As a matter of fact anyone who studies with care the poetry written by Englishmen and Irishmen (and Americans) in the interval between 1822 and the advent of Tennyson will find it haunted almost everywhere by Shelley. His influence on our *poets* is from the first incomparably greater than Wordsworth's or Byron's.

society and have it all out with them as with wind and
cloud, seas and floods, before his grand Acquittal, which
is nothing less than a stripping of all things stark naked
(politicians and winter trees) to reconcile them in that
which alone he will accept as final pardon in universal
love. As the clearest-eyed of his critics has written,
though not of him:

> When to the new eyes of Thee
> All things by immortal power,
> Near or far,
> Hiddenly
> To each other linkèd are,
> That thou canst not stir a flower
> Without troubling of a star—

Then, sings Francis Thompson,

> O seek no more!
> Pass the gates of Luthany, tread the region Elenore.

Yes: and as we cannot stir a flower without troubling
of a star, I suppose that today no-one can turn a stone
in public life without troubling that large political
shelter towards which its revealed vermin scurry.
Shelley wrote at the end of a great war: and he cursed
things in themselves accursed. But he hoped:

> Saturn and Love their long repose
> Shall burst, more bright and good
> Than all who fell, than One who rose,
> Than many unsubdued:
> Not gold, not blood, their altar dowers,
> But votive tears and symbol flowers.
>
> Oh, cease! must hate and death return?
> Cease! must men kill and die?

Cease! drain not to its dregs the urn
  Of bitter prophecy.
The world is weary of the past,
Oh, might it die or rest at last!

IV

One has, to be useful to you, to deal with Shelley in relation with our times, which happen to be not dissimilar from his own: and today I must content myself mainly with trying to convince you that, whatever Shelley had missed to do when he perished off Via Reggio at the age of thirty, *ineffectual* is the falsest word that has been—the falsest word that can be—applied to him. I merely wish today to establish that: and I am sure it ought to be established in your minds, Gentlemen, being convinced that our true poets are prophets, and that, of all our prophets, amid our present discontents Shelley still exerts over the mass of Englishmen an incomparable power which has to be consented with , or to be conciliated, or—if you are unwise enough to reject the first of these ways and unpractical enough to neglect the second—to be coerced. And in this last I am neither wicked enough to wish nor fool enough to promise you any good fortune.

V

It skills nothing that in Shelley's life-time, in the short time granted to him, he failed. Of course he failed. Momentary failure was a doom implicit in his attempt. But let me, after quoting to you one of the innominate host who caught fire from his torch, to run with it, I refer you to a passage, too long to be quoted here, written by an accepted poet—James Thomson, of *The City of Dreadful Night;* who belike more than once passed Luke Daniel on the inhospitable pavement— each with an equal Shelley in his heart—and trod it out to a more tragical end. James Thomson has never yet come to his own—if there be any such place: but his name is at any rate far more familiar than my poor Luke Daniel's. In his fine poem *Shelley*, James Thomson sees in a Vision the Archangel Raphael standing with the heavenly host above the gulf of space in which our planet spins, and hears his voice speaking. I ask you to turn to the passage beginning:

> A voice fell past me like a plummet cast
>   To fathom that unfathomable sea;
> A voice austerely said—"At last, at last
>   The measure of the world's iniquity
> Brims God's great urn; at last it all must be
>   Poured out upon the earth in blood and tears
> And raging fire, for years and years and years."[1]

and to read on. It will at once acquaint you with some great verse by a poet who has never yet had his meed and will persuade you (I think) that Shelley did *not* fail. You will have, in your generation, to realise that, albeit in another way than Thomson's; and if you happen to belong to the governing class (whatever that class may happen to be), or to a class contending for government (and this you can scarcely escape), you will have to deal with it as a quick and vivid fact, at once beautiful and highly dangerous if wrongly faced or wrongly handled. For Thomson's mere protest is the significant thing; far more significant than the grounds upon which he denied Shelley's failure or the words in

[1] See James Thomson's Poetical Works, vol. ii, pp. 246 ff., *Shelley*.

which he uttered that denial. Shelley, though not seldom goaded into wrath by the tyrants, as Christ was goaded by the Pharisees, had as truly "pitied both the tyrant and the slave" as Byron had hated the one and scorned the other. Shelley *had* preached a cure, however impracticable and even mischievous it might seem to the lords of the earth—Sidmouth, Castlereagh, Canning, preoccupied with the immediate short-sighted business of driving the symptoms under. You and I, living at our remove of time from these politicians, can see that, dealing with the moment on the panic of self-preservation, they were expediently successful, and that they won by a cleverness we can admire even after discounting their enormous advantage in commanding the law, the justiciary, the magistracy, with the Horse Guards at call. But the last thing to be killed in this world is resentment of injustice: and the fire in Thomson's heart represented the surviving resentment of millions.

The world carried on upon the old wheels, more or less. There was a crust scarfed over that which had been driven under; and upon that scoriac crust men sat and read Mill *On Liberty*, Buckle's *History of Civilisation*, Arnold's *Culture and Anarchy*, Mrs. Humphrey Ward's *Robert Elsmere*, and all that sort of thing. It was a period in which Seeley's *Ecce Homo* and his *Expansion of England* inevitably took their turn (after a due interval) as "epoch-making" books. Since all must die, it can never be a matter of indifference whether there be a God or not: and, if there be, what he is likely to be like: as, to quote the *mot* of the cynic, a large number of the prosperous were eager to learn how, the while our Empire expanded, they might profitably contract.

I pray you, Gentlemen, not to mistake me as decrying the Victorian age—of which indeed I am a fragmentary and inconsiderable survivor. A poet of the younger generation, Mr. William H. Davies, has confessed, as a student of birds, that

> oft times their private lives
> Have spoilt the joy their music gives.

I would not too sharply, too literally, press this home upon you. Yet I confess that when some of you bring to me, for sympathy, verse and essays outspoken in contempt of your poor father's age, I think of an evening in a college garden when I tried to save a robin from his son bent on parricide, and as you read on confidently, I murmur to myself Mr. Davies' concluding stanzas:

> So, when I see this robin now,
> Like a red apple on the bough,
> And question why he sings so strong,
> For love, or for the love of song?—
> Or sings, may be, for that sweet rill
> Whose silver voice is never still—
> Ah, now there comes this thought, unkind,
> Born of the knowledge in my mind:
> He sings in triumph that last night
> He killed his father in a fight;
> And now he'll take his mother's blood—
> The last strong rival for his food.

The Victorian age will come to be recognised in due time for a very great age, uttering thoughts with a freedom at this moment—it is the truth whether you like it or not!—at this moment forbidden to you by Governmental order. If, as young men, you will listen to me, I would exhort you to winning back the general right of free speech before chatting of *vers libres*.

But the Victorian age had built itself, for its while, into defences across which Shelley could be studied by field-glass and periscope, and reported as ineffectual, however seraphic. And just then came along the Darwinian hypothesis, to be interpreted pretty swiftly into struggle-for-life, competition, Nature's first law; with all the Churches crying the odds and making their usual book on the winners.

And so inevitably came the War.

And so inevitably at the close of it comes back Shelley. The choice before any one of you, Gentlemen, today is sharp but exceedingly simple. I shall try to aid it in my next lecture; but assuredly I shall have nothing subtle to tell you. For even were subtlety within my compass, I hold that, just now, it would merely impair my argument and distract your attention upon irrelevancies or upon things, at best, of secondary relevance: whereas I want you to see the spirit of Shelley naked as I see it—naked as a sword and therefore effectual as a sword. I suppose the finest piece of criticism ever written upon him to be Francis Thompson's famous essay. Yet Thompson starts off upon an irrelevant attempt to relax Pluto's brow; that is, his Church's —the Church of Rome's—disapprobating frown upon Shelley. I dare say he felt the urgency to make this plea. His fellow-Catholics, as Cardinal Newman told them, have ever occupied a somewhat false attitude towards literature—or at any rate an attitude which great writers have never accepted nor are ever likely to accept: while their bias towards over-praising any poet who happens to belong to their own faith is always a little tiresome and not seldom more than a little ludicrous. Poetry, of her simply willing dignity and with perfect sweetness, will serve religion and philosophy when either truly needs her. She is at once too high a princess and priestess and too gentle a minister to allow a thought of jealousy to distract the sweet and pensive methods of her service. But she has her henchmen yet: fierce and prompt to assure any priest or philosopher, who tries to bully their lady, that they will see him damned first.

Our concern, then, with Shelley today is one which makes trivial any question of the degree of his acceptability to any college of priests.

As students of poetry and its technique, again, we shall have something to say; but not so as to convey that he was *vox et præterea nihil:* which is, for all their polemics, the impression which Arnold and Swinburne agree in conveying with their combined dispraise and praise. Still more trivial, of course, is all the personal gossip—all the "chatter about Harriet"—fetched for us and offered to us by those sutlers and campfollowers of literature who search yesterday's battlefields to strip the fallen for marketable relics. Lastly, I propose to bring no flowers: to show you the sword against tyrants, not to wreathe it with olive boughs: to present you the naked blade, with its edge of choice. Here it is, the last legacy of his greatest poem:

Demogorgon. Spirits, whose homes are flesh: ye beasts and
    birds,
  Ye worms, and fish; ye living leaves and buds;
  Lightning and wind; and ye untameable herds,
  Meteors and mists, which throng air's solitudes:—
A Voice.   Thy voice to us is wind among still woods.
Demogorgon. Man, who wert once a despot and a slave;
  A dupe and a deceiver; a decay;
  A traveller from the cradle to the grave
  Through the dim night of this immortal day:

All.   Speak: thy strong words may never pass away.
Demogorgon. This is the day, which down the void abysm
    At the Earth-born's spell yawns for Heaven's despotism,
        And Conquest is dragged captive through the deep;
    Love, from its awful throne of patient power
    In the wise heart, from the last giddy hour
        Of dead endurance, from the slippery, steep,
    And narrow verge of crag-like agony, springs
    And folds over the world its healing wings.

Gentleness, Virtue, Wisdom, and Endurance,
These are the seals of that most firm assurance
    Which bars the pit over Destruction's strength;
And if, with infirm hand, Eternity,
Mother of many acts and hours, should free
    The serpent that would clasp her with his length;
These are the spells by which to reassume
An empire o'er the disentangled doom.

To suffer woes which Hope thinks infinite;
To forgive wrongs darker than death or night·
    To defy Power, which seems omnipotent;
To love, and bear; to hope till Hope creates
From its own wreck the thing it contemplates;
    Neither to change, nor falter, nor repent;
This, like thy glory, Titan, is to be
Good, great and joyous, beautiful and free;
This is alone Life, Joy, Empire, and Victory.

SHELLEY (II)

I

LET us steadily remember, Gentlemen, that the true test of genius lies in its durability; in its strength to withstand age and weather, to outlive fashion, circumstance, and vicissitudes of taste, to emerge from disrepute and neglect, to submit to the touch of Time, yet abide ineffaceably itself. This property of endurance it would seem to attain, less by virtue of immobility than by a sort of organic persistence, subtly adapting itself to mean, as life itself means, something always immensely important while yet not quite the same. We all feel of Shakespeare, for example, that Ben Jonson's line

He was not of an age, but for all time

has justified itself and will go on justifying itself, but—if we can trust the experience of three centuries—not at all in the way Ben Jonson had in his mind, but because, although godlike, Shakespeare's genius has almost infinite variableness and shadow of turning.

Now Shelley's is a far stiffer, less pliant, more positive genius than Shakespeare's, who "never condemned." It is more intellectual, and at times intellectual to the dangerous point of priggishness. It is (as I shall try to show) in some ways far more spiritual.

But it is—other considerations apart—so far less
catholic as it is less human. It yearns far more over
humanity, but is less humane; less brotherly, while
preaching brotherhood as mankind's one salvation; the
reason being that whoso hates, though he preach hate's
very opposite (as Shelley did), by the very act of hating
narrows himself down to his foe and to that extent, becomes *like him*. Though he invoke the sublimest powers
of earth, sea and air, as Shelley did, he has consented to
enter a close ring and fight with his elected adversary
for a creed. Shelley condemned, as Shakespeare did not
or did never save by implication; Shelley preached, as
Shakespeare did not.

Now although preaching be a stiffer and narrower
trade than dramatic poesy, and the pulpit therefore a
more ephemeral platform than the stage; although, for
example, the magnificent sermons of Donne, hammered
out of stubborn metal red-hot with passion, are today
almost forgotten, or at any rate are in practice treated
by us as negligible in comparison with many a passage
of Shakespeare far less thoughtful, far less passionate
(and Donne, I should tell you was, in massiveness of
genius, almost Shakespeare's match, and surely his
equal in masculinity); nevertheless a preacher of genius,
if he be sincere, in the right sense poetical—that is,
creative—and prophetical—that is, an utterer of catholic argument—will find the world come round to him.
This has happened again and again to Isaiah. With
how changed an ear did we, in these late times, listen to
the voice of one reading to us the chapter beginning
"Comfort ye, comfort ye my people, saith your God,"
or that other chapter beginning "For Zion's sake will I
not hold my peace, and for Jerusalem's sake I will not
rest, until the righteousness thereof go forth as bright-

ness, and the salvation thereof as a lamp that burneth"!
With how new and incisive an accent it cut to our
hearts! With what weight of recovered meaning to
drive the edge home!

It has happened many times to Isaiah. It has happened more than once even to a very different preacher
—Juvenal. It has happened to Shelley. He means today—or should mean to us if we have any sense in our
heads—something more momentous, more imperative,
than he meant to us a few years ago, when we worshipped such things as *The Skylark* or "When the lamp
is shattered" for their mere beauty,—if not absolutely,
at most in a semi-detached way; when that their beauty
was their truth was all we knew about them and all we
needed to know; when we could enjoy even the Titanic
theme of *Prometheus Unbound* at our academical ease.
But time—a century of time—has brought us back to
the original rebellious Shelley by reproduction of circumstances and of misery: an exhausting war, a dis-
tracted Europe; loans, paper-money, mad prices,
guerilla wars, anarchy, pestilence, famine: profiteers
growing fat, military exploiters enjoying the chance of
their lives, fishers in troubled waters hooking up old
boots enough to trade off and equip unemployed armies
for fresh expeditions; and the infants who should live
to recreate and renew this world's great age, coming to
birth only to perish of starvation on their mothers' laps—

> Continuo auditæ voces, vagitus et ingens
> Infantumque animæ flentes in limine primo.

II

All this, as I tried to show in my previous lecture,
has the rather brutal advantage of driving us back upon

Shelley's first intention: of forcing our eyes upon what he himself meant by what he wrote and disengaging it from the secondary merits or degrees of merit or defect over which Matthew Arnold and Swinburne squabbled in their comfortable intervening age.

Let us consider some of these qualities, to put them aside for a moment, but on a promise to reinvoke them; for it may seem paradox, but is simple truth, that we can only see how great they are, and how significant, when we have cleared Shelley's main purpose and then bring them back as its inseparable enforcements; that they lose their real import for us if we exalt them into a place above and apart from that.

And let us begin with Shelley's lyrical quality. Swinburne tells us roundly that "Shelley outsang all poets on record but some two or three throughout all time: his depths and heights of inner and outer music are as divine as Nature's and not sooner exhaustible. He was alone the perfect singing god: his thoughts, words, deeds, all sang together. . . . Of all forms or kinds of poetry the two highest are the lyric and the dramatic, and as clearly as the first place in the one rank is held among us by Shakespeare, the first place in the second is held—and will never be resigned—by Shelley." On the other hand we have Matthew Arnold telling us that "the right sphere for Shelley's genius was the sphere of music not of poetry; the medium of sounds he can master, but to master the more difficult medium of words he has neither intellectual force enough nor sanity enough." A living Professor of English Literature, after setting these two judgments side by side, exclaims "Here is indeed divergence, and with a vengeance!—not between critics merely, but between critics who are also excellent poets. . . . Further argument is not needed," he goes on, "to convince us of the irreconcilable nature of the quarrel between the majority and minority respecting Shelley's place among the poets."

I am not sure that you and I, at all events, cannot find some reconciliation of the quarrel so far as it touches Shelley's lyrical gift. In Swinburne's panegyrics, as in his cursings, qualifications were apt to disappear. It was (if I may put it so) "little Algy's way"; and if we allow him to stun us into accepting for an axiom that Shelley's lyrical ear was impeccable, we do wrong. It was native and most marvellous, as Shakespeare's dramatic sense was native and most marvellous. But the both were extremely rapid writers: and as the both could afford many heavy mistakes, the both undoubtedly made them. If, for instance, nothing survived of Shelley but *A Vision of the Sea* (published in 1820 along with *Prometheus Unbound*), or if it came to us as the work of an unknown writer, what verdict should we pass on the lyrical expertness of such lines as these? . . .

> One after one
> The mariners died; on the eve of this day,
> When the tempest was gathering in cloudy array
> But seven remained. Six the thunder has smitten,
> And they lie black as mummies on which Time has written
> His scorn of the embalmer; the seventh, from the deck
> An oak-splinter pierced through his breast and his back,
> And hung out to the tempest, a wreck on the wreck. . . .

Should we not say, and with justice, that the metre is uncouthly handled, clotted with consonants, and—worse—that, even were it capably handled, the metre itself is undignified and below its subject?

I confess then, taking a grip on my courage, that when I read Mr. Swinburne's rapture over such a line as

Fresh spring, and summer, and winter hoar,

I have my doubts. "The music of this line," says Mr. Swinburne, "taken with its context—the melodious effect of its exquisite inequality—I should have thought was a thing to thrill the veins and draw tears to the ears of all men whose ears were not closed against all harmony by some denser and less removable obstruction than shut out the song of the Sirens from the hearing of the crew of Ulysses." Now that sort of talk is mere bullying, and I had rather prove myself a fool in public than take bullying from any man. I *know* that my ear is not "closed against all harmony": and I know, if any critic take that tone with me, the place to which I commend his departure. But let me read you the context—just ten lines in all.

O world! O life! O time
On whose last steps I climb,
    Trembling at that where I had stood before;
When will return the glory of your prime?
    No more—Oh, never more!

Out of the day and night
A joy has taken flight;
    Fresh spring, and summer, and winter hoar,
Move my faint heart with grief, but with delight
    No more—Oh, never more!

Heaven knows I want no better; still, Swinburne's argument, easy enough to be sustained in print, comes to nothing at all when a good reader so modulates the speaking voice that, at will, it emphasises or makes nothing of the pause, the irregularity, which according to Swinburne is a thing to draw tears to the eyes. Let it, I say: and let us treat the entire thing as holy.

Nevertheless, knowing how rapidly Shelley wrote, and how he left his MSS. (this poem was published posthumously by Mrs. Shelley in 1824) I confess to a suspicion that, after all, Shelley in the rush of inspiration, left a one-syllabled epithet for "Summer," to be filled in later.

"Fresh spring and summer, [?] and winter hoar." What does it matter? you will ask. Well it matters a little, in two ways. I am speaking (or supposed to be speaking) to an audience of young men; and I would warn you against accepting the authority of any critic, be he poet or not, who talks as a bully. Suspect him even when he talks as a pundit. One of the most severely beautiful of living poets—Sir William Watson—chose to fall foul, the other day, of Milton's exquisite line:

And Tiresias and Phineus, prophets old

—which he called "strangely wayward." Now Milton was a classical scholar, and the line as Milton wrote it, is, *classically accented*, perfect. Sir William Watson writes, however:

I do not forget that Milton was an accomplished musician and that it is one of the devices of musicians to torture us with a discord in order that they may assuage us with its resolution: and this may have been what Milton here intended. But it is surely unfortunate to have so framed the line that the reader stops to wonder if Milton really dictated it in its present form or thus:

And Phineus and Tiresias, prophets old.

I forbear from comment.[1] Again I find in **Mr.**
Robert Bridges' *Essay on Keats* a note on a line of Shel-
ley's which has puzzled many—Heaven knows why.
He says:

> There is, in fact, one line of Shelley, which is particularly
> admired for a very beautiful rhythm, which he probably did
> not intend—

> And wild-roses, and ivy serpentine

> where Shelley, I should suppose, stressed *wild-roses* like
> primroses.

I do not suppose so. I suppose that Shelley drew
one long utmost monotonous accent over the three
syllables of *wild-roses*. But let me read you four stanzas
of the poem and for a better purpose:

> I dreamed that, as I wandered by the way,
>   Bare Winter suddenly was changed to Spring,
> And gentle odours led my steps astray,
>   Mixed with a sound of waters murmuring
> Along a shelving bank of turf, which lay
>   Under a copse, and hardly dared to fling
> Its green arms round the bosom of the stream,
>   But kissed it and then fled, as thou mightest in dream.

> There grew pied wind-flowers and violets,
>   Daisies, those pearled Arcturi of the earth,
> The constellated flower that never sets;
>   Faint oxslips; tender bluebells, at whose birth
> The sod scarce heaved; and that tall flower that wets—

---

[1] Though I would interject here that Arnold's *obiter dictum*—"Shelley
is not a classic, whose various readings are to be noted with earnest
attention"—is merely false. Shelley *is* a classic, and his words *are* to
be noted with the *most* earnest attention.

Like a child, half in tenderness and mirth—
Its mother's face with Heaven's collected tears,
When the low wind, its playmate's voice, it hears.

And in the warm hedge grew lush eglantine,
 Green cowbind and the moonlight-coloured may,
And cherry-blossoms, and white cups, whose wine
 Was the bright dew, yet drained not by the day;
And wild roses, and ivy serpentine,
 With its dark buds and leaves, wandering astray;
And flowers azure, black, and streaked with gold,
Fairer than any wakened eyes behold . . .

Methought that of these visionary flowers
 I made a nosegay, bound in such a way
That the same hues, which in their natural bowers
 Were mingled or opposed, the like array
Kept these imprisoned children of the Hours
 Within my hand,—and then, elate and gay,
I hastened to the spot whence I had come,
That I might there present it!—Oh! to whom?

The measure here is grave and disposed. Many
poets have trodden it. But observe how charmingly
the foot of the born lyrist takes liberties with the beat.
Mark in the very next line after that long-drawn stress
of "wild roses" how audaciously, how beautiful, the
beat is checked with quite unexpected cæsura:

 And wild roses, and ivy serpentine,
 With its dark buds and leaves, wandering astray—

Let us pause a moment to mark also how the second
stanza echoes in very cadence Perdita's catalogue of
her flowers in *The Winter's Tale:*

  Faint oxslips; tender bluebells, at whose birth
  The sod scarce heaved. . . .

And now Perdita
>   Violets dim,
>   But sweeter than the lids of Juno's eyes
>   Or Cytherea's breath; pale primroses,
>   That die unmarried, ere they can behold
>   Bright Phœbus in his strength—a malady
>   Most incident to maids; bold oxlips and
>   The crown imperial; lilies of all kind,
>   The flower-de-luce bring one. ¹

Even so Beatrice Cenci's most sorrowful spinning song with its prelude deepens an echo upon the Clown's song in *Twelfth Night* with Orsino's prelude:

>   O, fellow, come, the song we had last night.
>   Mark it, Cesario, it is old and plain;
>   The spinsters and the knitters in the sun
>   And the free maids that weave their thread with bones
>   Do use to chant it: it is silly sooth,
>   And dallies with the innocence of love,
>   Like the old age—

and, thus introduced, the Clown sings his ever lovely

>   Come away, come away, death,
>   And in sad cypress let me be laid—

Even so, but more tragically—tragically as Ophelia, though with a difference—says and sings Beatrice Cenci, with a touch, too, of Amiens in her song:

>   Brother, sit near me; give me your firm hand,
>   You had a manly heart. Bear up! Bear up!
> [*To her mother*]
>   O dearest Lady, put your gentle head
>   Upon my lap, and try to sleep awhile:

---

¹ Which it is not, by the way, being an iris. " ᴾ*old* oxlips "—they are "*faint* oxlips" in Shelley. (So easy is it, as Herodotus would say, for men to hold different opinions on the most ordinary topics!)

Your eyes look pale, hollow and overworn,
With heaviness of watching and slow grief.
Come, I will sing you some low, sleepy tune,
Not cheerful, nor yet sad; some dull old thing,
Some outworn and unused monotony,
Such as our county gossips sit and spin,
Till they almost forget they live: lie down!
So, that will do.   Have I forgot the words?
Faith!   They are sadder than I thought they were.

False friend, wilt thou smile or weep
When my life is laid asleep?
Little cares for a smile or a tear,
The clay-cold corpse upon the bier!
    Farewell!   Heigho!
    What is this whispers low?
There is a snake in thy smile, my dear;
And bitter poison within thy tear.

Sweet sleep, were death like to thee,
Of if thou couldst mortal be,
I would close these eyes of pain;
When to wake?   Never again.
    O World.   Farewell!
    Listen to the passing bell!
It says, thou and I must part,
With a light and a heavy heart.

III

It is when he turns from other men's measures to
follow the lilt, to be drawn into the whirl, the ecstasy, of
his own sweet pipings—when, like Waller's Gratiana, he

beats the happy pavement
By such a star made firmament—

that we get the Shelley we know: the incomparable, the
pard-like spirit; the fated, the intoxicated young god.

Liquid Peneus was flowing,
　　And all dark Tempe lay
In Pelion's shadow, outgrowing
　　The light of the dying day,
　　　Speeded by my sweet pipings.
The Sileni, and Sylvans, and Fauns,
　　And the Nymphs of the woods and the waves,
To the edge of the moist river-lawns,
　　And the brink of the dewy caves,
And all that did then attend and follow,
Were silent with love, as you now Apollo,
　　With envy of my sweet pipings.

I sang of the dancing stars,
　　I sang of the dædal Earth,
And of Heaven—and the giant wars,
　　And Love, and Death, and Birth,—
　　And then I changed my pipings,—
Singing how down the vale of Mænalus
　　I pursued a maiden and clasped a reed.
Gods and men, we are all deluded thus!
　　It breaks in our bosom and then we bleed:
All wept, as I think both ye now would,
If envy or age had not frozen your blood,
　　At the sorrow of my sweet pipings.

　　Those of us your elders, Gentlemen, in whom sorrow
and age have not quite frozen their blood, can recall
the first shock of that upon their youth, the rushing
revelation of sheer beauty: and I hope it exercises no
less a magic upon you.   One can understand, of course,
Swinburne's fervent championship—one could scarcely
pardon anything short of idolatry in the poet who had
returned the echo in *Atalanta in Calydon*.

And Pan by noon and Bacchus by night,
 Fleeter of foot than the fleet-foot kid,
Follows with dancing and fills with delight
 The Mænad and the Bassarid;
And soft as lips that laugh and hide
The laughing leaves of the tree divide,
And screen from seeing and leave in sight
 The god pursuing, the maiden hid.

Swinburne, moreover, was a flaming revolutionary republican (of a school-boy debating-society type: he never really grew up), predisposed therefore to back up the subversive Shelley, apart from loyalty to poetical discipleship. Let us grant that: as also let us grant in Arnold a certain reasoned antipathy to Shelley's doctrine, together with a certain constitutional shrinking from excess of any kind. Still I have to muse over a certain sourness in his famous essay on Shelley. For it is sour; and, with all its skill as a piece of writing, it does not contrive to hide a certain amount of positive unfairness. "And so we have come back again, at last," he writes, after forty odd pages of polite detraction, "to our original Shelley." Two pages and a quarter remain. Of this space, a page and a half are devoted to citing two witnesses (Miss Rose and Captain Kennedy) to assure that Shelley was charming in looks and converse (which everyone knew without Miss Rose's or Captain Kennedy's help) and a sort of dinner-table commentary that "feminine enthusiasm may be deemed suspicious, but a Captain Kennedy must surely be able to keep his head." So we come to the last paragraph, which runs:

To all this we have to add the charm of the man's writings—of Shelley's poetry.

Well, yes, one would have thought so! Shelley's poetry—or "the man's" if you have arrived at preferring that term as more descriptive—Shelley's poetry is, when you come to think of it, the main reason why we are talking about Shelley instead of about somebody else.

It is his poetry, above everything else, which, for many people, establishes that he is an angel.

Have you ever sat in a drawing-room and listened to a middle-aged lady taking away a servant girl's character? She talks just like that.

We have arrived then, at the climax, at the final word on Shelley's poetry. Here it is:

> *Of his poetry I have not space now to speak.*   But let no one suppose that a want of humour and a self-delusion such as Shelley's have no effect upon a man's poetry. The man Shelley, in very truth, is not entirely sane, and Shelley's poetry is not entirely sane either. The Shelley of actual life is a vision of beauty and radiance, indeed, but availing nothing, effecting nothing.

So the essay concludes with an iteration of the too-famous dictum on Shelley, which had first decorated the final paragraph of an essay on Byron.

> And in poetry, no less than in life, he is "a beautiful and *ineffectual* angel, beating in the void his luminous wings in vain."

This time, the word "ineffectual" is italicised, so that the reader may make no mistake.

I have called the essay "sour": but I have a suspicion that "soured" would be the juster word. For Arnold, poet of *The Strayed Reveller* and of the songs in *Empedocles* must (one would say) have loved Shelley in his time, and with a whole heart. Nay, we have proof of

Shelley

it: for of *The Scholar Gipsy* itself, as again of *Thyrsis*, the very accent is Shelley's:

> Still nursing the unconquerable hope,
>> Still clutching the inviolable shade,
>>> With a free onward impulse brushing through,
>>> By night, the silver'd branches of the glade. . . .
> But fly our paths, our feverish contact fly!
>> For strong the infection of our mental strife,
>>> Which, though it gives no bliss, yet spoils for rest;
>> And we should win thee from thy own fair life,
>>> Like us distracted, and like us unblest.
>>> Soon, soon thy cheer would die,
> Thy hopes grow timorous, and unfix'd thy powers,
>> And thy clear aims be cross and shifting made;
>> And then thy glad perennial youth would fade,
> Fade, and grow old at last, and die like ours.

Set that, I say, against a stanza of *Adonais:*

> Peace, peace! he is not dead, he doth not sleep—
> He hath awakened from the dream of life—
> 'Tis we, who lost in stormy visions, keep
> With phantoms an unprofitable strife,
> And in mad trance, strike with our spirit's knife
> Invulnerable nothings.—*We* decay
> Like corpses in a charnel: fear and grief
> Convulse us and consume us day by day,
> And cold hopes swarm like worms within our living clay.

—and tell me if you can that Arnold had not at some time drunk thirstily of Shelley's magic potion, which leaves no man identically the man he was before.

IV

The truth is that, for causes not beyond conjecture (but not here to be discussed), the potion in time soured

on Arnold's memory.   But what are his exact words?
"The right sphere for Shelley's genius was the sphere
of music."   Now that, taken literally, is flat nonsense;
and Arnold must on second thoughts have known it.
It was just his way of saying a thing here, of conceding
what he knew at least as well as anyone else—the fact
that Shelley is a superlatively melodious poet.   He goes
on, "the medium of sounds he can master"—"does"
would have been a handsomer word—"but to master
the more difficult medium of words he has neither intellectual force enough, etc."

If this were true it had yet been charitable to add,
"or perchance he was not granted time enough": for
Shelley, as you know, perished before his thirtieth
birthday, and in the last two years of his life poured out
lyric after lyric (most of them foretasting immortality
before this mortal should put on incorruption) with a
fevered haste as if driven by some second sense that
his days were short:

> But at my back I always hear
> Time's wingèd chariot hurrying near.

But is it true that Shelley failed to master words?
I think I can guess at the half-truth which Arnold had
in his mind and momentarily mistook for the genuine
truth.   I believe it was, consciously or unconsciously,
dwelling on Keats for comparison.

The gods gave to Keats a briefer time even than to
Shelley.   Yet, during it, by comparison, Keats sought
the right word *deliberately*, even with extraordinary
deliberation, as though surely, of set purpose, moving toward the high mastery of Dante or of Shakespeare.

Take, for an instance or two:

The moving waters at their priestlike task—

A laughing schoolboy, without grief or care,
Riding the springy branches of an elm.

High prophetess, said I, purge off
Benign, if so it please thee, my mind's film.

Solitary thinkings, such as dodge
Conception to the very bourne of heaven.

To cease upon the midnight with no pain.

But we talk of Shelley. Before you accept such a diagnosis as Arnold's of the causes of the disease, will you restore the horse to his proper position before the cart and first ascertain for yourselves if the disease exists? Will you, for a simple test, turn to some lovely lyric, such as "When the lamp is shattered," and observe with what economy of epithet, with what direct use of words or sentences used in apposition, and thereby with what art concealing art, the exquisite emotional effect is attained?

When hearts have once mingled
Love first leaves the well-built nest;
    The weak one is singled
To endure what it once possessed.

O Love! who bewailest
The frailty of all things here,
    Why choose you the frailest
For your cradle, your home, and your bier?

V

In *Prometheus Unbound* you will find a song (by the sixth spirit) in a metre which is basically a simple, even a common one, as common as Christy Minstrelsy.

Ah, sister! Desolation is a delicate thing:
  It walks not on the earth, it floats not on the air,
But treads with lulling footstep and fans with silent wing
    The tender hopes which in their hearts the best and
    gentlest bear. . .

Now at Bracknell, in April, 1814—that is, in his
twenty-second year—Shelley composed some stanzas
which experiment upon this metre with the most fla-
grant and (to my mind) the most delicate pauses,
stresses, cadences, undulations. I read a portion of the
poem to you, in a previous lecture, on Byron. But
because it illustrates Shelley's metrical audacity, and at
the same time exhibits him in the act of learning and
in process of attaining, at twenty-one, that mastery
over words which Arnold denies him, and lastly because
I have ever found it, in spite of some juvenile lapses,
hauntingly sorrowful, hauntingly beautiful, I shall conclude today by attempting to read you the whole. It
has no title.

Away! the moor is dark beneath the moon,
  Rapid clouds have drank the last pale beam of even:
Away! the gathering winds will call the darkness soon,
  And profoundest midnight shroud the serene lights of
  heaven.

Pause not! The time is past! Every voice cries, Away!
  Tempt not with one last tear thy friend's ungentle mood:
Thy lover's eye, so glazed and cold, dares not entreat thy
    stay:
  Duty and dereliction guide thee back to solitude.

Away, away! to thy sad and silent home;
  Pour bitter tears on its desolated hearth;
Watch the dim shades as like ghosts they go and come,
  And complicate strange webs of melancholy mirth.

The leaves of wasted autumn woods shall float around thine
    head:
The blooms of dewy spring shall gleam beneath thy feet:
But thy soul or this world must fade in the frost that binds
    the dead,
    Ere midnight's frown and morning's smile, ere thou and
    peace may meet.

The cloud shadows of midnight possess their own repose,
    For the weary winds are silent, or the moon is in the deep:
Some respite to its turbulence unresting ocean knows;
    Whatever moves, or toils, or grieves, hath its appointed
    sleep.

Thou in the grave shall rest—yet till the phantoms flee
    Which that house and heath and garden made dear to
    thee erewhile,
Thy remembrance, and repentance, and deep musings are
    not free
    From the music of two voices and the light of one sweet
    smile.

SHELLEY (III)

I

IT happened on the 19th of June, 1822,—the day when news of Leigh Hunt's arrival in Italy reached Shelley at Casa Magni, and started him preparing his small yacht for the cruise from which he was never to return alive—that another and a very different Englishman mounted a stout cob at Kensington, to take holiday jogging the road through Edgware, Stanmore and Watford, to St. Albans.

I suppose, indeed, that among notable men of the time you could hardly choose a pair more dissimilar, in temperament, habit and person, than Shelley and William Cobbett; than the "pard-like spirit" whose mortal face remains fixed in our imagination as immortally young, ardent, beautiful—in motion so pard-like, or so like a very Ariel, that Trelawny at the close of their first meeting looked up to ask "Where is he?" and was answered "Who? Shelley! Oh, he comes and goes like a spirit, no one knows when or where"; than (shall we borrow so much as is true from Arnold's famous unfortunate sentence?) this angel ballasting, for his last voyage, his luminous wings with a volume of Sophocles and a volume of Keats on either hip; and that other farmer-like, positive, cynically-mouthed fellow turned sixty, trotting the home counties in dust-coloured coat, drab breeches and gaiters, and reining up by a gate to run his eye over so many acres of barley or of swede turnips and calculate their autumn yield in pounds, shillings and pence.

Yet the one dissimilar was in exile, as the other dissimilar had been twice in exile, through persecution; and for reasons which, however colourably—nay, excusably—differentiated at the moment by circumstances and passion, can be detected by us, at our remove of almost a hundred years, as truly identical: this one reason, this *vera causa*, being that both men had spoken scorn of the Government for its inhuman and stupid and callous (if not venal) handling of that public disease which every long War, through inversion of right values among civilised men, by hasty taxation, hasty loans, hasty profiteering, hasty measures against profiteering; by hasty expedient wages flung to this or that selected or improvised industry without reference to industry in general, above all by the easy and fatal flood of paper-money, inevitably brings with ruin in its train.

II

When he sailed on his last cruise, Shelley left behind him a prose pamphlet in manuscript (it was published for the first time a few weeks ago by the Clarendon Press) containing this passage, which I shall read to you with but one explanatory comment:

But in the habits and lives of this new aristocracy [that is, of the profiteers who, in the Napoleonic struggle as in our time, happy warriors! turned their country's necessity to glorious gain] created out of an increase in public calamities, and whose existence must be determined by their determination, there is nothing to qualify our disapprobation. They eat and drink and sleep and, in the intervals of these things performed with most vexatious ceremony and accompaniments, they cringe and lie. They poison the literature of the age in which they live by requiring either the antitype of their own mediocrity in books, or such stupid and distorted and inharmonious idealisms as alone have the power to stir their torpid imaginations. Their hopes and fears are of the narrowest description. The domestic affections are feeble, and they have no others.

Cobbett, riding toward St. Albans amid the full tide of hay-harvest, notes that——

the weather is fair and warm; so that the public-houses on the road are pouring out their beer pretty fast, and are getting a good share of the wages of these thirsty souls. It is an exchange of beer for sweat; but the tax-eaters get, after all, the far greater part of the sweat; for, if it were not for the tax, the beer would sell for three-halfpence a pot, instead of fivepence. Of this three pence-halfpenny the Jews and jobbers get about two pence-half-penny.

But now observe how trustful all the while are these two denouncers of her social evils upon the perennial fecundity of England and the renewed miracle of her summer's prime. An intelligent American has left it on record after his first visit to Europe that, of all the wonders promised him, two so far surpassed all promise so that all fore-told praise faded like a breath before the visible reality—the collected masterpieces of Velasquez in the gallery of Madrid, and the tumultuous pageantry of our early English summer. Well, you all know Shelley's poem, written in his last days and beginning:

    I dreamed that, as I wandered by the way,
      Bare Winter suddenly was changed to Spring . . .

and I ask you to correlate in your minds that poem with this passage wherein Cobbett concludes the diary of his short holiday tour.

I have traversed to-day what I think may be called an average of England as to corn-crops. Some of the best, certainly; and pretty nearly some of the worst. My observation as to the wheat is, that it will be a fair and average crop, and extremely early. . . . The barley and oats must, upon an average, be a light crop. The peas a light crop; and as to beans, unless there have been rains where beans are mostly grown, they cannot be half a crop; for they cannot endure heat. . . . Beans love cold land and shade. The earliness of the harvest (for early it must be) is always a clear advantage. This fine summer, though it may not lead to a good crop of turnips, has already put safe into store such a crop of hay as I believe England never saw before. Looking out of the window, I saw the harness of the Wiltshire wagon-horses (at this moment going by) covered with the chalk-dust of that county; so that the fine weather continues in the west. The sainfoin hay has all been got in, in the chalk countries, without a drop of wet. . . . The grass crops have been large everywhere, as well as got in in good order. The fallows must be in excellent order . . . such a summer is a great blessing. . . . It is favourable for poultry, for colts, for calves, for lambs, for young animals of all descriptions, not excepting the game. The partridges will be very early. They are now getting into the roads with their young ones, to roll in the dust . . . and, in short, this is one of the finest years that I ever knew.

III

Love of England breathes in every line of that; the more eloquently because Cobbett indulges in no heroics and probably while he wrote was quite unconscious of the *why* of it; of the depth of passion expressing itself in an interest alert for every item—an intimate, accepted love, faithful down to trifles; even as a mother will warn her child not to get his feet wet, all unaware that she does it because her soul is bound up in his welfare and, watching over it, like One watching over Israel, she slumbers not nor sleeps. Nor will any of you, I imagine, who have read the history of those times with intelligence, doubt that either the unpractical Shelley (as we will agree for the moment to call him) or the impracticable practical man Cobbett, as they loved their country—and it may be by that sole virtue—divined a better cure for her disease than ever did Sidmouth or Castlereagh; that Shelley and Cobbett—Shelley with his insistence that the ultimate cure is social understanding, mutual charity, and that hatred and oppression are poisons without effect but to inflame; Cobbett with his intellectual diagnosis of the mischief evident in paper-money and in theories of "over-production"—that these were right in the main, and that Sidmouth, Castlereagh, with their fellow-politicians, were disastrously wrong. The most of us can see this, at a hundred years' remove. But it by no means follows that—similar as the conditions and the circumstances are—we, who could give so sound advice to the dead, can apply it to ourselves today. Men grope their transitory life through a cloud of phenomena; and it has been observed that many a wise professor, after letting his voice break in lecture, over the generosities of a Socrates, a Regulus, a Garibaldi or a Lincoln, will return to his rooms and accinge himself straighway to the next immediate dirty job, even of University politics.

Still, these examples of the past remain for us, whether or not we take the trouble to learn from them:

and I would seek this morning, having called up these two spirits, to enquire—quite apart from politics, merely for our instruction as students of literature—why Shelley remains a force today, while the more combative Cobbett (right as he was on many practical points, such as the paper currency) has faded back to be recollected as a merely historical figure; or (if that be an over-statement) has come to be read by far fewer than his admirably virile prose deserves. The reason lies, I suggest, not only in the superior resonance of poetry over prose. There is, to be sure, a tremendous accent, seldom to be accomplished by prose, in such lines as those which conclude *Prometheus Unbound:*

> To suffer woes which Hope thinks infinite;
> To forgive wrongs darker than death or night·
> To defy Power, which seems omnipotent;
> To love, and bear; to hope till Hope creates
> From its own wreck the thing it contemplates;
> Neither to change, nor falter, nor repent;
> This, like thy glory, Titan, is to be
> Good, great and joyous, beautiful and free;
> This is alone, Life, Joy, Empire, and Victory.

Never would I willingly diminish for you the magnificent power of that accent. But to what, when we seek back, does it owe its magnificence? Surely not to words alone, to any trick of rhythm or of eloquence: surely rather because, as Longinus has told us, *sublimity is the echo of a great soul;* and because, as Aristotle insists, your poet works by illustrating, by revealing, through the particular, the Universal. I have read you an extract from Shelley's pamphlet. The prose is good on the whole, and he clinches his paragraph excellently. "Their hopes and fears are of the narrowest description.

Their domestic affections are feeble, and they have no others"—We hear the argument closed as with two snaps of a double lock. Yet the prose is no better than the prose some scores of Englishmen could write, and habitually wrote, in those days, though it be better than any within the compass of living Englishmen— save, perhaps, some half-a-dozen.

(Let us take heart over this, however. M. Anatole France, discussing Stendhal's wooden style, has told us —and no opinion on this subject deserves more respect —that *all* Frenchmen wrote ill in Stendhal's time: so there is hope for us—seeing how French prose has pulled itself together—that we in our turn may recover.)

We get most easily, I think, to the root of the question by considering—not that, given the theme, Hazlitt or Southey, each on his side, would have written on it better—but that quite a number of able contemporaries (and I instance Sydney Smith and Lord Brougham) could have been counted upon to write at least as well, and could have been counted upon more confidently. For an example, turn up Brougham's account, in the *Edinburgh Review*, of Dundas and his Scots time-servers, and study the grave mastery of its satire. He is handling a crisis in the artificial game of politics, and he handles it with caressing solemnity:

It was a crisis to try men's souls. For a while all was uncertainty and consternation; all were seen fluttering about, like birds in an eclipse or a thunderstorm; no man could tell whom he might trust; nay, worse still, no man could tell of whom he might ask anything. It was hard to say, not who were in office, but who were likely to remain in office. Our countrymen were in dismay and distraction. It might truly be said they knew not whither to look or which way to turn.   Perhaps it might be more truly said that they know not *when* to turn. . . .

I suggest to you that the Shelley whose prose can barely hold its own against Brougham's accomplished art—the Shelley we have to match against Sydney Smith, or Frere or Canning or Macaulay—is not, for purpose of ours, the incomparable man who wrote *Prometheus Unbound*.

IV

Let us compare the prose pamphlet with another manuscript left behind in his desk when he put out for that last cruise: that most noble fragment *The Triumph of Life*, in which he handles that most difficult of measures, the *terza rima*, as it has never been handled in English, before or since.   Listen to the cadence of it, and beneath the cadence recognise the authentic note, the "echo of a great soul"——

> As in that trance of wondrous thought I lay,
> This was the tenour of my waking dream:—
> Methought I sate beside a public way
>
> Thick strewn with summer dust, and a great stream
> Of people there was hurrying to and fro,
> Numerous as gnats upon the evening gleam,
>
> All hastening onward, yet none seemed to know
> Whither he went, or whence he came, or why
> He made one of the multitude, and so
>
> Was borne amid the crowd, as through the sky
> One of the million leaves of summer's bier;
> Old age and youth, manhood and infancy,

Mixed in one mighty torrent did appear,
Some flying from the thing they feared, and some
Seeking the object of another's fear;

And others, as with steps towards the tomb,
Pored on the trodden worm that crawled beneath,
And others mournfully within the gloom

Of their own shadow walked, and called it death;
And some fled from it as it were a ghost,
Half fainting in the affliction of vain breath:

But more, with motions which each other crossed,
Pursued or shunned the shadows the clouds threw,
Or birds within the noonday aether lost,

Upon that path where flowers never grew,—
And, weary with vain toil and faint for thirst,
Heard not the fountains, whose melodious dew

Out of their mossy cells forever burst;
Nor felt the breeze which from the forest told
Of grassy paths and wood-lawns interspersed

With overarching elms and caverns cold,
And violet banks, where sweet dreams brood, but they
Pursued their serious folly as of old.

What I would have you consider for the moment is
not any adventitious beauty in those lines: for indeed
the beauty of great and sincere poetry can never be
separated as adventitious, treated as ornament. I
want you to consider, rather, how they bring all back—
all the futilities and fears out of which wars are bred and
festered; all the delusions of hatred; all the expedients of
paper-money and false economies; with a reminder of
the Universal, that in chasing these things or allowing
himself to be coaxed by them astray from the essentially

simple business of life—from working at his trade, hoping, loving his wife and children, doing his best for them, and humbly, in intervals of rest, seeking his God —man but pursues an ancient and solemn folly—that so he "walketh in a vain shadow and disquieteth himself in vain."

And I would ask you to consider this, today, for a particular reason. They tell me that the working men of this country just now, when they read serious books, choose for the most part books on Economics: that in the Workers' Educational Association, for example, courses on Economics are ousting the study of Literature. I think—if I may be allowed a glance at certain old enemies of our English Tripos—that some of the reproach of this rests upon a generation of literary lecturers who went about the country announcing to the proletariat that Chaucer's literary career was divisible into three periods, and otherwise (in Carlyle's phrase) feeding the worker's belly with the east wind. But anyhow I tell you, and with conviction, that no man can usefully study Economics or any like "science" unless he bring to it some proportionate view of life as a whole: that nowhere, so far as I am aware, can he learn that proportionate view but in the great authors; and that, *if he get this right, or so far as he gets this right*, he has learnt the qualifying imagination which alone fits him to handle human affairs. A little knowledge is not a dangerous thing, *if it be the right sort of knowledge*. We all possess a very little knowledge, for that matter: and, that little carries no more risk than a decent man ought to run for the sake of his kind. As I reported to you once of the ninth book of *Paradise Lost*, I say to you now of Shelley's *Hellas* or of that fragment *The Triumph of Life;* that "anyone who can master it so as to rise to the height of its argument and incorporate all its beauties in himself, will become, by virtue of that single achievement, a cultivated man," at least to the extent of having his eyes open to the truth that man cannot live by bread alone—nay, that, even if he could, he ought not to live upon bread wrung from the starvation of Europe.

> Shakespeare was of us, Milton was for us,
>   Burns, Shelley, were with us—they watch from their graves!

It appears to me plain as daylight that no so-called labour-movement can arrive at good by forgetting these prophets whose voices follow through the market and whisper, recalling us; that, forgetting their teaching it merely exchanges one Smiles *On Self-Help* for another, a Victorian for a Georgian materialism.

V

It will be for you, Gentlemen, going forth from your preparation here, to combat this materialism; some of you by direct teaching in the schools, but all by that influence which, when everything is said, an educated man exerts upon his fellows. Well I know (since numbers of you make me the repository of their literary opinions)—well I know, and whisper no secret to the reeds,—that the name of Shelley commands enthusiasm in most of you, adoration in many, and something near idolatry in not a few. And I am glad; because it means bravery, and you can scarcely invoke a name more potent, a name more like a sword. But a middle-aged man of letters may all too easily, if less cynically than Browning's Ogniben, "have known *Four*-and-twenty leaders of revolts"; and it is precisely because I wish the weapon well that I would spend a few moments trying to hone it for your use.

VI

You will not commit the folly of doubting that the true sword of Shelley is his poetry, and its true edge the lyric. I daresay Matthew Arnold's prophesy that Shelley's prose would outlive his verse is to you quite incredibly foolish. Well, it *was* an egregious utterance: and yet Matthew Arnold, with all his caprices, was poet and critic too, and should not be mistaken for a fool. I suggest that we seek what gnat had stung him, to poison the author of *Thyrsis* against the author of *Adonais*.

Well—to begin with—to Arnold, as we know, conduct made up three-fourths of life. I have no doubt that it made up at least as much as that to Shelley's father, Sir Timothy, as *he* saw it after his lights. But —even as Mr. Saintsbury confessed, the other day, in his *Notes from a Cellar Book*, that he had "always been sorry for gin"—I have always been a little sorry for Sir Timothy Shelley. *He* did not invent the name given him at the font; and truly, if any one of you will suppose himself a Sussex baronet, religiously and formally disposed, bearing that absurd name and owning a considerable stake in the country, to have your son and heir sent down from Oxford for publishing an atheistical tract is at the least an unsettling and vexatious experience. And when this insubordinate youth bolts off to consort with people of inferior social pretensions, of violent opinions and deplorable habits, the tension is not eased. It increases—I am still asking you to put yourselves for a moment in Sir Timothy's place—when this son makes an undesirable marriage, tires of it, and elopes with the daughter of a philosopher whose interest in this experimental application of his theories turns out to be, on his part, not easily sublimated above a cash basis, and so ruthlessly cuts the knot that the first poor heroine (and victim) of his knight-erranty wanders out to drown herself. No—put it as you will—there are sordid elements in the story which no decent baronet could help feeling as injurious to a family name. And if any one say that these sordid elements, however disgusting to the poet's father, were no concern of Matthew Arnold's, I answer, first, that a doctrinaire community such as the Godwins' has an exasperating effect upon the normal man, and he bursts out with "What a set!" impulsively (even as some unregenerate in this audience exclaim it upon Golder's Green or Letchworth, blameless cities of the plain): and next, that Matthew Arnold's outburst was directly provoked by a book of professed authority, which coated the naked facts over with sentimental excuses; and that, ungrateful as the process may be, it becomes, on such a challenge, the business of honest criticism to wipe the facts clear. If you read between the lines, you will detect that nine-tenths of Arnold's apparent disparagement of Shelley, when it is not actually directed upon Shelley's indiscreet admirers, springs out of irritation with them. I don't maintain that for exemplary ciriticism; but it is what we feel like.

You have to add, I am afraid, that Shelley passed on to these apologists an incredible lack of humour; which he himself displayed in his relations with men and still more evidently in his relations with women: that at times this lack in him appears quite innocent and charming, as when at the age of nineteen he posts off to Dublin

with an "Address to the Irish People" in his pocket:
but in the dreadful letter to his wife, written on his
journey of elopement, it is, while equally evident, certainly not charming, and if innocent all the more inhuman. And it persists. For many quite whole-hearted
lovers of Shelley it poisons a great part of *Epipsychi-
dion*, written in 1820. The part of devil's advocate is
hateful to me, and I wish to get through with it as rapidly as possible. The truth is, Shelley's personal
attractiveness, operating perversely upon a whole literature of apology, has promoted him to the post of
whippingboy for the whole "Romantic Movement":
that he, poor self-tortured spirit, has been made to
bear individually the punishment for frailties general to all the Romantics from Rousseau down, and
specially for the one malady most incident to the whole
movement.

VII

Our main problem in life reduces itself after all to
this—that we have, each throughout his life in a hardly
intelligible world, to be reconciling individuality with
duty, the liberty of our own spirit with the claims of a
social state. Now the obvious danger (by which I
mean, not any certain risk of persecution, but an inward
risk to truth)—the besetting danger to one who bravely
stands up for his individual soul—may be summed up in
one word, *egoism:* and when that egoism turns pedantic,
it becomes a very lively danger indeed.

Take the passion of love, for example. I suppose that
every imaginative youth has felt in his time—and felt
for good—the impulse expressed in that sentence of
St. Augustine's which Shelley chose for the epigraph

to *Alastor*—"*Nondum amabam, et amare amabam, quære-bam quid amarem, amans amare*"; but when the apologist tells us that the poet's aspiration for love is for something perfect which, if to be reached at all, can only be reached in this sublunary sphere through a series of experiments, of which (when we consider the shortness of life) two or more may even be allowed to run concurrently, why then without subscribing to all Lord Eldon's observations on this subject, I fall back on a remark of Dr. Johnson's, reported by Boswell from a moment of easy unbuttoned confidence during travel (the date is 1777):

> In our way, Johnson strongly expressed his love of driving fast in a post-chaise.   "If (said he) *I had no duties, and no reference to futurity*, I would spend my life in driving briskly in a post-chaise with a pretty woman."

For a second example, others have found this besetting egoism of the Romantics more ludicrously if less harmfully evinced in their interpretation of nature by making her sublimest convulsions coincident and correspondent with a transport, a mood, or any temporary indisposition, of their own.   These Romantics are indeed, one and all, terribly at ease in the Alps with their thunderstorms: and again one recalls, as from a distance, the words of Marcus Aurelius that such people may make for themselves private retiring places, by sea-shores or on mountains, but the true man is he who, mixing with his fellows, gently maintains the independence of his soul.

Such, Gentlemen (I repeat), from Rousseau downwards have been the perils of romanticism.   It was, and is, easy to make fun of them as (for example) Frere and Canning did.   It was, and is, easy to mock at these

men as frantic egoists, as sensuous drifters; to quote
against the Germanic poets chasing the "blue flower"
of romantic love Rivarol's smart criticism that "Cats
do not caress us; they caress themselves upon us." But
the wise man will, upon a second thought, recall to mind
that it is easy to walk the way of convention, that the
way of trespass from it in search of something quick and
better is dangerous, vagrant, leading anywhither—may
be to limitless error. But the way, though it lead to the
pit, is the way seeking life; whereas the way of convention lies between dead walls and leads nowhere, but to
very dusty deaths. Say that these men made ruin of
their lives and brought ruin on others; say that their discovered sympathy with rock, mountain and stream was
fantastic and selfish, their sympathy with human-kind
loose in theory and disastrous in any number of particular instances that can be cited. Still the result has been
that through the poetry of their time, we see nature in
lovelier outlines, clearer colours, as with laved eyes, and
our fellow-men, if not as trees walking, at least better
than the stems and fruit of gibbets.

VIII

Shelley has much to teach us yet. If he can teach us
the root of his matter—that human society will never
be reformed but on some law of love and understanding
—he will come in time to an even greater kingdom than
he yet inherits. I wish with my heart that he could
march from it tomorrow out of Cambridge to kill the
false gospel taught promiscuously just now by false
interpreters of a Cambridge man's teaching—the doctrine that mutual injury rather than mutual help is the
foundation of public and private prosperity.

Well, it may be that the official mind (which is created out of the conventional mind, and to that appeals for sanction) will resent the counter-attack of a gospel of mutual help as fiercely as it did a hundred years ago and nineteen hundred years ago, and by similar devices. For that sort of mind learns nothing and forgets nothing. But on two points let us clear our minds of cant.

For the first—let us not pretend, of anybody persecuted in our time as Shelley was persecuted in his, that he is truly persecuted for any private infirmities of will or of conduct. To such infirmities within its own circle the official mind has always been generous, even to a fault. A balance sheet of illegitimacy, for instance, drawn between descendants of the court and ministers of George IV and those of the men whom these courtiers and ministers publicly hounded on pleas of morality would, I think, repay persual. These victims were punished, not for their frailties, but *through* their frailties *for* their opinions.

On the other hand, and for the second point, let us be equally clear with ourselves that the true miseries of Shelley's life, as of Byron's, came not of external contrivance; that their real tortures were not of the sort that any bullying or persecution can inflict on a brave man (and Byron and Shelley were brave men), but ensued upon the passionate error or errors in their own breasts: for, as I have hinted, when once the path of obedience is felt to be false, the ways of error in pursuit of something better may ramify endlessly. I ask you to imagine for a moment that Byron and Shelley had succeeded in persuading men, and to proceed to imagine a happy middle-age, or a mellow sunset of life, for either of them. The late Professor Dowden (if I read him

rightly) prognosticated such an autumnal close for
Shelley, if only the gods had not loved him too well and
killed him young. For my part, my imagination refuses
any such picture—let be the idleness of the speculation.
In a previous lecture I read you a lyric, written in 1814,
of which the key-line, perhaps, is this

Duty and dereliction guide thee back to solitude. . .

and that most haunting lyric is classed among his Early
Poems. But let me read you now three stanzas on almost the same theme, written a bare year before his
death:

The serpent is shut out from Paradise.
    The wounded deer must seek the herb no more
        In which its heart-cure lies:
    The widowed dove must cease to haunt a bower
Like that from which its mate with feigned sighs
        Fled in the April hour.
    I too must seldom seek again
Near happy friends a mitigated pain.

Of hatred I am proud,—with scorn content;
    Indifference, that once hurt me, now is grown
        Itself indifferent;
    But, not to speak of love, pity alone
Can break a spirit already more than bent.
        The miserable one
    Turns the mind's poison into food,—
Its medicine is tears,—its evil good.

Therefore, if now I see you seldomer.
    Dear friends, dear *friend!* know that I only fly
        Your looks, because they stir
    Griefs that should sleep, and hopes that cannot die:
The very comfort that they minister

> I scarce can bear, yet I,
> So deeply is the arrow gone,
> Should quickly perish if it were withdrawn.

Did I say "*almost* the same theme?" It is the very same: as the fruit in the flower, as the bough in the shoot, fatally implicit in Shelley's own organic growth toward sorrow. Nay, it is the end of all men insatiate for joy.

IX

But he loved much. When all is said and done, he loved so much that to speak of sin in such a man and (God help us) of *our* forgiving it, were perilously nigh blasphemy. It is observable of many great men—of Coleridge, for example among Shelley's own contemporaries—that as receding time veils much, it more and more lifts *this* prominent; that, though circumstance put them on the wrong on a temporary quarrel—nay even so wrong as to be for the while beyond defence by very casuistry—they were right, after all, and right in a degree beyond their own guessing, because before trusting to others' charity they themselves used it towards the world. I think that over the grave of Shelley, any one who feels all the strain—the στοργή, as the Greeks called it—of such human compassion, must stand with a divided heart, desiring to strew lilies for a career cut short, timorous upon a second thought that

> He hates him much
> That would upon the rack of this tough world
> Stretch him out longer.

Yes: as Shelley wrote the last word on Keats, let us quote from Keats the words for our epitaph on Shelley:

"High Prophetess," said I, "purge off,
Benign, if so it please thee, my mind's film."—
"None can usurp this height," return'd that shade,
"But those to whom the miseries of the world
Are misery, and will not let them rest."

MILTON (I)

I

IN this and three following lectures, Gentlemen, I shall speak of John Milton, and especially of *Paradise Lost*. But although we shall be drawn on and delayed to linger upon many rarities in that most noble poem, my main purpose will not be to expound these; as neither shall I vex you with more dates and details of the poet's life than seem necessary, or at least relevant, to an argument which, with your leave, shall take its time and then only be summarised when we have done.

II

What is the word that comes uppermost when we think of Milton, the man and his work together? Suppose that for a start, I passed around a number of slips of paper, inviting each of you to write down the one epithet which seemed to him most characteristic, most compendious, and at the same time most nearly expressive. How would the votes go?

Well, I daresay "sublime" would carry the day: either that or "harmonious" (or some other word expressive of majestic verbal music). A few might hit on "prophetic." All these are good, and I shall recur to them. But I hope that one or two papers, being

88

opened, would agree with mine and reveal the word
"*solitary.*"

I believe that *loneliness*, if neither uppermost nor least
impressive, must be the common dominator with all of
us in our conceptions of Milton and of the poetry in
which he reflects himself. What is Wordsworth's first
word of him?

> Thy soul was like a Star, and dwelt apart. . . .

We deceive ourselves, even if, acknowledging this,
we trace it to our pity for his later blindness and exile.
These throw their shadows back on his earlier work: but
that earlier work dwells somehow in its own lonely
shadow and throws it forward:

> Or let my Lamp at midnight hour
> Be seen in som high lonely Towr,
> Where I may oft out-watch the *Bear*,
> With thrice great *Hermes*, or unsphear
> The spirit of *Plato* to unfold
> What Worlds, or what vast Regions hold
> The immortal mind that hath forsook
> Her mansion in this fleshly nook.

Now I ask you, still for a start upon our subject, to
move your thought onward to the time when, blindness
having overtaken him, he begins upon *Paradise Lost.*
What is he about to essay? He tells us. It is an

> adventurous Song
> That with no middle flight intends to soar
> Above the *Aonian* Mount, while it pursues
> Things unattempted yet in Prose or Rhime.

His blindness apart, how can we separate sublimity from
solitariness here? As an eagle, flying towards the sun

above all other birds, is alone, so a poet must be determined to be solitary as part of his intention to soar above the Helicon of others and to pursue in an upper æther

Things unattempted yet in Prose or Rhime.

Let us move on to the passage where, for once in this great impersonal epic, the personal Milton breaks forth —breaks out of conscious physical blindness and, on the very strength of its weakness, challenges a light unendurable by happier normal eyes. I mean of course the famous Invocation to Light which opens the Third Book of *Paradise Lost*. Everyone knows it: many of you, I doubt not, have it by heart: the most of you, I dare say, have felt not only its intrinsic beauty, but its exquisite appropriateness, coming just where it does. Throughout the first two Books the poet has been trafficking with his theme through the mirk of Hell, and thereafter through the profounder dark of Chaos and Night, out of which, heartened by promise, Satan—the apostate Angel—Lucifer

Springs upward, like a pyramid of fire,

aloft through glimmering dawn, dubious twilight, into the Upper Universe all radiant with light streaming from the battlements of Heaven. As the poet and his readers follow him aloft and front it too, "it is but natural," says Masson, they should "feel the novelty of the blaze and be delayed by the strange sensation."

I cannot offer to read that passage to you as it should be read. I shall merely try to repeat it for my purpose; indicating by pauses (if I can) how cnosen qualities— sublimity, majesty, music, prophecy—nay and Milton's

physical blindness itself—are one by one subsumed into
this great dignity of solitude.

Hail, holy light, offspring of Heav'n first-born!
Or of th' Eternal Co-eternal beam
May I express thee unblam'd?   Since God is light,
And never but in unapproachèd light
Dwelt from Eternitie, dwelt then in thee,
Bright effluence of bright essence increate!
Or hear'st thou rather pure Ethereal stream,
Whose Fountain who shall tell?   Before the Sun,
Before the Heavens thou wert, and at the voice
Of God as with a Mantle didst invest
The rising world of waters dark and deep
Won from the void and formless infinite.

Thee I revisit now with bolder wing,
Escap'd the *Stygian* Pool, though long detain'd
In that obscure sojourn, while in my flight
Through utter and through middle darkness borne
With other notes than to th' *Orphean* Lyre
I sung of *Chaos* and *Eternal Night*,
Taught by the heav'nly Muse to venture down
The dark descent and up to re-ascend,
Though hard and rare: thee I revisit safe,
And feel thy sovran vital Lamp; but thou
Revisit'st not these eyes, that rowle in vain
To find thy piercing ray, and find no dawn;
So thick a drop serene hath quencht their Orbs,
Or dim suffusion veild.
                              Yet not the more
Cease I to wander where the Muses haunt
Cleer Spring, or shadie Grove, or sunnie Hill,
Smit with the love of sacred song; but chief
Thee *Sion*, and the flowrie Brooks beneath
That wash thy hallowd feet, and warbling flow,
Nightly I visit: nor sometimes forget

Those other two equal'd with me in Fate,
So were I equal'd with them in renown,
Blind *Thamyris* and blind *Mæonides*,
And *Tiresias* and *Phineus*, Prophets old;
Then feed on thoughts that voluntarie move
Harmonious numbers; as the wakeful Bird
Sings darkling, and in shadiest covert hid
Tunes her nocturnal Note.
                              Thus with the Year
Seasons return, but not to me returns
Day, or the sweet approach of Ev'n or Morn,
Or sight of vernal bloom, or Summer's Rose,
Or flocks, or herds, or human face divine;
But cloud in stead, and ever-during dark
Surrounds me, from the chearful waies of men
Cut off, and for the Book of knowledg fair
Presented with a Universal blanc
Of Nature's works to mee expung'd and ras'd,
And wisdome at one entrance quite shut out.

So much the rather thou, Celestial light
Shine inward, and the mind through all her powers
Irradiate; there plant eyes; all mist from thence
Purge and disperse; that I may see and tell
Of things invisible to mortal sight.

The main word, you perceive, is of blindness; of blindness groping, aching, back toward light remembered.
But consider how melody—melody of Sion's brooks,
melody of the hidden "darkling bird"—melts into it;
consider how prophecy, through Tiresias and Phineus,
is compelled into it: consider how all these at the end
compressed back upon the inner soul, *there* find the light
to match the divine light, sublimity to challenge sublimity. It is only in solitude or darkness that the bright-
est light can be read, as it is only through smoked spec-

tacles that our eyes can endure the extreme flames of
astronomy. Hear, for illustration, Shelley's word on the
apprehensive genius of Coleridge, palsied between vision and fleshly weakness——

> You will see Coleridge—he who sits obscure
> In the exceeding lustre and the pure
> Intense irradiation of a mind,
> Which, with its own internal lightning blind,
> Flags wearily through darkness and despair—
> A cloud-encircled meteor of the air,
> A hooded eagle among blinking owls.

—the difference, of course, between Milton and Coleridge being that the one conquered and put forth his
strength, that the other failed of will, and sank. But the
moral of both is Blanco White's famous sonnet—that
only the hooded eye can speculate on intensest light, as
only when dark draws in upon him can man even surmise the stars.

> Mysterious Night! when our first parent knew
>   Thee from report divine, and heard thy name,
>   Did he not tremble for this lovely frame,
> This glorious canopy of light and blue?
> Yet 'neath a curtain of translucent dew,
>   Bathed in the rays of the great setting flame,
> Hesperus with the host of heaven came,
> And lo! Creation widened in man's view.
>
> Who could have thought such darkness lay concealed
>   Within thy beams, O Sun! or who could find,
> Whilst fly, and leaf, and insect stood revealed,
>   That to such countless orbs thou mad'st us blind!
> Why do we then shun Death with anxious strife?
> If Light can so deceive, wherefore not Life?

III

When I was of your age, Gentlemen,—an undergraduate at the sister University—I sat sometimes in a Lecture Theatre less comfortable (as I remember) than this, but in many respects so similar that the recollection of it has daunted me, more than once or twice, on entering by the door yonder. For I came to hear, and I sat and listened to, the very voice of a man who might (I say it with conviction) not presumptuously have compared himself with Milton, as Milton compared himself with blind Mæonides——

> equal'd with [him] in Fate,
> So were I equal'd with [him] in renown.

Fate, even in these few years, has so juggled with the fame of John Ruskin that the teachings for which he was then worshipped but a little this side of idolatry seem forgotten as a flame up a chimney, whereas those which his contemporaries merely derided, accounting him a crank, astray and wandering from his mission— the gospel he preached in *Unto This Last*, for instance —burn on today as a fire that slowly eats into the core of a great log on the hearth. After such vicissitudes, such oscillation of valuing in so brief a while no one can say precisely where men's judgment of John Ruskin will finally set up its rest. And prose is prose: poetry is poetry. For that reason, if for no other, John Ruskin will never be estimated alongside John Milton. But I avow to you that in many ways he was even such a man; that essentially he was a comparable man; and that fate (if not renown) so nearly equalled the two as to invite, and excuse, a brief comparison.

IV

For a comparison, then, somewhat in the manner of Plutarch:

John Ruskin was born in London—at 54, Hunter Street, Brunswick Square—on February 8, 1819; his father being a well-to-do wine-merchant of Scottish descent, by his own exertions well-educated, valuing literature and the arts. This worthy man had married a cousin somewhat older than himself and of his own straitish evangelical sect; and this woman, being with child, vowed the vow of Hannah—"Lord . . . if thou wilt . . . remember me, and not forget thine handmaid, but wilt give unto thine handmaid a man child, then I will give him unto the Lord all the days of his life." So a man child was born to her, and (the appetite growing by what it feeds on) in her exaltation she hoped that he would live to be a bishop.

This prayer was not granted, or not literally: although the child, denied childish toys, rekindled the hope from time to time by mounting a chair and preaching sermons to his parents across the back of it. Very soon there supervened a tendency to compose verses. The parents shifted their hopes: he might, *faut de mieux*, live to be a great poet. They whipped him sometimes, just as often as they thought it good for him: to the child it appeared a puzzle that they should keep a good table (which they could well afford) and fare richly, while inflicting so much self-denial upon him. It was not greed in him, but a genuine intellectual puzzle. He loved them devotedly: he failed in no filial duty throughout his life, and was nursing his mother when she died at the age of ninety.

How often, looking around, is one moved to cry out

upon parents, "God! why, after feeding their children and making them happy, cannot they leave them alone!" But the Ruskins with aching care were all the while protecting and preparing this sacrificial child. They were "giving" him—their only one—and making him meet to be given. Their worldly prosperity increasing, they moved out to Herne Hill, where he played alone in a fine garden, and was (as the phrase goes) privately educated. You may read all the sad story in *Præterita*. The father's culture inclining to a connoisseurship of drawings in water colour, the child is set to acquire this art under tuition of Copley Fielding and Harding: "to wash colours smoothly in successive tints, to shade cobalt through pink madder into yellow ochre for skies," etc. He is taken for an annual holiday with his Papa and Mamma, at first about Great Britain on the wine-selling business, afterwards abroad. He goes through the callow love-fever incident to sheltered youth. He is at length launched upon Christ Church, Oxford, and from Oxford upon the "grand tour" of Italy. The trouble is, that this dedicated son, instead of being the the mere clod or the vain prig on which his parents' practice would have worked little harm one way or another, turns out to be a real prophet of genius. He comes back—eager, to accomplish, and sensitive—to wrestle with the world of which he sees the evil, without having learnt—without having even surmised—that understanding which many an ordinary boy picks up by genial converse with his father's stablemen. He came home to face and fight a real world in which he had to be tortured and beaten, praised for that which he accounted of no worth, and, as soon as his argument came to seriousness, laughed at by every soul he strove to save. So, having spent a large patrimony in poor service of his fellows, he lingered out his last days in a life's defeat, and died, most lonely, in the chair in which he had stood to delight his parents with childish sermons. This was in 1900: but the real agony of his life had been passed some years before I heard him. It had actually ended some eleven or twelve years before, in 1878; when on the verge of a serious mental sickness, having to write a note on an exhibition of Turners in Bond Street, the desolate man penned this note.

Oh, that some one had told me, in my youth, when all my heart seemed to be set on these colours and clouds, that appear for a little while and then vanish way, how little my love of them would serve me, when the silence of lawn and wood in the dews of morning should be completed; and all my thoughts should be of those whom, by neither, I was to meet more!

V

Now will you mark the parallel and forgive the length to which I have drawn the lower line?

John Milton, like Ruskin, was a Londoner and very much of a Londoner: born well within sound of Bow Bells and almost beneath the shadow of the belfry—the date, December 9th, 1608. His father, too, like John Ruskin's, was

a citizen
Of credit and renown,

doing prosperously as a scrivener at the sign of the Spread Eagle in Bread Street, Cheapside, and dwelling comfortably above and behind his place of business. (A scrivener's business, one may explain, consisted partly in the drawing up of wills, marriage settlements, deeds, and the like, partly—and, one suspects, more profitably—in arranging loans upon mortgage.)

John Milton the father had lofty designs for John Milton the son, even as John Ruskin the father had lofty designs for John Ruskin the son. "From the first"—to quote Masson—"there is proof that his heart is bound up in his son John, and that he had conceived the highest expectations of what that son would turn out to be be. A portrait of the poet, as a sweet, serious roundheaded boy at the age of ten"—I suppose "round-headed" here to be purely descriptive and void of any proleptic intention—"still exists, which his father caused to be done by the foreign painter then most in fashion, and which hung on the wall of one of the rooms in the house in Bread Street. Both father and mother doted on the boy and were proud of his promise." They planned him for Holy Orders and to become a bishop. . . . I hope, Gentlemen, that my comparison already begins to look a little better than Fluellen's—"there is a river in Macedon; and there is also moreover a river at Monmouth . . . 'tis alike as my fingers is to my fingers, and there is salmons in both."

John Milton anticipated John Ruskin again in being given a good sober Scottish tutor; from whose supervision he passed to St. Paul's School, then located hard by Bread Street. From St. Paul's, at sixteen, he came up here, to Christ's College, and here he abode seven years.

There was no hurry in the preparation of John Milton. It is uncertain at what date he disappointed his parents by announcing that he would have none of Holy Orders. The decision, whenever taken, showed wisdom: for those were the days of Archbishop Laud; and under

Laud's church-rule the temper of Milton, never docile, could have found no place. But although he will have no eye on any episcopate,[1] he is by this time as sure as ever his parents had been, and even surer, that a high destiny awaits him. He is shaping himself to it. He intends, in fine, to be a great Poet. For what has Ben Jonson said?—"Every beggarly Corporation affoords the State a Mayor, or two Bailiffs, yearly: but"—quoting Petronius—"*Solus Rex, aut Poeta, non quotannis nascitur*"—"the King and the Poet, these two, cannot be raised by annual husbandry." And what has Tasso said, that proud bard? "*Non c'è in mondo chi merita nome di creatore, se non Iddio ed il Poeta*"—"in this Universe is no one deserving the name Creator save God himself and the Poet."

So, at twenty-three, our poet goes down from Cambridge, admired by all and nicknamed *The Lady* "on account of his fair complexion, feminine and graceful appearance, and a certain haughty delicacy in his tastes and morals"; carrying great expectations, but not to be hurried towards realising them, albeit this fine deliberation be attended by some private misgivings. We may read it all confessed, the misgivings together with the proud conscious claim, in the sonnet he wrote on leaving Cambridge.

> How soon hath Time, the subtle thief of youth,
>   Stoln on his wing my three-and-twentith year!
>   My hasting dayes flie on with full career,
> But my late spring no bud or blossom shew'th.
> Perhaps my semblance might deceive the truth
>   That I to manhood am arriv'd so near;

---

[1] Save a dour one. Let us remind ourselves of *Lycidas* and his angry derangement of metaphors:

> Blind mouthes! that scarce themselves know how to hold
> A Sheep-hook. . . .

And inward ripenes doth much less appear,
That som more timely-happy spirits indu'th.
Yet, be it less or more, or soon or slow,
  It shall be still in strictest measure eev'n
  To that same lot, however mean, or high,
Toward which Time leads me, and the will of Heav'n.
  All is, if I have grace to use it so,
  As ever in my great task Master's eye.

VI

His father, having retired from London and business
(in or about 1632, in his seventieth year), had taken a
country house at Horton in Buckinghamshire. Thither
our doubly dedicated young man withdrew, and there,
for another five years and eight months (July, 1632–
April, 1638) he went on strictly meditating the apparently thankless Muse. This was all very well; but even
a destined Isaiah has—as the unregenerate say—to get
a move on, sooner or later. He was, in fact, beginning
to write gloriously: but to cold appearance, he was nearing his thirtieth year and, so far, had not done a hand's
turn of verifiable work. His Cambridge friends began
to grow impatient for some fulfilment of the promise
on which they had pinned belief; and so, and yet more
naturally, did the father. We know that even before
leaving Cambridge, Milton had written the Ode *On the
Morning of Christ's Nativity*, and that to these medita-
tive years belong *L'Allegro*, *Il Penseroso*, *At a Solemn
Music*, *Comus*, *Lycidas*—things imperishable. But
these were not published—although *Comus* had been
acted, winning great favour; and he aspired far beyond
these. Meanwhile he continued "wholly intent, through
a period of absolute leisure, on a steady perusal of the
Greek and Latin writers, but still so that occasionally I

exchanged the country for the city, either for the purpose of buying books or for that of learning anything new in Mathematics or in Music, in which I then took delight." These, you will agree, were innocent purposes to take a young man of his age up to London. But I cannot doubt that the account is strictly truthful.

If you consider the lines in *L'Allegro*——

> Towred Cities please us then,
> And the busie humm of men,
> Where throngs of Knights and Barons bold
> In weeds of Peace high triumphs hold,
> With store of Ladies, whose bright eyes
> Rain influence, and judge the prize
> Of Wit, or Arms. . . .

I think you will almost certainly adjudge this to be second-hand experience derived from books; remoter, even, than the banquet which in *Paradise Regained* Satan spread for Christ, obviously combining recollections of Petronius with personal reminiscences of a Lord Mayor's feast in London Guildhall.

> He spake no dream; for, as his words had end,
> Our Saviour lifting up his eyes beheld
> In ample space under the broadest shade
> A Table richly spread in regal mode,
> With dishes pil'd, and meats of noblest sort
> And savour—Beasts of chase, or Fowl of game
> In pastry built, or from the spit, or boyl'd,
> Gris-amber-steam'd; all Fish, from Sea or Shore,
> Freshet or purling Brook, of shell or fin,
> And exquisitest name, for which was drain'd
> *Pontus*, and *Lucrine* bay, and *Afric* coast.
> Alas how simple, to these Cates compar'd
> Was that crude Apple that diverted *Eve!*

I really make no doubt, Gentlemen, that you will find the true Milton rather in the youth, acquainted with our Chapel of King's College and aspiring in *Il Penseroso*——

> But let my due feet never fail
> To walk the studious Cloysters pale,
> And love the high embowèd Roof
> With antick Pillars massy proof,
> And storied Windows richly dight,
> Casting a dimm religious light.
> There let the pealing Organ blow
> To the full voic'd Quire below,
> In Service high and Anthems clear
> As may, with sweetness, through mine ear
> Dissolve me into ecstasies
> And bring all Heav'n before mine eyes. . . .

Nor again is it wayward criticism (I suggest to you) that when in *L'Allegro* Milton bids us

> to the well-trod stage anon,
> If *Jonson's* learnèd sock be on,
> Or sweetest *Shakespear*, fancies childe,
> Warble his native Wood-notes wilde.

—the invitation is a reader's rather than a playgoer's. Exquisitely descriptive as this "warbling," these "native woodnotes," may be of *A Midsummer Night's Dream* or of *As You Like It*, read and remurmured and tasted over in the library where, we are told, he loved to sit somewhat aslant in an elbow chair with a leg thrown over one of its arms—I confess they seem to me as little reminiscent of the actual playhouse as those correspondent ones in *Il Penseroso*, wherein reading, and no more than reading, is plainly intended—

Som time let Gorgeous Tragedy
In Specter'd Pall com sweeping by,
Presenting *Thebs*, or *Pelops* line,
Or the tale of *Troy* divine;
Or what (though rare) of later age
Ennobled hath the Buskind Stage.

I ask you to consider well that Milton's father allowed
him perfect freedom on these London visits—as indeed,
if he had not, the youth would have claimed it for himself. In Mr. Birrell's good phrase "Milton was always
determined, whatever else he was or might become, to
be his own man." Over a chastity sensitive as a girl's
he had buckled the harness of a strong purpose, and so
was doubly proof. But I want you to understand that
this was the same John Milton who wrote later, in
Areopagitica——

He that can apprehend and consider vice with all her
baits and seeming pleasures, and yet abstain, and yet dis-
tinguish, and yet prefer that which is truly better, he is the
true wayfaring Christian. I cannot praise a fugitive and
cloistered virtue, unexercised and unbreathed, that never
sallies out and seeks her adversary, but slinks out of the
race, where that immortal garland is to be run for, not
without dust and heat. Assuredly we bring not innocence
into the world, we bring impurity much rather; that which
purifies us is trial, and trial is by what is contrary. That
virtue therefore which is but a youngling in the contemplation of evil, and knows not the utmost that vice
promises to her followers, and rejects it, is but a blank virtue, not a pure.

Yes, indeed:

Milton! thou shouldst be living at this hour:
England hath need of thee: she is a fen
Of mineral waters . . .

VII

Forgive me that I dwell so much on this self-dedicated youth; and bear with me while I continue (as I shall) to lay stress on Milton's isolation: for indeed, if you will wait, I am piling up material against my later argument. But I have elected, having a general theory to unfold later, to choose a subject of which every personal detail may speciously tell against me.

Let us have it, all fair and square. No man can charge idleness upon this youth who in these years wrote *L'Allegro, Il Penseroso, Arcades, Comus, Lycidas,* and the rest. His noble sonnet on *Shakespeare*——

What needs my *Shakespear* for his honour'd Bones . . .

had appeared anonymously in the second or 1632 edition of the Shakespeare Folio as a commendatory verse. His *Comus* had been performed and had won deserved applause on the greensward by Ludlow Castle. *Lycidas* had seen print in 1638, signed "J. M." at the end of a collection of obituary poems contributed by thirty-two friends and published by the Cambridge University Press in memory of Edward King. But the most of his poems remained in manuscript: and we have to lay our account with the cold fact that up to the age of thirty-two (and, it may be, later) Milton had not earned a penny for himself.

VIII

We need not make very much of this: as we need not, when we come to it, waste our emotion over the more notorious fact that *Paradise Lost* brought just ten pounds to its author during his lifetime, and eight additional pounds to his widow, who parted with the copy-

right. *Et sunt commercia cœli!* Tears over that will
do more credit to our hearts than to our historical sense:
for authors did not look, in those days, to earn a living
by their books. They published for fame, or in conten-
tiousness, or to authenticate their writings against
piratical printers and garbling copyists, or for a variety
of reasons which you may trace for yourselves by following the bibliography (say) of Donne's Poems, of Bacon's
Essays, of Burton's *Anatomy*, or of Sir Thomas Browne's
Religio Medici. They did not write for a competence.
Shakespeare, as we know, was a good man of business:
he never found it possible to collect his plays for publication or bothered the players for leave to collect them.
If we go back a century or a couple of centuries from
Milton, we find that mere copying of MSS. commanded
far higher prices than authorship ever obtained for some
hundreds of years under the printing press. If we go
forward a century and read of the eighteenth-century
men commemorated in Johnson's *Lives of the Poets*,
we may trace how the patron and the jail between them
were still coping with an economic theory that literature,
being priceless, would be insulted by a decent payment.

So, you see, when we have accepted Milton's conse-
cration to the high calling of poetry, we need not be
astonished that at thirty-two he had not earned a penny.
Still for you and me that cold fact, as I have called it,
naturally reflects the mind to Milton's father, and how
he took it.

IX

He took it very well; and for this and another reason
I am glad to pause on a few words about him.

He was, as we have seen, a scrivener; prosperous,
and now retired out of London. But, like Ruskin's

father, he was a man of liberal and cultivated taste. "For one thing," says Masson of the household in Bread Street, and the description may travel to Horton, "music was perpetual in it"——

The scrivener was not only passionately fond of music, but even of such note himself as a musical composer, that, apart altogether from the fame of his great son, some memory of him might have lingered among us to this day. Madrigals, songs, and psalm tunes of his composition are to be seen yet in music-books published before his son was born, or while he was but in his boyhood, and not in mere inferior music-books, but in collections in which Morley, Wilbye, Bull, Dowland, Ellis Gibbons, Orlando Gibbons, and others of the best artists of his day were his fellow contributors.

In particular one may name Ravenscroft's *Whole Book of Psalms*, a rather famous compendium of church music published in 1621, in which two tunes called "Norwich" and "York" are by John Milton the elder. York tune remains a favourite to this day, and is (I believe) the one to which we yet sing Tate and Brady's "O God of Hosts, the mighty Lord" (No. 237 in *Hymns Ancient and Modern*).

I shall have something to say in another lecture about these old song books, and about Milton as an eminently musical poet. Just here I content myself with stressing the fact that music conditioned all his youth, and specially that his father taught him to sing tunably and to play upon the organ—an accomplishment to which he returned for solace in his blind old age.

Experience and observation have both taught me that parents desire their children to be like themselves, only

better; and that Providence usually and beneficently
frustrates the first part of that desire. It appears evident the elder Milton, seeing that his son declined to be
a bishop and (even more firmly) to be become a lawyer,
longed to make a musician of him. But I quoted Mr.
Birrell just now to the effect that our poet was always
determined, whatever else he was or might become, to
be his own man. Let me append to this Masson's most
probable conjecture, that he had at Horton, "learnt to
be master, and more, in his father's house"—his father,
let me remind you, being well over seventy.

Now to his father, sometime in this Horton period,
Milton addressed a poem, with a few words on which I
shall today conclude. He wrote it—this poem *Ad Pa-
trem*—in Latin hexameters; and "The decent obscurity
of a dead language" has to some extent veiled their importance in the story of John Milton's life. But listen
to these lines.

> Nec tu perge, precor, sacras contemnere Musas
> Nec vanas inopesque puta, quarum ipse peritus
> Munere mille sonos numeros componis ad aptos,
> Millibus et vocem modulis variare canoram
> Doctus Arionii meritò sis nominis hæres.
> Nunc tibi quid mirum si me genuisse poëtam
> Contigerit, charo si tam propè sanguine juncti
> Cognatas artes studiumque affine sequamur?
> Ipse volens Phœbus se dispertire duobus,
> Altera dona mihi, dedit altera dona parenti;
> Dividuumque Deum, genitorque puerque, tenemus.
>
> Tu tamen ut simules teneras odisse Camœnas,
> Non odisse reor. Neque enim, pater, ire jubebas
> Quà via lata patet, quà pronior area lucri,
> Certaque condendi fulget spes aurea nummi;
> Nec rapis ad leges, malè custoditaque gentis
> Jura, nec insulsis damnas clamoribus aures.

Sed, magis excultam cupiens ditescere mentem,
Me, procul urbano strepitu, secessibus altis
Abductum, Aoniæ jucunda per otia ripæ,
Phœbæo lateri comitem sinis ire beatum.
Officium chari taceo commune parentis;
Me poscunt majora. Tuo, pater optime, sumptu
Cum mihi Romuleæ patuit facundia linguæ,
Et Latii veneres, et quæ Jovis ora decebant
Grandia magniloquis elata vocabula Graiis,
Addere suasisti quos jactat Gallia flores,
Et quam degeneri novus Italus ore loquelam
Fundit, barbaricos testatus voce tumultus,
Quæque Palæstinus loquitur mysteria vates.
Denique quicquid habet cælum, subjectaque cælo
Terra parens, terræque et cælo interfluus aër,
Quicquid et unda tegit, pontique agitabile marmor,
Per te nôsse licet, per te, si nôsse libebit;
Dimotâque venit spectanda Scientia nube,
Nudaque conspicuos inclinat ad oscula vultus,
Ni fugisse velim, ni sit libâsse molestum . . .
　At tibi, chare pater, postquam non æqua merenti
Posse referre datur, nec dona rependere factis,
Sit memorâsse satis, repetitaque munera grato
Percensere animo, fidæque reponere menti.
　Et vos, O nostri, juvenilia carmina, lusus,
Si modò perpetuos sperare audebitis annos,
Et domini superesse rogo, lucemque tueri,
Nec spisso rapient oblivia nigra sub Orco,
Forsitan has laudes, decantatumque parentis
Nomen, ad exemplum, sero servabitis ævo.

Here it is in Masson's rendering: which deserves, in my opinion, more praise than it has ever received.

Do not thou, I beseech, persist in contemning the Muses,
Thinking them vain and poor, thyself the while to their
　bounty

Owing thy skill in composing thousands of sounds to the
  verses
Matching them best, and thy cunning to vary the voice of
  the singer
Thousands of trilling ways, acknowledged heir of Arion.
Why shouldst thou wonder now if so it has chanced that a
  poet
Comes to be son of thine, and if, joined in such loving
  relation,
Each of us follows an art that is kin to the art of the other?
Phœbus himself proposing a twin bequest of his nature,
Gifted one half to me, with the other gifted my parent,
So that, father and son, we hold the god wholly between us.
Nay, but, pretend as thou mayest to hate the delicate
  Muses,
Lo! my proofs that thou dost not. Father, thy bidding
  was never
Given me to go the broad way that leads to the market of
  lucre,
Down where the hope shines sure of gold to be got in
  abundance;
Nor dost thou force to the Laws and the lore of the rights
  of the nation
Sorely ill-kept, nor doom my ears to the babble of asses;
Rather, desiring to see my mind grow richer by culture,
Far from the city's noise, and here in the depths of retire-
  ment
Lapt at my own sweet will amid Heliconian pleasures,
Letest me walk all day as Apollo's bosom companion.
Needless here to mention, the common kindness parental;
Greater things claim record. At *thy* cost, worthiest father,
When I had mastered fully the tongue of the Romans, and
  tasted
Latin delights enough, and the speech for which Jove's
  mouth was moulded,
That grand speech of the Greeks which served for their
  great elocution,

Thou 'twas advised the vaunted flowers of Gaul in addition
Thereto the language in which the new and fallen Italian
Opens his lips with sounds that attest the Barbarian inroads.
Yea, and the mystic strains which the Palestine prophet
  delivers.
Further, whatever the heaven contains, and under the
  heaven
Mother Earth herself, and the air betwixt earth and the
  heaven,
Whatso the wave overlaps, and the seas ever-moveable
  marble,
Thou giv'st me means for knowing, thou, if the knowledge
  shall please me.
Science, her cloud removed now offers herself to my gazes
Nakedly bending her full-seen face to the print of my kisses,
Be it I will not fly her nor count her favours a trouble. . .
So my father dear, since the perfect sum of your merits
Baffles equal return, and your kindness all real repayment,
Be the mere record enough, and the fact that my grateful
  remembrance
Treasures the itemed account of debt and will keep it for
  ever.
Ye too my youthful verses, my pastime and play for the
  present,
Should you sometimes dare to hope for eternal existence,
Lasting and seeing the light when your master's body has
  mouldered,
Not whirled down in oblivion deep in the darkness of Orcus,
Mayhap this tribute of praise and the thus sung name of
  my parent
Ye shall preserve, an example, for ages yet in the future.

X

But one thing remained for this vowed youth, as for
Ruskin, to be cope and crown in his preparation.   In the

month of April, 1638—his mother having died a year
before, and his old father at length giving consent—
Milton set out with a manservant upon that journey
which should be the dream of every young Englishman
who aspired to be an artist; and passed, through Paris;
thence, by the Mediterranean coast, to Italy—to Florence, to Rome.

MILTON (II)

I

I STARTED, a week ago, by reading the immortal Invocation to Light which opens the *Third Book of Paradise Lost*, and by drawing your attention to four points on which Milton would seem expressly to justify himself through his Epic, and his Epic through the man. They were—

1. Prophetic Sublimity ⎱ these two justifying the
2. Music   ⎰   work
3. His loneliness   ⎱ these justifying the
4. His physical blindness ⎰   workman

this last—the poignant physical affliction of blindness —giving the stab which releases the whole personal passionate outburst.

Now I grant that Milton's blindness so far causes and conditions his loneliness that to keep the two at all separate in our minds is not easy, as to keep them strictly separate would be pedantic: for, as I warned you in my very first lecture from this Chair, quoting Renan, *la vérité consiste dans les nuances;* and in literature, at any rate, it is only a pedant who boxes up genius, or the works of genius, in compartments, or classifies for any mortal purpose save handiness of treatment. Still I would have you keep the two so far distinct in your minds as not to attribute all his loneliness to his later blindness. For, a week ago, I was at some pains to show that his was an isolated youth from the start, through his parents' ambition: and I shall have to show you to-day how inner pride and outer circumstance isolated yet farther his middle life, long before blindness overtook him.

II

Indeed, in dealing with Literature I so distrust classifications, even for handiness, that I use even one so modest as the above for a mere scaffolding of the argument, and would entreat you, when the argument is done, to clear the scaffolding away and forget it.

Or, since we had something to say last time about John Ruskin, may I employ here a figure of the sort that used to be dear to Ruskin's heart? Some of you may remember (from the notes to your Aristophanes) that the Greeks were used to brand certain breeds of their race-horses with this or that letter of their ancient alphabet; and that in particular there was a certain Corinthian strain marked with a Koppa (or ϙ) and claiming, for original sire, no less a stallion than Pegasus. Now Pegasus, as you also know, was the winged horse of Song. He had slaked his thirst in Pirene: Pallas, goddess of Wisdom, had caught him, bridled him, broken him (for the which meed the Corinthians stamped the figures of the pair on their coinage: the goddess on the obverse, the winged horse on the reverse; with a Koppa, their City's initial letter): that he had saved Helicon for the Muses, and by impact of his hoof, upspringing toward heaven, had released their own fountain Hippocrene—the Horse's Well—to gush perpetually down the mountain-side. So now, if only for a fancy and to help our memory, let us harness up these four scions of Pegasus (*κοππατίοι*) in our minds; three at first—Prophecy, Music, Loneliness; afterwards, in due time, tracing up Blindness—the insight of Blindness—to complete our four-in-hand. This, at any rate, is the team I am attempting to drive through our study of Milton: and since my words must be so far less swift than the charioteer's eye, you will forgive me for directing your notice by dull successions from one to another of the team, when the plunges of their gallop are almost actually—nay to appearance quite actually and vividly—simultaneous.

III

We left Milton in his thirtieth year, on the road to Italy. "It has been remarked," I read, "that Milton's chief enthusiasm in Italy was not art but music." I have not remarked this, and I find no evidence for it unless by "art" we are to understand painting alone. Certainly he is silent, so far as we know, about pictures; and as certainly he attended a concert in the palace of Cardinal Francesco Barberini, at which he heard the famous Leonora Baroni sing. For the rest, the lines which I read you last week from the epistle *To his Father* leave us in no doubt that Milton had made definite choice of Poetry of his first interest. He always, as we say, knew his own mind, and the names of the men with whom he consorted at Florence, in the chief Academies or Literary Clubs, are the names of men of letters. Beyond a doubt (as I hold) he was already determined upon a great Poem, though undecided upon his theme, and whether to build an Epic or a Tragedy. Certainly (as I shall presently show) he was so determined, and still so undecided, a year later.

Understand, pray—Milton revelled in Music, then and until the close of his days. You remember my quoting Masson's words; his father's house, at Horton, as in Bread Street, was always "full of music"—fuller than most houses, I grant you (being the house of an old composer), but not thereby, nor by any means, so sharply different from its neighbours as such a house would be in our own days. I will not say that we have utterly lost the art—the most gentle art—of chamber music. But if you consider the mass of the old music books preserved to us and dating from the late sixteenth and early seventeenth centuries, you will sigh for a delicate domestic joy almost, if not quite, departed. Take up one of the old four-part song books; spread it open upon the table: see how it falls apart, with two scores reading this way and the other two that way. Then call up the picture of your four singers standing up to it after supper—say hostess and daughter, host and guest—or four jolly men laying down tobacco pipes, facing two-and-two, and trolling "There is a Lady sweet and kind," or "Since first I saw your face I resolved to honour and renown ye," or "There was a Frog jumped into a Well," or solemnly—

> The man of life upright
>   Whose guiltless heart is free
> From all dishonest deeds
>   Or thought of vanity . . .

"'Twas merry in hall." Can you not hear it, picture it? the hearty yet mutually corrective pitch and pause of those choristers, who knew one another's foibles so well in their day; the intermittent touch of lute or virginal or *viol de gambo;* the candle-light on the board, the decanters and glasses pushed out of the way of the late-opened book; the lifted chins and those our fore-fathers' beards wagging in rhythm or in fugue

> My true love hath my heart, and I have his,
>   By just exchange one for another given. . . .

Yes, Milton had grown up attuned

> To hear the lute well toucht, or artfull voice
> Warble immortal Notes and *Tuskan* Ayre—

But it is surely with organ-music, rather, that our thoughts instinctively associate him: and this as well through his masterly command of speech, to make it suggest the full range of eloquent sound—from clear flute-note to diapason open and thundering—as because it was, as we know, his favourite instrument, taught him by his father.   You all remember Tennyson's alcaics—

> O mighty mouth'd inventor of harmonies,
> O skill'd to sing of Time or Eternity,
>   God-gifted organ-voice of England,
>   Milton, a name to resound for ages.

But will you listen to some verses far less well known, in which a poet of the last generation imagines the entry of the great organist, Samuel Wesley, into Heaven? And will you, mentally substituting our poet's name for that of Wesley, where it occurs, ask yourselves if we may not, in many a passage of *Paradise Lost* foretaste even so celestial a welcome for John Milton?

> When Wesley died, the Angelic orders,
>   To see him at the state,
> Pressed so incontinent that the warders

Forgot to shut the gate.
So I, that hitherto had followed
　　As one with grief o'ercast,
Where for the doors a space was hollowed,
　　Crept in, and heard what passed.
And God said:—"Seeing thou hast given
　　Thy life to my great sounds,
Choose thou through all the cirque of Heaven
　　What most of bliss redounds."
Then Wesley said:—"I hear the thunder
　　Low growling from Thy seat—
Grant me that I may bind it under
　　The trampling of my feet."
And Wesley said:—"See, lightning quivers
　　Upon the presence walls—
Lord, give me of it four great rivers
　　To be my manuals."
And then I saw the thunder chidden
　　As slave to his desire;
And then I saw the space bestridden
　　With four great bands of fire;
And stage by stage, stop stop subtending,
　　Each lever strong and true,
One shape inextricable blending,
　　The awful organ grew.
Then certain angels clad the Master
　　In very marvellous wise,
Till clouds of rose and alabaster
　　Concealed him from mine eyes.
And likest to a dove soft brooding
　　The innocent figure ran; ˏ
So breathed the breath of his preluding,
　　And then the fugue began—
Began; but, to his office turning,
　　The porter swung his key;
Wherefore, although my heart was yearning,
　　I had to go; but he

Played on; and, as I downward clomb,
I heard the mighty bars
Of thunder-gusts, that shook heaven's dome,
And moved the balanced stars.—*T. E. Brown*.

Now the poem of Milton's which earliest translates his passion for actual organ-music into poetry that really resembles it; not merely confessing the passion as *Il Penseroso* confesses it, in the lines I quoted last week—

There let the pealing Organ blow
To the full voic'd Quire below,
In Service high and Anthems clear
As may, with sweetness, through mine ear
Dissolve me into ecstasies
And bring all Heav'n before mine eyes . . .

but infusing it, as by throbbing pulse of the organ itself, until we feel the instrument and its singer to be one, that its true love hath its heart and it has his, and all (as Browning tells through the mouth of Abt Vogler)—

All through my keys that gave their sounds to a wish of my soul,
All through my soul that praised as its wish flowed visibly forth,
All through music and me:

—that poem is, of course, the short one entitled *At a Solemn Musick;* which I invite you to consider for this reason and for another to which, after reading the lines, I shall presently come. Conjecture assigns them to 1634 or thereabouts—say four years before Milton started on his Italian tour. They probably followed soon upon *Arcades:* for they come next after *Arcades* in the volume of Milton MSS. preserved in the Library of Trinity College here; and the volume contains no fewer than four drafts of this piece, "exhibiting," says Masson, "in perhaps a more extraordinary manner than any other extant specimen of Milton's autograph, his extreme fastidiousness in composition, his habit of altering, correcting, rejecting, erasing and enlarging, till he had brought a piece to some satisfactory perfection of form." But now take the lines themselves—observe how the flute note begins, and how, gradually, the pipes open and swell to their power—

At a Solemn Musick

Blest pair of *Sirens*, pledges of Heav'ns joy,
Sphear-born harmonious Sisters, Voice and Vers,
Wed your divine sounds, and mixt power employ,
Dead things with inbreath'd sense able to pierce,
And to our high-rais'd phantasie present
That undisturbèd Song of pure concent,
Ay sung before the saphire-colour'd throne,
To him that sits thereon,
With Saintly shout and solemn Jubily,
Where the bright Seraphim in burning row
Their loud uplifted Angel trumpets blow,
And the Cherubick host in thousand quires
Touch their immortal Harps of golden wires,
With those just Spirits that wear victorious Palms,
Hymns devout, and holy Psalms
Singing everlastingly;
That we on Earth with undiscording voice
May rightly answer that melodious noise;
As once we did, till disproportion'd sin
Jarr'd against nature's chime, and with harsh din
Broke the fair musick that all creatures made
To their great Lord, whose love their motion sway'd
In perfect Diapason, whilst they stood
In first obedience, and their state of good.
O may we soon again renew that Song,

And keep in tune with Heav'n, till God ere long
To his celestial consort us unite,
To live with him and sing in endless morn of light!

I said that I held, in brief reserve, another reason for quoting these lines. But surely you see it? Surely you perceive that here, four years before his Italian tours; that here and in such lines as these of *Lycidas*—

So *Lycidas* sunk low, but mounted high,
Through the dear might of him that walked the waves ...
And hears the unexpressive nuptiall Song,
In the blest Kingdoms meek of joy and love,
There entertain him all the Saints above,
In solemn troops, and sweet Societies,
That sing, and singing in their glory move,
And wipe the tears for ever from his eyes.

—surely (I say) you perceive that Milton, before his Italian journey, had fairly mastered his style, fairly mastered the organ-music of speech? What occupied him now, as I shall next try to make plain, was architectonic —the *structure* of his great poem, whether in form of Tragedy or of Epic: and what he sought earnestly now, to decide his choice between these two consecrated forms, was a worthy Subject.

IV

But here we must pause for a minute or so, to fetch him back from Italy. From Rome he travelled to Naples, with the intent to cross thence to Sicily, and extend his tour to Greece. At Naples, however, news overtook him of political troubles at home; troubles in Scotland, and civil war in England imminent thereupon, if not inevitable. He turned back. The decision was prompt, but the retreat leisurable. He spent another two months at Rome, a second two months in Florence: made an excursion to Lucca, crossed the Apennines, passed through Bologna and Ferrara to Venice, where again he lingered a month. [Here, by the way, let me interpose that Milton not only acquainted himself with the outward aspect of these cities, but consorted with many of the most distinguished Europeans of that day—

πολλῶν δ' ἀνθρώπων ἴδεν ἄστεα καὶ νόον ἔγνω.]

From Venice, after despatching to England by sea the books he had collected in his wanderings, he proceeded to Verona and Milan; thence, over the Pennine Alps, to Geneva; rested there a week or two; and thence (again through Paris) pushed home for England and Horton, which he reached early in August, 1639, to find all well and rejoicing over his return.

Now actually he arrived close under the fore-cast shadow of an event—the outbreak of the Great Civil War—which was to postpone for another twenty years the grand purpose to which all his youth had been devoted: and he knew the stroke to be overhanging. But there is evidence that Milton behaved as (and it has fallen to our lot in our time to observe it) so many men do under the last fatal hurry of an uncontrollable event. Restlessly, and as though time were now all-important after long indecision, he fell to choosing the Subject of his projected masterpiece, scribbling and covering sheets of paper with lists of possible themes and titles.

V

I spoke casually, just now, of certain Cambridge papers in Milton's autograph. If you will go to Trinity

College Library, you may see with your own eyes even such a paper as I have just mentioned, in Milton's own handwriting—a list of projected Subjects, ninety-nine in all, with notes here and there on their possibilities. They are mainly Biblical Subjects, and the Fall of Man in various forms of presentment has clearly a dominant hold in his mind. But here are some others. *Naboth falsely witnessed against; Elijah bringing the Rain; Hezekiah Beseiged; Herod Massacring,* or *Rachel Weeping, Christus Patiens; Christ Risen; Hardiknute Dying in his Cups; Athelstan Exposing his Brother to the Sea and Repenting; Macbeth*—"beginning at the arrival of Malcolm at Macduff. The matter of Duncan may be expressed by the appearing of his ghost."

Macbeth! Some reasons which explain Milton's design, and even in part excuse his audacity in proposing a theme handled by Shakespeare thirty years before, were discussed in *The Nineteenth Century* for December, 1891, by that most learned scholar Mr. John W. Hales, and you may find the paper reprinted in his volume entitled *Folia Litteraria.* Today, however, we are not concerned with speculation on Milton's *Macbeth.* The point I ask you to note in all these entries—for I propose to say a good deal upon it in my Third Lecture—is that he is indexing all these themes as subjects for *tragedy,* and, where he annotates, is obviously considering them as tragical themes. There is no doubt at all that, at this time—say about 1639—Milton intended his great poem to be a Tragedy, not an Epic.

VI

Soon after his return to England the household at Horton was broken up; his brother and his brother's

wife, with one child, removing to Reading, the aged
father accompanying them. Some little while before
this removal Milton himself had taken lodgings in London, over a tailor's shop in St. Bride's Churchyard,
Fleet Street (some of you may like to know that it stood
on a part of the site of the present *Punch* Office). A
little later, wanting more room for his books, he moved
to a "garden house" in Aldersgate Street. In one or
other of these lodgings he made out the list now in
Trinity Library; and so we see him, waiting on the
Muse, seated alone, in the loneliness of London. Yet
that loneliness was not so complete as he might well
have wished: for besides his brother at Reading (who
later took the Royalist side, in time turned Roman
Catholic under James II, and lived to become Sir Chris-
topher Milton, and a Judge) he had a surviving sister,
Anne, who had married one Edward Phillips of the
Crown office in 1624, had been left a widow in 1631 with
two young sons, had married again, and was now dwelling near Charing Cross. It was considered that the
boys Edward and John might well go to their uncle to
be schooled. The younger, aged nine, boarded with
him: Edward, aged ten, came daily. Now Milton held
strong theories about Education, and subsequently
printed them in a Tract addressed to Master Samuel
Hartlib: but he seems to have enjoyed it in operation
only a little more than his pupils. He could scarcely
have enjoyed it less than they. He was a strong flogger.

VII

So we come back to his loneliness, which now heavily
deepens, and continues to deepen, creeping about him
like a darkness before ever the actual darkness de-

scended. We mistake if we think of Milton as naturally
morose, or as ungentle, ungenial, unsociable, ascetic.
He ate and drank delicately, being fastidious and tem-
perate in all things (until he took to pamphleteering,
and hooked his boarding-irons alongside Salmasius and
other controversialists, when his language became such
as—well, such as we should hardly look for from the
sort of gentleman that Christ's College had called a
lady). But he loved good wine, and the good converse
that befits it—as witness his sonnet.

To Mr. Lawrence

Lawrence, of vertuous Father vertuous Son,
　　Now that the Fields are dank, and ways are mire,
　　Where shall we sometimes meet, and by the fire
Help wast a sullen day; what may be won
From the hard Season gaining: time will run
　　On smoother, till *Favonius* re-inspire
　　The frozen earth; and cloth in fresh attire
The Lillie and the Rose, that neither sow'd nor spun.

What neat repast shall feast us, light and choice,
　　Of Attick tast, with Wine, whence we may rise
To hear the Lute well toucht, or artfull voice
　　Warble immortal Notes and Tuskan Ayre?
He who of these delights can judge, and spare
To interpose them oft, is not unwise.

He had had friends; not many; but two young and dear
ones: of whom one, Edward King, had (as you know)
died early, to live eternally in *Lycidas*. Of the death of
the other, Charles Deodati, he had heard a rumour
abroad, but did not learn the particulars until he reached
England. Deodati was son of an Italian physician

naturalised in London and (one gathers) an old friend and neighbour of the Milton household. The youth had taken his medical degree; and had started in practice in the north of England—near Chester, it is believed. He had been Milton's one confidant, mainly by letter, during the Horton days. He had died in London, little more than four months after Milton's start upon his tour: but no news of this would seem to have reached Milton until he was making back with a heart (as he himself tells us) impatient to rejoin his friend and pour out his soul in talk of Italy—so dear to the one through ancestry, and to the other, now, by knowledge. "Knowst thou that Land? . . ." But not only was Deodati dead: he had died under tragic circumstances to which a few letters and a cluster of burial entries in the registers of St. Anne's, Blackfriars, give some faint clue. The old father, Dr. Theodore Deodati, had married, at sixty-four, a second wife. A step-motherly war had broken out. It drove Philadelphia, a daughter by the first marriage, from the house; and with Charles, newly returned from the north, she took refuge in lodgings; where a fever, or the plague in some form, caught and destroyed them both, in August, 1635, but a few weeks after the wife of an elder brother, also concerned in the quarrel, had died in childbirth.

Everyone knows *Lycidas:* few read the Latin *Epitaphium Damonis* in which Milton commemorated this other friend, Charles Deodati. A good Latinist would, I think, condemn its Latin; which, scorning the unscholarly vulgate and seeming to aspire even to the Virgilian of the Eclogues, can truly be beaten, for Virgilian, by any clever sixth-form boy of our day. I suppose it to be of a seventeenth century quasi-Augustan pattern in Latin composition. I quote a few lines only—

Ite domum impasti; domino jam non vacat, agni.
Pectora cui credam? quis me lenire docebit
Mordaces curas, quis longam fallere noctem
Dulcibus alloquiis, grato cum sibilat igni
Molle pirum, et nucibus strepitat focus, at malus Auster
Miscet cuncta foris, et desuper intonat ulmo?
Ite domum impasti; domino jam non vacat, agni.

But here again I have recourse to Masson's hexameter rendering—

Go unpastured, my lambs: your master now heeds not your bleating.

—that is the refrain—

Whom shall I trust with my thoughts?   Or who will teach me to deaden
Heart-hid pains?   Or who will cheat away the long evening
Sweetly with chat by the fire, where hissing hot on the ashes
Roasts the ripe pear, and the chestnuts crackle beneath, while the South-Wind
Hurls confusion without, and thunders down on the elm-tops?

There is nothing, of course, in the *Epitaphium* comparable with the grace of *Lycidas:* and yet the Latin, helped by its refrain (though that he borrowed from the Eclogues), has a sob in it which somehow is not felt in *Lycidas:* a στοργή of friendship which *Lycidas* in its perfection either misses or—more likely—classically avoids.

So, at thirty-one, Milton had lost his only two coæval and intimate friends, and both shockingly.   And so he comes to the edge of the year 1640—the year of the Long Parliament—which, as I suppose, through politics,

tore across the personal affections of Englishmen a rent
more fatal than England had known before or has
known since. Whatever else Civil War may mean (and
I pray, not idly, that none of us may live to learn), it
must mean that you feel a possible half of your fellow-
countrymen to be your direct enemies, hot and em-
bittered: that for social amenity you substitute hatred
toward that possible half; and worse—that you live in
guardful suspicion; that, of any man you meet on the
public thoroughfare you know not, though he smile, if
he be a friend, or conceal a dagger under his clock.
Every day increases suspicion, and all suspicion isolates.

The Civil War broke out; and on top of its outbreak
Milton took a step which intensified the misery of isolation at least tenfold: for you cannot marry a wife for
comfort and be left by her with no worse loss than lack
of the comfort you sought. Everyone knows the story
of poor Mary Powell; perhaps because no one has quite
solved the mystery of it. The War had broken out in
1642. About Whitsuntide, 1643, Milton made a sudden dash into leafy Oxfordshire, and returned to Aldersgate with a bride of seventeen, he being then thirty-five.
As his nephew Phillips put it, "he took a journey into
the country, nobody about him certainly knowing the
reason, or that it was any more than a journey of recre-
ation: but home he returns a married man, that went
forth a bachelor." Considered merely as a raid, or (to
borrow one of his own phrases) a "brief model" of marriage by capture, this might pass for an exploit, the more
gallant because he had taken his spoil in the very heart
of the enemy's camp—Mary's father being a Royalist
Oxfordshire squire, with an old estate, a mansion, "a
carriage and what not" (Masson) and a considerable
quantity of debts. Research, I regret to say, has dis-

covered that among these was one of £500 to Mr. John Milton; and if this at all explains the mystery—if the poor girl went for better or worse in discharge or in consideration of that debt—why then silence is best.

But of marriage, even though it be effected by capture, the delicate problem of translating passion into companionship remains invariable. Of Milton we are told that "though keenly alive to the subtle charm of a woman's personality, [he] was unpractised in the arts of daily companionship. He had an ideal. . . . One of his complaints was that his wife was mute and insensate, and sat silent at his board." But later, of another wife, this exacting man complained because she *wouldn't* sit silent. She sang: and, as he remarked, "she had a good voice, but no ear." So, we may conjecture, when the third Mrs. Milton tuned her nocturnal note, her lord sat darkling or in shadiest covert hid. "It must"—I resume the quotation from Mr. Birrell—"have been deadly dull, that house in Aldersgate Street. Silence reigned, save when broken by the cries of the younger Phillips sustaining chastisement."

After a month she left him. In the violence of his indignation he penned his famous tract—*The Doctrine and Discipline of Divorce restored to the good of both sexes;* and this doctrine being abhorrent to friends and foes alike, he lived for two years the loneliest man, perhaps, in London. Then his wife came back, knelt at his feet and was forgiven—nobly, generously forgiven—and very soon his roof was sheltering the whole family of Powells, ruined in the King's cause. Mary died in childbed, in 1652.

Had he any friends—friends in the true sense—during the years that followed? Yes, certainly Andrew Marvell, his assistant in the Latin Secretaryship, was one. Both were essentially men of high thought, and men of style. As Mr. Asquith reminded the English Association the other day, men of style abounded in that seventeenth century, but Marvell was remarkable among them. As I shall show later, a like problem in poetry occupied the minds of both, and both were experimenting upon it. And Milton had recommended Marvell for his post. Yes, Wordsworth is right: Marvell was one of those who "called Milton friend."

VIII

But how came Milton on the 21st of February, 1653, to ask that Mr. Andrew Marvell might be appointed to assist him?

Because he himself was by this time blind.

Blindness—total blindness: and upon that, in 1660, loss of place, exile, persecution, hiding. . . . Think of it all!

Ah, but what of the great work that we saw him—so long ago and after so long a preparation—on the eve of writing? Almost twenty years have passed: Milton has now turned fifty: and not a line of it is written. "Is that also lost, then?"—Since for a man conscious of power, dedicated to use it so as ever in his "great task Master's eye," to be robbed of his work, or to know *that* lost through default, is a worse hell than blindness. Then is that also lost?

No: for see! This man—sans light, sans friends, sans hope, sans everything: this man—

> though fall'n on evil dayes
> On evil dayes though fall'n, and evil tongues,
> In darkness, and with dangers compast round,
> And solitude—

this indomitable man seats himself in his shabby leath-
ern chair as in a throne, throws a leg over its arm in the
old negligent boyish attitude, and begins to speak our
great English epic.

MILTON (III)

I

IN his pamphlet entitled *The Reason of Church Government*, published in 1641 (that is, when he was nearing 33), Milton avows to the world that he has for some time been minded by encouragement of his friends, "and not less by an inward prompting which now grew daily upon me, that by labour and intense study (which I take to be my portion in this life) joined with the strong propensity of nature, I might perhaps leave something to aftertimes as they should not willingly let it die. These thoughts at once possessed me and these other: that if I were certain to write, as men buy leases, for three lives and downward, there ought no regard be sooner had than to God's glory by the honour and instruction of my country." He dwells upon the patriotic motive: he intends not hardly "to arrive at the second rank among the Latins" but

to fix all the industry and art I could unite to the adorning of my native tongue. . . to be an interpreter and relater of the best and sagest things among mine own citizens throughout this Island in the mother-dialect; that what the greatest and choicest wits of Athens, Rome, or modern Italy, and those Hebrews of old, did for *their* country, I, in my proportion, with this over and above of being a Christian, might do for mine; not caring to be once named abroad, though perhaps I could attain to that, but content with these British Islands as my world, whose fortune hath hitherto been that, if the Athenians, as some say, made their small deeds great and renowned by their eloquent writers, England hath had *her* noble achievements made small by the unskilful handling of monks and mechanicks.

He goes on to say that he has been dubious in what form to shape his grand theme—whether in Epic or Tragedy or Lyric. I ask your forgiveness for extracting a few sentences only from a passage which Milton himself makes apology for having condensed.

"Time serves not now," he says, "and perhaps I might seem too profuse, to give any certain account of what the mind, at home in the spacious circuits of her musings, hath liberty to propose to herself through highest hope and hardest attempting; whether the *Epick* form whereof the two poems of Homer, and those other two of Virgil and Tasso are a diffuse, and the Book of Job a brief model. . . . Or whether those *Dramatick* Constitutions, wherein Sophocles and Euripides reign, shall be found more doctrinal and exemplary to a nation. . . . Or if occasion shall lead to imitate those magnific *Odes* and *Hymns* wherein Pindarus and Callimachus are in most things worthy, some others in their frame judicious, in their matter most and end faulty; but those frequent Songs throughout the Law and The Prophets beyond all these, not in their divine argument alone, but in the very critical art of composition, may be easily made appear over all the kinds of *Lyrick* Poetry to be incomparable."

II

Thus Milton reports himself to be hesitating whether to choose Epic, Tragedy or Lyric for his form. But the MS. in Trinity College Library (written about this time or a little earlier) tells us that, for the form, he had actually chosen Tragedy; and that for his subject, *The Fall of Man* had laid compelling hold on him, superseding the theme of *King Arthur*, which, as his Latin poem *Manso* and the *Epitaphium Damonis* plainly tell, had engaged his thought during his Italian tour. *Paradise Lost* not only heads the list in the Trinity MS., it is thrice repeated: and each time a draft of the dramatic scheme follows the title. The first is brief; it runs——

The Persons: Michael; Heavenly Love; Chorus of Angels; Lucifer; Adam, Eve with the Serpent; Conscience; Death, Labour, Sickness, Discontent, Ignorance, with others, Mutes, Faith; Hope; Charity.

He scores this out and writes another parallel with it.

The Persons: Moses [Michael or Moses was first set down then Michael deleted]; Justice, Mercy, Wisdom; Heavenly Love; the Evening Star, Hesperus; Lucifer; Adam; Eve; Conscience; Labour, Sickness, Discontent, Ignorance, Fear, Death, Mutes; Faith, Hope, Charity.

This again is scored out, and a third draft follows, almost a *scenario*:

Paradise Lost: The Persons: Moses prologises, recounting how he assumed his true body; that it corrupts not because of his [having been] with God in the Mount: declares the like of Enoch and Eliah, besides the purity of the [place] that certain pure winds, dews and clouds preserve it from corruption; whence [ex]horts to the sight of God; tells they cannot see Adam in the state of innocence by reason of their sin.—(Act 1) Justice, Mercy, Wisdom, debating what should become of Man if he fall. Chorus of Angels sing a Hymn of the Creation.—(Act 2) Heavenly Love; Evening Star;

Chorus sing the Marriage Song and describe Paradise.—
(Act 3) Lucifer contriving Adam's ruin. Chorus fears for
Adam, and relates Lucifer's rebellion and fall.—(Act 4)
Adam, Eve, fallen; Conscience cites them to God's exami-
nation. Chorus bewails and tells the good Adam hath lost.
—(Act 5) Adam and Eve, driven out of Paradise, presented
by an Angel with Labour, Grief, Hatred, Envy, War,
Famine, Pestilence, Sickness, Discontent, Ignorance, Fear,
Death entered into the world: mutes to whom he gives their
names, likewise Winter, Heat, Tempest etc.; Faith, Hope,
Charity comfort him and instruct him.

Chorus briefly concludes.

This draft—in which, as you perceive, each Act ends
on grand chorus—is left standing. Later, we come on
a fourth and yet more elaborate one, with the Acts simi-
larly ending in choruses. To read it through would take
more time than we can spare here. It does little beyond elaborating or altering details, and it concludes
"Compare this with the former Draft."

III

Having now established that Milton first cast *Paradise Lost* in the form of a Tragedy, I shall this morning ask you to examine it with me upon three
points:

(1) The first: What persuaded him to alter his mind
and make an Epic? This, being capable of a personal
and adventitious answer, will be found (I foresee)
comparatively unimportant.

(2) The second—and for us, as students of literature
touching the heart of the argument: How did that
change of form affect the poem? this again raising the
question, Is the Epic form alive today or effete?

(3) The third—which I shall postpone to another

hour: How far has *Paradise Lost* triumphed over omens apparently against it, and by what sleight or skill?

First, then, for the reasons that persuaded Milton to turn his planned Tragedy to Epic.

I think I can convince you that he did so unwillingly. To begin with, he had his Aristotle's *Poetics* by heart, and believed in the scheme of old Greek tragedy as the only true pattern. For not only have we the drafts in the Trinity MS. all scaled to this pattern: not only have we the prejudice implicit, yet earlier, in a significant grudging parenthesis in *Il Penseroso*.

> Som time let Gorgeous Tragedy
> In Scepter'd Pall com sweeping by,
> Presenting *Thebs*, or *Pelops* line,
> Or the tale of *Troy* divine;
> Or what (though rare) of later age
> Ennobled hath the Buskind Stage.

We have it—after more than thirty years—exhibited in practice by *Samson Agonistes*, and in theory confirmed by the preface to that drama. A quotation from Aristotle's famous definition of Tragedy underscores the title of Samson[1]; and the preface, after premising that, of the plot "they only will best judge who are not unacquainted with Aeschylus, Sophocles and Euripides, the three tragic poets unequalled yet by any, and the best rule to all who endeavour to write Tragedy," goes on boldly to accept as a precept that Unity of Time which can with difficulty be read into a casual observation which Aristotle certainly never meant to be a rule.[2] "The circumscription of time,"

---

[1] Samson, we may note, is twice entered on the Trinity list of projected dramas.

[2] *Poetics*, c. 5, ἡ μὲν ὅτι μάλιστα πειρᾶται ὑπὸ μίαν περίοδον ἡλίου εἶναι ἢ

adds Milton, "wherein the whole drama begins and ends, is, according to ancient rule and best example within the space of twenty-four hours."

We have here, then, an Aristotelian "more loyal than the king": and those of you, Gentlemen, who have done me the pleasure to read the *Poetics* through with me in private class, remembering the comparison between Epic and Tragedy with which that treatise (as we have it) concludes, will not doubt that Milton consented with Aristotle in preferring Tragedy as the higher of the two great serious forms of verse.[1]

"But what does it matter?" you may ask, adding, "Surely Milton never designed these dramas for actual presentation on the stage?"

My retort is that he certainly did; and that therefore it matters a great deal.

For consider. In the first place, two of his earlier compositions, dramatic in form, had already been staged and acted—*Arcades*, in 1633 (?), as "part of an Entertainment presented to the Countess Dowager of Derby at Harefield by some Noble Persons of her Family,"

μικρὸν ἐξαλλάττειν = "Tragedy endeavours to keep as nearly as possible within one circuit of the sun or something near that." Aristotle lays down no law here, but is merely (as Bywater puts it) dealing with the practice of the theatre in his time.

[1] Here is the passage. I use Bywater's translation, altering it only when, towards the end, I come to the words καὶ ἔτι τῷ τῆς τέχνης ἐργῳ, which "in its poetic effect" seems to me to render too vaguely. "In the operation of its art" is quite literal and surely gets nearer to the meaning. Aristotle had disposed of an objection against Tragedy—that it is liable to be vulgarised by its actors—by answering that the value of a drama does not depend upon its casual interpreters: that any movement, however noble in intent, will be degraded if you entrust it to a cad; and that anyhow, the quality of a play persists into our reading of it and can be vindicated by our reading.

Bywater renders: "In the second place one must remember (1) that

and *Comus* on Michaelmas Night, 1634, as a masque at
Ludlow Castle before the Earl of Bridgewater, son-in-
law of the aforesaid Countess of Derby, and then Lord
President of Wales: the parts of the Two Brothers being
taken by two of his sons, Lord Brackley and young
Mr. Thomas Egerton, that of the lady by his fourteen-
year-old daughter, Lady Alice Egerton, whose pure
girlish voice, acknowledged to have been exquisite, we
can, with a little imagination, hear singing Lawes' music
(Lawes himself enacted the Attendant Spirit) in the
lovely Echo song:

> Sweet Echo, sweetest Nymph that liv'st unseen
>   Within thy airy shell
> By slow *Meander's* margent green,
> And in the violet imbroider'd vale
> Where the love-lorn nightingale
> Nightly to thee her sad Song mourneth well;
> Canst thou not tell me of a gentle Pair
> That likest thy *Narcissus* are?
>   O if thou have
> Hid them in some flowry cave,
>   Tell me but where,

Tragedy has everything that Epic has (even the Epic metre being
admissible), together with a not inconsiderable addition in the shape
of the Music (a very real factor in the pleasure of the drama) and the
spectacle. (2) That its reality of presentation is felt in the play as
read, as well as in the play as acted. (3) That the tragic imitation
requires less space for the attainment of its end; which is a great advantage, since the more concentrated effort is more pleasurable than one
with a large admixture of time to dilute it.—Consider the Œdipus of
Sophocles, for instance, and the effect of expanding it into the number of
lines of the *Iliad*. (4) That there is less unity in the imitation of the
epic poets, as is proved by the fact that any one work of thesis supplies
material for several tragedies. . . . If, then, Tragedy is superior in these
respects, *and over and beside these in the operation of its art (since the object
of each is to produce no chance pleasure but its own particular one), it is
clear that Tragedy excels in Epic by better achieving its end.*"

> Sweet Queen of Parly, daughter of the Sphear,
> So maist thou be translated to the skies,
> And give resounding grace to all Heav'ns Harmonies!

—"strains" says the listening Thyrsis

>   that might create a soul
> Under the ribs of Death.

May we not on the slope of Ludlow listen and so hear
it recreated, poured out from the heart of little Lady
Alice, long since dust?—and ponder with William
Barnes——

> The zummer aïr o' theäse green hill
> 'V a-heav'd in bosoms now all still,
> An' all their hopes an' all their tears
> Be unknown things ov other years.

But, to resume:—Milton had written two dramatic
pieces; both of which had been acted, and acceptably.

IV

Now you may urge that it is a far cry from a masque
such as *Comus* (even when we have allowed that *Comus*
differed from other masques of its time, and differed
successfully) to a set drama presenting, on a classical
model, Heaven and Hell, with the story of Adam's fall.
Then next I pray you remember: first, that the masque,
just then, was superseding the kind of play we sum-
marise in our minds as Elizabethan: that the Elizabethan or (if you will) the Shakespearean type had
pretty well worn itself threadbare in the hands of
Tourneur, Shirley, and far worse practitioners: that a
new form was wanted; and that if the new form at-

tempted to present even Heaven and Hell, the masque, which quite commonly coped with Olympus and all its gods, magniloquent in speech and floating in movement, had—with a little daring—the whole theatrical apparatus ready to hand.

Further, will you remind yourselves that Milton in 1640 was scarcely fifty years removed from the old morality play, and by only a little more from the miracle play? To think of harking back and taking a fresh start from these may seem absurd enough to us, who live almost three hundred years later. But let us put ourselves back in his time, and suppose ourselves debating how to replace an outworn dramatic convention with something at once different and yet faithful to artistic tradition. Supposing this, will you deem it an extravagant conjecture that Milton's mind seriously harked back over a short half-century? Does it even strike you,—reminding yourselves how much more diffident of itself English literature was then than it is now, how much humbler before the authority of the classics—as a hope only possible of occurrence to a thoroughly impracticable mind? Well then, even so, let us recall our knowledge of the man; that he had lived a dedicated and self-cloistered life, that he was always a somewhat impracticable fellow, proud and more than conscious of his powers; that he came to the drama as a mere scholar, without any of the apprenticeship through which, day in and day out, the easy natured Shakespeare, always willing to learn, had learned to beat the University wits and even Ben Jonson, at their own game; that he was so signally throughout life a *sic volo sic jubeo* fellow, and that he had already two amateur successes in the classical style to encourage him. Recollecting all this, can we, with positive evidence before us of his having planned *Paradise Lost* as a drama, pronounce it inconceivable, or even less than probable, that Milton meant to achieve on the actual stage something of the sort that Handel afterwards achieved in oratorio?

V

Then why did he change his mind?

I give you the answer to that in a dozen words. *In 1642 Parliament closed the Theatres; which remained shut until the Restoration.*

A Puritanical religion—that is, a religion which, hating art of all kinds that solace life and preluding with a fast, assures an infernal hereafter upon decent merry folk here who crave no future bliss if it involve a bigot's company—strikes first upon the theatre as inevitably as it will continue, if successful, to bludgeon anything and everything calculated to make glad the heart of man.

As it had been under the fathers of the Church from Tertullian to Augustine, so it happened again when Milton was a young man. "The unlawfulness of dramatic entertainments," says Masson, "had always been a tenet of those stricter English Puritans with whom Milton even then felt a political sympathy";' and Prynne's famous *Histriomastix*, in which he denounced stage-plays and all connected with them through a thousand quarto pages (1632), had helped confirm Puritanism in this tenet.

Say that Milton remained true to his belief in the drama. From the 2nd of September, 1642, when the Long Parliament passed its ordinance suppressing stage-plays, down to the very eve of the Restoration— that is, for close upon eighteen years—his dream of re-

creating our national drama had come to naught and
remained at naught, for the simple reason that the door
of every theatre stood closed and locked by law.
Therefore, I say, Milton turned from Tragedy to Epic.
Years after—in 1667 or thereabouts—when those doors
had been reopened as sluices to admit the mud and
garbage of Restoration Drama, the old man gallantly
assigned himself to his old task and wrote *Samson
Agonistes*; not *Samson Pursophorus* ("Samson the
Firebrand-bringer") as projected in the old Trinity
list, but Samson the Champion in bonds; blinded,
broken by the Philistines, even as the poet himself was
broken and blind; groping until his arms feel about the
twin pillars; and so, with heel planted on defeat, drawing them in until the walls bend, yield, crack; and still
the great muscles swell closer and closer embracing
their last triumph, only to relax under the downrush
of death.

VI

Yes: I shall have a word or two to say on *Samson
Agonistes*. But meantime we have *Paradise Lost*, a
tragedy turned into epic. Here, for a specimen, we
have, inserted in Book IV, the ten lines which Milton
had once shown to his nephew Edward Phillips "as
designed for the very beginning of the said tragedy"—
the lines in which Satan, first setting foot on earth,
addresses the Sun, "high in his meridian tower," fell
blazing over Eden.—

> O thou that with surpassing Glory crownd,
> Look'st from thy sole Dominion like the God
> Of this new World; at whose sight all the Starrs
> Hide their diminisht heads; to thee I call,
> But with no friendly voice, and add thy name,

O Sun, to tell thee how I hate thy beams,
That bring to my remembrance from what state
I fell, how glorious once above thy Spheare,
Till Pride and worse Ambition threw me down,
Warring in Heav'n against Heav'ns matchless King.

So we come to the question, What effect had Milton's change of design upon *Paradise Lost*, for good or evil? And with that question we touch the heart of the argument by which for seven years now, from this desk, I have tried and proved your powers of endurance. In season, and often (I fear me) out of season, still my plea has been that *we cannot separate art, and specially the literary art, from life—from daily life—even from this passing hour—and get the best out of either.*

Gentlemen, let us forbear to think of ourselves for a moment, since fortune has been kind to us, and given us—to each in his degree—some sense of literature and of the joy to be derived from it. Because we have that sense and prize it, and would increase it by whatever unlikely means, we are all met in this place today. There is no other excuse for us.

Let us think, rather of the millions in this country who awake, arise, go to their labour, eat, drink, and sleep again, without ever a notion of the sustenance, the solace, the spiritual food of life laid up for them in books: of the free granaries to which they might help themselves with both hands and yet never diminish our store by a fraction.

Well now, I do not invite you to grieve over things which, because they happened in the past, cannot be altered. Yet, I put it to you, there is much cause for regret that our literature, which took its origin in the proud scholarship of the Renaissance, has ever tended to be so aristocratic, to be written for the elect. That

it needed not to be so written, that the noblest literature of which our language is capable can be addressed
to a mixed audience in church or in theatre, or to a
public conceived in the author's mind as an audience of
common men, has been proved by the translations of our
Authorised Version of the Bible, proved by Shakespeare, proved by Bunyan, by Burns, by Dickens; yes,
and I will dare to say by Burke and by Shelley—for it
has been observed by me that many a man of humble
education catches fire from Burke or from Shelley long
before he can taste the last felicities of either.

You may wonder that I include Shelley. I include
him for this reason: that, of all the Romantics, the "ineffectual" Shelley abides today as the strongest living
influence: and if you ask me how this should be, I
answer that I cannot certainly tell, but very likely it is
because Shelley had so penetrating a conception of a
poet's duties to his generation that he stumped the
country with them after Peterloo: and if we choose to
smile at this as a ridiculous performance, I hope we
shall only do so after making very sure of our own sense
of humour. I hold it at least arguable that as a nation
we should have profited enormously by giving Shelley
audience in the days of Castlereagh and Sidmouth and
Eldon, and coming to an understanding at the time,
instead of closing the vent by persecution and waiting
until the ferment blew out the end of the cask; which is
our plight today. But I ask any of you (for this is the
point) if the matter of Shelley, which, ethereal or no,
was vital to its age, does not concern us more intimately
today than the matter of *Paradise Lost*: if, as affecting
us and in comparison with *Prometheus Unbound*, our
great national Epic—adorable always for its music, its
superb virtuosity—be worth very much for what it tells.

If you deem the above illustration too controversial, let me use a more harmless one. Go, if you will, next spring to the rotunda of sculpture in the Royal Academy: spend a quiet half-hour in contemplating the exhibits, and interrogate your soul. "Why are these things such things, and why are they here?" They are there mainly because nobody wants them anywhere else. The bust of the present keeper of the King's Conscience will, as likely as not, be there, because we have no temple just yet (as we ought to have) to enshrine our King's Conscience: because it is the "thing to do" to make a bust of the Lord Chancellor; and into what place of worship we consign it hereafter no man cares. So scores of painters are there exhibiting landscapes that record the pastoral beauty of this fairest of lands on the chance that some rich man may take a fancy to buy one, carry it off, and hang it somewhere on a nail. So is it again with a great number of the portraits. You know what happens. We say to one another, "So-and-so is getting up in years. Is it not about time we subscribed to present him with his painting in oils, in recognition of his long public service?" Then we grumble and subscribe; or, if he be dead, we may perchance reward him with a statue in the public gardens, where his back aspect may hit a nice graduation betweeen the bandstand and the English Channel; or his front surprise us against a shrubbery approached by a winding path.

VII

The moral of this is, that you may have great artists, great poets, great painters and sculptors: but you will never have a great era of art; you will never have the excellent joys of painting, sculpture, music, poetry "in

widest commonalty spread"; as you will ever keep your
man of genius constricted and tortured; so long as you
treat him as a freak, as a pet, as anything but an honest
workman supplying a social demand. If he be a high
master, he will yet be proud, as every high master deserves to be. God himself cannot make the best violins
save by employing Stradivarius. Let me quote here a
passage written the other day by Mr. Charles Marriott
on the art of a great modern sculptor, Rodin. He says,
and most truly—

Because he was a great artist, Rodin suffered in an
exaggerated form the disadvantage suffered by every artist
since the Middle Ages. He is cut off from his base. In a
sense it would be true to say that the disadvantage began
when "artist" came to mean anything but a supremely
gifted workman. Lack of general recognition is a symptom
rather than a cause of it. The great artist must always
work in moral and intellectual isolation, and it does not hurt
him to do so any more than it hurts the saint. What
hurts him, what hurt Rodin, and what the artist of the
Middle Ages never knew, is material isolation; to live and
work without some definite relation to the everyday lives of
his fellow creatures. The pecuniary relation, however
satisfactory in itself, is not enough. Even when it takes
the form of an important public commission, it suffers from
exactly the same disadvantage as "diplomatic relations."
It does not represent the unconscious will of the people. As
for the relation established by what is called "intelligent
appreciation," it might be said fairly that there is nothing worse for an artist. Unless he is inhumanly arrogant
it makes him an opportunist. One had only to see the
sidelong glance of the great old man, as he exposed a piece
to some cultured visitor, to recognise how eagerly he
waited upon suggestion.

If those words be true—as I believe them to be true

—do they not shed a most illuminating ray into our great Epic? There was a time in England when England demanded a theatre and London crossed over from the stairs to Southwark to behold it. Of that common demand was begotten a Shakespeare to satisfy it. Shakespeare was an artist working to be equal (and more, but first equal) to a vivid demand, as Burke afterwards wrought to be equal to an audience which he could visualise as the British Senate and address with a consciousness that every word spoken there carried sonorous echoes upon material weight. But with Milton we have a man, in Mr. Marriott's words, "cut off from his base." He would reform the theatre, and behold! of a sudden there was no theatre to reform.

VIII

I have been at pains, trying to be fair, to heap every circumstance of Milton's circumstantial loneliness upon you. Yet here, I assert, lies the secret of the solitude in which we feel ourselves—so to say—marooned as we meditate the wonderful poem, and listen to that exquisite music—as it were

> Breaking the silence of the seas
> Among the farthest Hebrides.

I challenge you, at any rate, to deny that when we listen to Shakespeare, even at his greatest, it is always to a fellow speaker intimate and winning, sure of an affectionate ear: that on the contrary, when we read *Paradise Lost* we feel no such genial fellowship: we yield rather to the wand in the grasp of a high compelling master. Nay, I am sure that most of you will concede this: and still, the point being so important, I ask your leave to stress it with help of a few admirable sentences printed anonymously, ten years ago, in the *Times Literary Supplement*.

A fit comparison with the state of mind induced by reading Milton's poetry may be found in one of the paintings on the ceiling of the Sistine Chapel—*the Creation of Adam*. Like Michaelangelo's Adam we have been touched to life by an immortal finger, and wake to find ourselves on the dizzy edge of a mountain: like the figure that shelters under the arm of the Most High, we are caught up and whirled by an irresistible power. The predominant feeling is one of awe. We are mastered by something so great that we cannot question, and think of complaint almost as of blasphemy. Our admiration is not asked, our adherence is not claimed; both are imposed upon us by a purpose too strong for common humanity to resist. We have not been appealed to by a friend; we have been commanded by a master.

Now I repeat my protest that in my two previous lectures nothing was blinked of the share which Milton's individual character—with its "honest haughtiness and self-esteem" as he himself puts it—with, as we may add, its intellectual purity, its obstinacy, its lofty arrogance—contributed to produce that effect. But that this does not wholly account for it, and possibly accounts for less than one-half, we may convince ourselves in a minute by taking almost any passage from Shakespeare, almost any passage from Milton, and setting them side by side. Listen first to Cordelia, comforting old Lear—

> O my dear father! Restoration hang
> Thy medicine on my lips: and let this kiss
> Repair those violent harms that my two sisters
> Have in thy reverence made! . . .
> Had you not been their father, these white flakes

Had challenged pity of them.   Was this a face
To be opposed against the warring winds?
To stand against the deep dread-bolted thunder?
In the most terrible and nimble stroke
Of quick, cross lightning? to watch—poor perdu!—
With this thin helm?   Mine enemy's dog,
Though he had bit me, should have stood that night
Against my fire.

Now hear Michael to Adam—

"So maist thou live, till like ripe Fruit thou drop
Into thy Mother's lap, or be with ease
Gatherd, not harshly pluckt, for death mature:
This is old age; but then thou must outlive
Thy youth, thy strength, thy beauty, which will change
To withered weak and gray; thy Senses then
Obtuse, all taste of pleasure must forgoe
To what thou hast; and, for the Aire of youth
Hopeful and cheerful, in thy blood will reigne
A melancholly damp of cold and dry
To waigh thy spirits down and last consume
The Balme of Life."
                              To whom our Ancestor:
"Henceforth I flie not Death, nor would prolong
Life much, bent rather how I may be quit
Fairest and easiest of this combrous charge,
Which I must keep till my appointed day
Of rendring up, and patiently attend
My dissolution."
                              Michael replied:
"Nor love thy Life, nor hate; but what thou livst
Live well: how long or short permit to Heav'n."

Solemn, most noble lines, and altogether majestic!
Yet at once we note how much more vividly—and
poignantly, because vividly—Cordelia speaks. And

next we note that the difference is not only difference between Shakespeare and Milton; that much of it lies in *the form of Art chosen*: that Cordelia speaks vividly because that form compels us to see every accessory gesture, to witness the kiss, to watch her fingers as they lift Lear's white locks, as they piteously trace the furrows down the worn cheek, pause when a criss-cross suggest the cross double cut of lightning, stray back to the thin helm, recoil to clench themselves in the cry—

> Mine enemy's dog,
> Though he had bit me, should have stood that night
> Against my fire.

Lastly we see how the form of the art, being so much more vivid; and the subject being so much more human and intense upon the human heart; force the speech to utter those strange unexpected, yet most befitting words—"Alas, poor perdu!"—force Cordelia to seek back and snatch, as it were out of girlhood, out of lost days of kindness, familiar tender images to coo them over that great head brought low

MILTON (IV)

I

WHEN Aristotle—worshipping Homer yet not overawed by Homer's authority—declared, in the last chapter of the *Poetics*, for Tragedy as a higher art on the whole than Epic, he had much to back his daring. Tragedy, even as Epic, dealt with gods, demigods, a few ancient and royal houses. Its human characters all owned something of divine descent and were by consequence exalted in dignity and passion as, circumstantially, by the spectacle of their deeds and downfalls. Tragedy, moreover, came straight out of religious observance and worked upon higher solemnities than Epic, which was a strain sung to the feast in a chieftain's hall, convivial rather than ceremonial; of the dais and the high table. Tragedy moved still around an altar. Yet even Aristotle, in his day, has to start with a defence against those who prefer Epic on the ground that it appeals to a more refined audience; their objection being to the intrusion of actors with their capers and gestures, intended to help out the meaning for common wits. Aristotle's answer amounts to this; that, if it be bad, we must curse the histrions and attach the blame neither upon the tragic writer nor upon the tragic form. And the answer is all very well and sufficient, so far as it goes. But there were two things Aristotle could not possibly foresee. The first was the social degradation of the theatre. I pass its spectacular decline in Rome, its fatal loss there of all religious and ancestral honour, its not unprovoked persecution by the Fathers of the Church, its exile from society for a thousand years. But I ask you to note that when at length the hussy returned to take men's hearts by storm again, she came back a vagrant, in tawdry finery soiled with her discreditable past. The practitioners of drama were still, by legal definition, "vagabonds" and liable to whipping; it offered in a furtive way allurements that no effrontery could pass off as religious; it trafficked neither with gods nor with demigods, but in human passions; it commanded neither temple nor municipal stage and chorus; it put up for the day in inn-courtyards, or found lodging among the disorderly houses of the Bankside, itself scarcely less disorderly. Not even a Shakespeare could efface the stigma of its old trade, or quite exempt even a *Hamlet* or a *Lear* from association in men's minds with cat-calls, nuts and oranges.

Aristotle could as little foresee all this as he could foresee that Epic, continuing respectable under tradition, keeping its proud trailing robe aloof from contact with the skirt of its royal sister turned drab, would increase in estimation by her decrease. But so it happened. Dryden (though himself a prolific writer of drama and critic enough to beware of touching the *Poetics* otherwise than gingerly) has to write—"The most perfect work of Poetry, says our master Aristotle, is Tragedy. . . . But . . . an heroick poem is certainly the greatest work of human nature." And to the first *édition de luxe* of *Paradise Lost* (published in

1688) he contributed the famous "pinchbeck epigram"
—as Mark Pattison calls it—

> Three Poets, in three distant Ages born . . . etc.

—in which the Epic poet is assumed to stand above all
others.

Again, in Addison's famous pages which he devoted
to criticising *Paradise Lost* you will find it tacitly assumed that Epic is the highest form of poetry.   When
we reach Dr. Johnson—who comes to *Paradise Lost*, not
only with no disposition to do it justice, but even with
hands by no means clean[1], we find him admitting
hardily that—

> By the general consent of criticks the first praise of genius
> is due to the writer of an epick poem, as it requires an
> assemblage of all the powers which are singly sufficient for
> other compositions.

In short—and partly no doubt through the success of
Paradise Lost—it became the tradition of the penniless
literary aspirant to set out for London (as Crabbe did)
with an Epic in his pocket.   What he found there was
not a public who needed him, but, with luck, a patron
who patronised him because in that age the rôle of
Mæcenas consorted with a British nobleman's ideal
construction of himself.   Yet there is evidence in
plenty that the great man's languid demand for Epic
Poetry (*with* a Dedication) not seldom turned into a
brisk defensive movement against the number of
clients ready to supply it: and if you study the "poetical remains" of the eighteenth century preserved for

---

[1] The great doctor could be very loud upon morals.   Johnson's share
in a conspiracy with the Scotch forger Lauder to blacken Milton as a
thief and a plagiarist has never to this hour been explained away.

us in volume after volume of Chalmers's monumental
collection, I doubt not your exclaiming, "Small blame
to him!" or of your sympathising with Horace Walpole
—an eminent victim long before he became fourth Earl
of Orford—who, suffering from gout in addition, calls
out upon Epic as "that most senseless of all the species
of poetic composition, and which"—his testiness, you
perceive penetrating to the relative clause—"and which
pedants call the *chef d'œuvre* of the human mind. . . .
When nothing has been impossible to genius in every
other walk, why has everybody failed in this but the
inventor, Homer? . . . Milton, all imagination, and
a thousand times more sublime and spirited [than even
Virgil], has produced a monster."

II

Although Aristotle had but one great Epic poet,
Homer, from whom to generalise, while he had a number of great exemplars in tragic writing and ranges
among them liberally for his precepts and illustrations;
and although Homer had lived so long ago, even in
Aristotle's time, and still there was no promise of any
true successor; let us not pertly blame the great man
for not divining and prophesying what time has made
so plain to *us*—that a great epic poem is the rarest of
all human achievements; that a literature and a language are blessed indeed and inexpressibly promoted
among languages, among literatures, if they possess but
one grand Epic Poet. Where is the literature—which
speaks, or has ever spoken a language—owning more
than one Epic poet unmistakably of the first rank?

Here let me in parenthesis, Gentlemen, stress that
word "unmistakably." A deal of stupid moralising
has been written at one time and another around the

fact that Milton in his lifetime received but ten pounds in money, and his widow but eight additional pounds, for the copyright of *Paradise Lost*. Let none of it get in our way between us and the equal certainty that *Paradise Lost*, published in 1667 (the year after the Great Fire), stepped easily and at a stride to its place in men's estimation as one of the world's great Epics. Some might decry it, others might exalt: but it was *that*, and admittedly, and from the first. The fame of it at once collected about his lodgings in Artillery Walk a conflux of visitors; "much more," reports Aubrey, "than he did desire." The story goes that Dryden laid the book down and exclaimed, "This man cuts us all out and the ancients too!" and the anecdote may or may not be veracious. But whether or not Dryden said it, *Paradise Lost* was reprinted in 1674 (the year of Milton's death); in 1688 appeared the first *édition de luxe*, published on a subscription started by Lord Somers; and for this edition, to be printed under its engraved portrait of Milton, Dryden wrote his famous epigram—

> Three Poets, in three distant Ages born,
> Greece, Italy, and England did adorn.
> The first in Loftiness of Thought surpass'd,
> The next in Majesty, in both the last:
> The Force of Nature could no farther go;
> To make a third she join'd the former two.

—a "pinchbeck epigram," an epigram flashily false at every point. But what concerns us is that Dryden wrote it, and that so eminent a critic could sound so confident a note of applause within a few years of Milton's death: as, when Mark Pattison proceeds to tell us that the Whigs cried up *Paradise Lost*, and the Tories had therefore to cry it down, for political reasons, it only concerns *us* that the applause and the detraction alike based themselves upon admission of its greatness. Here, at any rate, Addison and Dr. Johnson find common ground. I suppose no honest critic ever put greater pressure on the forgiveness of his conscience than did Johnson when he shared in the campaign (it was a campaign, and deliberate) of writing down Milton. But what does Johnson write in a postscript to Lauder's dishonest attack, *An Essay on Milton's Use and Imitation of the Moderns in his "Paradise Lost,"* published in 1750? Newton's great edition had just been published, and Johnson had noted, in the memoir prefixed, that Milton's granddaughter, Elizabeth Foster, was still alive and in poor circumstances, keeping a small chandler's shop in Cock Lane, Shoreditch. He writes promptly and generously—

That this relation is true cannot be questioned: but, surely, the honour of letters, the dignity of sacred poetry, the spirit of the English nation, and the glory of human nature, require—that it should be true no longer. In an age, in which statues are erected to the honour of this great writer, in which his effigy has been diffused on medals, and his work propagated by translations, and illustrated by commentaries; in an age, which amidst all its vices, and all its follies, has not become infamous for want of charity: it may be, surely, allowed to hope that the living remains of Milton will be no longer suffered to languish in distress. It is yet in the power of a great people, to reward the poet whose name they boast, and from their alliance to whose genius, they claim some kind of superiority to every nation of the earth; that poet, whose works may possibly be read when every other monument of British greatness shall be obliterated; to reward him—not with pictures, or with medals which, if he sees, he sees with contempt, but—with tokens of gratitude, which he, perhaps, may even now consider as not unworthy the regard of an immortal spirit.

That is talking. That is how great men should salute great antagonists as they pass, and so dignify the brief while between us and the grave.

III

But, to return to Aristotle: though he found no significance in the fact that Homer had remained without successor to the Epic mantle, yet he might (one thinks) have surmised a warning in the argument he was at pains to counter—the argument that Epic in his day had come to address an intellectual public and must therefore be of an order superior to Drama, which addresses any and every one and thereby makes itself vulgar ($\phi o \rho \tau \iota \varkappa \acute{\eta}$). For a form of art which has arrived at catering for intellectuals only—and Homer certainly addressed no such audience—is an art for the few in any nation of men. We should not therefore condemn it, perhaps. But the truth remains, history certifying that great Epic writers tend, in modern times, to be lonely men. There is nothing in the least lonely about Homer: You can, with a very small amount of imagination, hear the fed men-at-arms "having put from themselves the desire of meat and drink," murmuring responses to him all adown the long hall. But surely when we picture Virgil to ourselves, it is as a lonely schol rly man, refining his verse with interminable secret pains. The Middle Ages, anyhow, chose to regard him as a wizard, and you will find it difficult to reconcile that conception with sociability or with any service of Epic to the wine-cup. To Dante Virgil was a companion, indeed, and a guide; but austere, tall be-

yond all ordinary height, not flesh and blood. And
Dante was even a lonelier man than Virgil; and Milton
loneliest of the three. High, rarefied intellectuals all,
and in progression less and less sensitive in their verse
to human passion, human frailty!

IV

We find ourselves here on the edge of a difficult
question. "Can Epic be written again in these days?
or has it rarefied itself away into a lost art?—lost, albeit
though so grand, so tremendously imposing."

I decline the speculation. Poetry for me has always
been the stuff the poets have written—just that and no
more: and criticism the business of examining that, of
sifting out (if one can) gold from dross. But with rules
and definitions I take leave to have no concern at all,
nor curiosity concerning any such commerce. Rules
are made to be broken, by the artist who can; definitions to be valued by any critic who cares. And in
these animadversions of mine upon Milton and *Paradise Lost* I beg you not for a moment to suppose me as
regretting that he did not make a Tragedy of it. Here
it is—our grandest Epic—and a poem for which, however
late we come to a full appreciation, everyone of us who
speak in English ought to be proudly thankful.

I will not even say that a man attempting Epic in
our days *must* be a lonely man, although I think that he
must, and although I note that the grandest Epic effort
of this generation has been made by Mr. Charles
Doughty; and that of writers now living you will with
difficulty name one lonelier or one whose fame is less
commensurate with his worth. But I will say that,
while finding it happily impossible to imagine a time
when delight in the *Iliad*, the *Odyssey*, the *Æneid*, the

Divine Comedy shall have perished among men, I cannot persuade myself but that the manufacture of great Epic must become harder and harder yet, and its rare visitations diminish out and pass into a tale that is told— that is, unless some genius shall arise to bow and bend its grand manner to narrate the nobler deeds of men conspicuous for virtue among their fellow-men of which our own later age has supplied examples, say in Lee, Lincoln, Gordon.   At present its own nobility obliges it; and our very reverence binds the tradition upon it that it must traffic with the gods, or with the heroic origins of a nation, or with both.   Our civilisation has reduced the multitudinous, warm-breathing companionable gods of Greece and Rome—*tot circum unum caput volitantes deos*—to one God; a God removed beyond vision and far out of reach of those tender intimate railleries which a Greek might use as a lover towards *his* Olympians; an Almighty, moreover; and by that almightiness capable of nullifying any scientific process from cause to effect, and nullifying thereby any human story concerning Him: while, as for national origins and antique heroes, science steadily dissipates the romantic aura about them, to substitute a fog of its own.   The mythology—or what there ever was of a mythology— behind Beowulf is not only no longer ours; it has so far faded out of the mind of our race that, in comparison with Greek fable, it awakes little curiosity and can scarcely, for any length of time, keep a hold on our interest.

Let us take this matter of national origins first, and remember that we are dealing with Milton.   Milton at first proposed King Arthur for the hero of his *magnum opus*: and I would in passing remind those foolish people who run themselves down as Anglo-Saxons, that

if they claim (as, if they do, I am sure they mistake
themselves) to belong to that very old fiasco, they can
not at any rate claim the heroic shade of Arthur for
a kinsman, or his Table Round as recording any compliment to their ancestry save as a proud contemporary
protest.   Well, Milton at first intended to commemo-
rate King Arthur.   But actually and although he
wrote a history of Britain, Milton, with his classical propensity and Italianate upbringing, had no local sense
of England at all.   He was a Londoner—a great Londoner—whose travel in this country reached just so far
north of London as Cambridge, and just so far west as
Horton in Buckinghamshire.   In intimacy with the
genius loci of any spot in rural England—which, after
all, remains the true England—with the palimpsest,
the characters, faint but indelible, which her true
lover traces on Berkshire or Sussex downs, along the
edge of Cambridgeshire fens, over Dartmoor or the wild
Yorkshire country, or up the great roads to the Roman
Wall—in this knowledge a page of Drayton, or even
a half-line of Shakespeare, will put Milton down.   One
recalls the magniloquent use he makes of place-names—

> City of old or modern Fame, the seat
> Of mightiest Empire, from the destined walls
> Of *Cambalu*, seat of *Cathaian Can*,
> And *Samarchand* by *Oxus*, *Temirs* throne,
> To *Paquin*, of *Sinaean* kings, and thence
> To *Agra* and *Lahore* of great *Mogul*
> Down to the golden *Chersonese*, or where
> The *Persian* in *Ecbatan* sat, or since
> In *Hispahan*, or where the *Russian Ksar*
> In *Mosco*, or the Sultan in *Bizance*,
> *Turchestan*-born . . .

or

> From *Arachosia*, from *Candaor* east,

> And Margian to the *Hyrcanian* cliffs
> Of *Caucasus*, and dark *Iberian* dales,
> From *Atropatia* and the neighbouring plains
> Of *Adiabene*, *Media* and the south
> Of *Susiana* to *Balsara's* hav'n . . .

with the rest of it. But of homelier English place-names, as ancient as the most of these and as delicately syllabled, he will not condescend to make one single catalogue. Of the Epic origins they enwrap by the thousand I suppose this fastidiously Italianate Englishman to have been either unaware, or, if aware, disdainful. For him the Mount of St. Michael, Caragluz, is not nameworthy in itself. Its vision in *Lycidas* looks seaward and southward

> toward *Namancos* and *Bayona's* hold;
> Look homeward Angel now, and melt with ruth—

but he does his wafting with dolphins!

V

On the theological story of *Paradise Lost* I shall be very brief. If our English springs could boast of Naiads; or Newmarket Heath had ever, in legend, been scoured by Centaurs; if our dim past (into which Milton sought in youth for a theme) had possessed a tolerable theogony for its background; I daresay he would not have had recourse to Judaic suggestion or, if you will, to Judaic inspiration, for his theme. But, as it happened, he did; and the result is curious.

Men of the eighteenth century praised him for the grandeur of his conception; and his detractors, too, of that century took him on that ground. Neither Addison nor Johnson can ever get far away from the prepossession that here, whatever we may think of him, was a tremendous fellow who took hold of the pillars of

heaven and hell.   Encomiast and detractor alike have
always this at the back of their criticism.

Now it has been said that miracles, like curses, come
home to roost.   We pass to another century, and find
Mark Pattison writing thus—

There is an element of decay and death in poems which we
vainly style immortal. Some of the sources of Milton's
power are already in process of drying up.   I do not speak of
the ordinary caducity of language, in virtue of which every
effusion of the human spirit is lodged in a body of death.
Milton suffers little as yet from this cause.   There are few
lines in his poems which are less intelligible now than they
were at the time they were written.   This is partly to be
ascribed to his limited vocabulary, Milton, in his verse,
using not more than eight thousand words, or about half the
number used by Shakespeare.

(And one remembers that *Paradise Lost* is easily the
most learned poem in our language, and that Shakespeare by repute was an indifferently learned man!)
Pattison goes on—

The defects of English for purposes of rhythm and harmony are as great now as they ever were, but the space that
our speech fills in the world is vastly increased, and this
increase of consideration is reflected back upon our older
writers.

But if, as a treasury of poetic speech, *Paradise Lost* has
gained by time, it has lost far more as a storehouse of divine
truth.   We at this day are better able than ever to appreciate its form of expression, its grace of phrase, its harmony of
rhythmical movement, *but it is losing its hold over our
imagination*.

And thereupon Pattison, as a thoughtful nineteenth
century agnostic, proceeds to tell us that, while it
would have been a thing incredible to Milton that the

hold of Jewish scriptures over the imagination of English men and women could ever be weakened, "this process . . . has already commenced." But years pass and with their passing men shift their point of judgment. As we look at the matter today, who cares a penny that Milton's theory of the Creation was right or was wrong? We are no more concerned to believe in it than to believe that Pallas Athene sprang to birth in full armour through a crack in the skull of Zeus. For us, as a reported tale, *Paradise Lost* has surely receded as far back into fiction as anything in the *Odyssey*. We grant all its premises. We ask only if, those premises granted, our artist be sincere and true to his art. I will put the question to you in this way—such questions being always raised best on a definite illustration— Does it in the least alter the effect of *Paradise Lost* upon our minds whether we believe or not that God made the world in six days and rested on the seventh, when Milton can command us up from the perfected work in the train of imagined Deity by lines such as these?—

> So Ev'n and Morn accomplish't the Sixt day:
> Yet not till the Creator from his work
> Desisting, though unwearied, up returnd;
> Up to the Heav'n of Heav'ns, his high abode,
> Thence to behold this new created World
> Th' addition of his Empire, how it shew'd
> In prospect from his Throne, how good, how faire,
> Answering his great Idea. Up he rode
> Follow'd with acclamation . . .
>   the Earth, the Aire
> Resounded, (thou remember'st for thou heardst)
> The Heav'ns and all the Constellations rung,
> The Planets in their stations list'ning stood,
> While the bright Pomp ascended jubilant.
> *Open, ye everlasting Gates*, they sung,

Open, ye Heav'ns your living dores; let in
The great Creator from his work returnd
Magnificent, his Six days' work, a World!

We come back to the old objection that, while Milton
masters us, he does not win us: he overawes, he as-
tounds, but he does not charm. The young, they say,
do not easily come to like him.

But let us examine. I think we all—but especially
the young—love spirituality in a poem, and rightly love
it. Now to be intensely spiritual a man must first be
humble: and Milton was not a humble man. He greets
us in an attitude uncompromisingly, if not quite affect-
edly, stiff and classical; as who should say, "Though I
tell of Heaven and of Paradise, and though I speak with
the tongues of men and of angels, I propose to do it in
the Greek formula because that is the only right way—
'Sing, Heavenly Muse!'" Moreover, Milton himself
so distinctly visualises "things invisible to mortal
sight" that when he comes to communicate these mys-
teries he tells us all—the geography of Paradise, the
construction of the bridge over Chaos, the measure-
ment of Mulciber's fall in terms of our own days and
seasons. But he who accurately describes a sublime
thing tends hereby to lessen it in our minds. Im-
mensity cannot be measured and remain immense; in
poetical dealing with mystery the part is, and must be,
greater than the whole.

VI

A critic, hitherto anonymous, has said—

Shakespeare had other methods. Edgar's purely ficti-
tious description of the cliff at Dover begins with details—
the crows and choughs no bigger than beetles, and so forth.
They leave us cold, until the last sentence comes:

I'll look no more,
Lest my brain turn and the deficient sight
Topple down headlong.

And at that we shudder. "For all beneath the moon," he
adds, "would I not leap upright"; and though we know
there is no cliff, we crouch with him, dizzy. Humanity
recognizes and admits the limitations of its speech, and of its
common weakness; and humanity replies to the admission
with a thrill. It will strive to soar to unimaginable heights
with Shelley, because it knows that Shelley is struggling,
groping, yearning himself. Milton, the master, sweeping
us along on his mighty pinion, seems sometimes to block the
prospect with his own knowledge.

An illustration might be taken from painting. There are
pictures so masterly, so complete, that they are like commands. "I will show you," the artist seems to say, "what
you could never see for yourself. There it is; and there is
nothing more to see." And from the mighty, masterly
work we turn aside to some modest picture by a lesser man,
and find in it nothing perhaps, of the splendour we have just
left, but an outlet, a loophole of escape, in which the artist
seems to say: "I could see no further. I do not know
what is beyond." Thus he gives us not only the dear touch
of bounded humanity, but the sense of mystery, of the
immanence of the unknown and the unknowable, which
bounded humanity, for all its greed of knowledge, hugs close
in secret. In poetry the same effect is obtained not only
by such direct means as Shakespeare used in the passage
quoted, but by the reticences, the phrases which admit, as it
were, that speech cannot express what is meant, the half-
words, half-sighs, like "The rest is silence," or "She should
have died hereafter."

There would have been a time for such a word.
Tomorrow, and tomorrow, and tomorrow
Creeps in this petty pace from day to day

And all our yesterdays have lighted fools
The way to dusty death. . . .

lines which do no more than point to the infinite, and leave it infinite still. In Milton, bent as he was upon mapping out the infinite, explaining the strange, there are no such phrases. There are few, even, of those lines, of which there are many in Shakespeare, in Keats, in Wordsworth, which seem, as if by direct inspiration, to mean far more than the words say, to open the doors and set the mind wandering in ways not realised.

No motion has she now, no force;
  She neither hears nor sees;
Rolled round in earth's diurnal course,
  With rocks, and stones, and trees.

The actual meaning of these words is as nothing compared with their effect upon the mind of the reader. It is not a verse as Abt Volger might say, but a star. [*The Times* Literary Supplement.]

But after all, these are questions of literary tact. And who will brutally blame some uncertainty of tact upon a blind man, who speaks, but can read no response, no sympathy, no quick answer in the eyes of his fellows: to whom returns not

Day, or the sweet approach of Ev'n or Morn,
Or sight of vernal bloom or Summer's Rose,
Or flocks, or herds, or human face divine?

VII

The redemption after all, and last high vindication of this most magnificent poem are not to be sought in its vast conception or in its framing, grand but imperfect as Titanic work always has been and ever will be. To find *them* you must lean your ear closely to its angelic language, to its cadenced music. Once grant that we have risen—as Milton commands us to rise—above humankind and the clogging of human passion, where will you find, but in *Paradise Lost,* language fit for seraphs, speaking in the quiet of dawn in sentry before the gates of Heaven?

And the secret of it?

I believe the grand secret to be very simple. I believe you may convince yourself where it lies by watching the hands of any good organist as he plays.

It lies—Milton had other secrets of course—but the main secret lies in the movement, the exquisitely modulated slide of his cæsura. Listen to it—

> Father, thy word is past, man shall find grace;
> And shall grace not find means, that finds her way,
> The speediest of thy wingèd messengers,
> To visit all thy creatures, and to all
> Comes unprevented, unimplor'd, unsought,
> Happie for man, so coming; he her aide
> Can never seek, once dead in sins and lost;
> Attonement for himself or offering meet,
> Indebted and undon, hath none to bring:
> Behold mee then, mee for him, life for life
> I offer, on mee let thine anger fall;
> Account mee man; I for his sake will leave
> Thy bosom, and this glorie next to thee
> Freely put off, and for him lastly die
> Well pleas'd

or

> The Birds thir quire apply; aires, vernal aires
> Breathing the smell of field and grove, attune
> The trembling leaves, while Universal *Pan*

> Knit with the *Graces* and the *Hours* in dance
> Led on th' Eternal Spring.   Not that faire field
> Of *Enna*, where Proserpin gathering flours
> Her self a fairer Floure by gloomie *Dis*
> Was gatherd, which cost *Ceres* all that pain
> To seek her through the world; nor that sweet Grove
> Of *Daphne* by *Orontes*, and th' inspir'd
> *Castalian* Spring might with this Paradise
> Of *Eden* strive;

or

> Som natural tears they drop'd, but wip'd them soon;
> The World was all before them, where to choose
> Thir place of rest, and Providence thir guide;
> They hand in hand with wandring steps and slow,
> Through *Eden* took thir solitarie way.

That is how I see Milton, and that is the portrait I would leave with you—of an old man, lonely and musical, seated at his chamber organ, sliding upon the keyboard a pair of hands pale as its ivory in the twilight of a shabby lodging of which the shabbiness and the gloom molest not him; for he is blind—and yet he sees.

ANTONY AND CLEOPATRA

I

I REJOICE that the Board which regulates our English Tripos has so promptly and boldly admitted the two great plays, *Measure for Measure* and *Antony and Cleopatra* into the list of those chosen for specific study: and I rejoice for two reasons, on the minor of which let me first say a few words.

Their inclusion seems to me—if I may use a word which promises to become too common—a sort of "gesture"; signifying that in casting the old, bad Tripos behind us, we have done with addressing ourselves coyly to potential schoolmasters and schoolmistresses, and propose to speak out to men and women. It is in part a chance that the inauguration of our new School of English up here has coincided with the return of young men from experiences that have made them impatient of humbug; as also that it coincides with a great enfranchisement of women and their return—or the return of the younger ones—from services in field or in hospital, which must have taught them, too, to look on life with wide-open eyes. Before this happened I said here, from this place, that if anyone is to study English literature in a University, English Literature with its whole content is the open field. A student may choose it or leave it alone, but

whoso chooses it must take it as frankly (say) as any
student who enters on a course of anatomy.

II

I am to speak to you this morning of Shakespeare's
Antony and Cleopatra: and the best I can do is, after all,
to encourage you to read the play, or to help you to
enjoy it just a little better as you read. Say that I am
to examine you upon it. What questions can I set
upon this, or upon any masterpiece of literature that
directly test your possessing the soul of the play?
Indirectly, unless I am a fool, I shall get at the quality
of your understanding through your answers to my
questions. But *directly* of its meaning how little can
I ask without tempting you to vague æsthetics? While
if I question you upon the date of the play, or upon
various readings of the text, I invite you to miss the
whole point of it.

And yet, if examinations were rightly conducted, to
test your acquaintance with the methods by which
great artists make great literature, and that understanding of them which is the true and capital and joyous reward of critical study, where can we find a drama
more illustrative than this *Antony and Cleopatra*? For
we have to our hand in North's *Plutarch*—itself one of
the most delightful of classics—the very page that gave
Shakespeare his material; the life of Marcus Antonius
out of which he built this play (and not this play only,
but a part of *Julius Cæsar*, and almost the whole of
Timon to boot); the very words that Shakespeare took
and transmuted into poetry, often by the deftest, most
economical touch. If you happen to know Greek, you
have the earlier pleasure of watching how North turns
the prose of Plutarch into English no less charming: but

you need no Greek for the deeper, subtler and withal more instructive pleasure of assisting while Shakespeare conjures sound English prose into superb English poetry under your eyes.

Let me first take the famous account of Cleopatra's first meeting with Antony.   Here is North's version of Plutarch:

For Cæsar and Pompey knew her when she was but a young thing, and knew not then what the world meant: but now she went to Antonius at the age when a woman's beauty is at the prime, and she also of best judgement.   So, she furnished her self with a world of gifts, store of gold and silver, and of riches and other sumptuous ornaments, as is credible enough she might bring from so great a house, and from so wealthy and rich a realm as Egypt was.   But yet she carried nothing with her wherein she trusted more than in her self, and in the charms and enchantment of her passing beauty and grace.   Therefore when she was sent unto by divers letters, both from Antonius himself, and also from his friends, she made so light of it and mocked Antonius so much, that she disdained to set forward otherwise, but to take her barge in the river of Cydnus, the poop whereof was of gold, the sails of purple, and the oars of silver, which kept stroke in rowing after the sound of the music of flutes, howboys, citherns, viols, and such other instruments as they played upon in the barge.

Let us halt here, for a moment, to note something the commentators miss.   In the play Enobarbus omits the opening sentence of this passage, because it has already, in an earlier scene, been dramatically suggested by Cleopatra herself, who is shameless in private talk with her servants Iras, Charmian and the young man Alexas:

Did I, Charmian,
Ever love Cæsar so? . . .
My salad days,
When I was green in judgment: cold in blood,
To say as I said then!

Enobarbus has but to give a description; and this is how
he begins it:

I will tell you.
The barge she sat in, like a burnish'd throne,
Burn'd on the water: the poop was beaten gold;
Purple the sails, and so perfumèd that
The winds were love-sick with them; the oars were
silver,
Which to the tune of flutes kept stroke and made
The water which they beat to follow faster,
As amorous of their strokes.

Let Plutarch and North resume:

And now for the person of her self she was laid under a
pavilion of cloth of gold of tissue, apparelled and attired like
the goddess Venus, commonly drawn in picture: and hard by
her on either hand of her, pretty fair boys apparelled as
painters do set forth God Cupid, with little fans in their
hands, with the which they fanned wind upon her. Her
ladies and gentlewomen also, the fairest of them were
apparelled like the nymphs nereids (which are the mer-
maids of the waters) and like the Graces, some steering
the helm, others tending the tackle and ropes of the barge,
out of the which there came a wonderful passing sweet
savour of perfumes, that perfumed the wharf's side, pestered
with innumerable multitudes of people. Some of them
followed the barge all alongst the river-side: others also ran
out of the city to see her coming in. So that in the end
there ran such multitudes of people one after another to

see her, that Antonius was left post alone in the market-
place, in his imperial seat to give audience: and there went a
rumour in the people's mouths, that the goddess Venus was
come to play with the god Bacchus, for the general good of
all Asia.

Now let us see how it goes into verse—

> For her own person,
> It beggar'd all description; she did lie
> In her pavilion, cloth-of-gold of tissue,
> O'er-picturing that Venus where we see
> The fancy outwork nature: on each side her
> Stood pretty dimpled boys, like smiling Cupids,
> With divers-colour'd fans, whose wind did seem
> To glow the delicate cheeks which they did cool,
> And what they undid did.

Agrippa.   O, rare for Antony!

Enobarbas.   Her gentlewomen, like the Nereides,
> So many mermaids, tended her i' the eyes,
> And made their bends adornings: at the helm
> A seeming mermaid steers: the silken tackle
> Swells with the touches of those flower-soft hands,
> That yarely frame the office.   From the barge
> A strange invisible perfume hits the sense
> Of the adjacent wharfs.   The city cast
> Her people out upon her; and Antony,
> Enthroned i' the market-place, did sit alone,
> Whistling to the air; which, but for vacancy,
> Had gone to gaze on Cleopatra too,
> And made a gap in nature.

III

Let me pause for a moment upon this passage, and a
good example of a paradox constantly observable in
Shakespeare's fitting together of description and
thought.

The paradox is this. In handling a thought he ever
inclines to put it in the concretest form; as conversely,
his most vivid visualisations are ever shading off into
thought. For an instance or two—"Sleep that knits
up the ravell'd sleave of care" (which beats even
Sancho Panza's "How excellent a thing is sleep! It
wraps a man round like a cloak"), or,

> Golden lads and girls all must,
> As chimney-sweepers, come to dust

or

> And unregarded age in corners thrown

or

> And all our yesterdays have lighted fools
> The way to dusty death. Out, out, brief candle!

—or, in this play,

>   'Tis paltry to be Caesar;
> Not being Fortune, he's but Fortune's knave,
> A minister of her will: and it is great
> To do that thing that ends all other deeds;
> Which shackles accidents and bolts up change;
> Which sleeps, and never palates more the dug,
> The beggar's nurse and Cæsar's.

I say it is the great paradox in Shakespeare's handling of language that while he never touches a general-
isation but he must visualise it and force us to see it
thus in concrete images, he scarce ever describes a thing
but, where other describers would hold to particulars,
he shades us off into a thought, or tells the actual thing
and straightway glides to some image of it; reflected in
the mind as it were glassed on water, "following
darkness like a dream."

So here, in this famous passage of Cleopatra upon Cydnus, her sails perfume the air as in Plutarch, but so (as not in Plutarch) that the winds were love-sick with them: and again the silver oars keep time, as in Plutarch, but so (as not in Plutarch) they made

> The water which they beat to follow faster,
> As amorous of their strokes.

IV

Still all this is descriptive writing—a purple patch in a drama—and, after all, not so much better than Plutarch's, if you ask *me*—and, anyhow and however well executed, not the real test of a *dramatist's* quality. If you ask my opinion, I say that North is even a trifle better than Shakespeare—prose against verse—in describing the approach of the barge with the attendants—

> Some steering the helm, others tending the tackle and ropes of the barge, out of the which there came a wonderful passing sweet savour of perfumes, that perfumed the wharf's side, pestered with innumerable multitudes of people.

Again, if you will, we will call it a draw between the prose which leaves Antony "post alone in the market-place, in his imperial seat to give audience," and the verse which so graphically sets him and leaves him enthroned whistling to the air which

> but for vacancy,
> Had gone to gaze on Cleopatra too,
> And made a gap in nature

—and so does not, after all, treat Antony any better than does the crowd, but, like the crowd, edges off to follow a curiosity and a conceit.

It is not, I say, upon *description* that we can test a dramatist. His traffic lies not in word-pictures, though he may use them profitably now and again, to lift his play. He deals rather—as Aristotle pointed out—with men and women in action, *doing* things: and it is in a passage concerned with action that we must properly seek a dramatic artist, to judge his handling of his material.

Here, then, is the material supplied by Plutarch and North as preliminary to Antony's self-slaughter—

When Antonius saw that his men did forsake him, and yielded unto Cæsar, and that his footmen were broken and overthrown: he then fled into the city, crying out that Cleopatra had betrayed him unto them, with whom he had made war for her sake. Then she being afraid of his fury, fled into the tomb which she had caused to be made, and there locked the doors upon her, and shut all the springs of the locks with great bolts, and in the meantime sent unto Antonius to tell him that she was dead. Antonius, believing it, said unto himself: What dost thou look for further, Antonius, sith spiteful fortune hath taken from thee the only joy thou hadst, for whom thou yet reservedst thy life? when he had said these words, he went into a chamber and unarmed himself, and being naked said thus: "O Cleopatra, it grieveth me not that I have lost thy company, for I will not be long from thee: but I am sorry, that having been so great a captain and emperor, I am indeed condemned to be judged of less courage and noble mind, than a woman!" Now he had a man of his called Eros, whom he loved and trusted much, and whom he had long before caused to swear unto him, that he should kill him when he did command him: and then he willed him to keep his promise. His man drawing his sword, lift it up as though he had meant to have stricken his master: but turning his head at one side, he thrust his sword into himself, and fell down dead at his master's foot.

As prose this passage has many merits.   Every non-inflected language finds trouble over its pronouns: and our Elizabethans inclined (perhaps wisely) to let that trouble take care of itself.   We should be shy nowadays, of writing "whom he had long before caused to swear unto him, that he should kill him when he did command him"; but the meaning is perfectly plain and easy and no more ambiguous (say) than the meaning of St. Matthew xxvii. 43, in the Authorised Version—"He trusted in God; let him deliver him now, if he will have him."   North, following Plutarch, tells the story straightforwardly, with liveliness and some simple dignity.

Now watch the poet.   His eye travels down the page and, first of all, lights on the two commanding words—the name of the servant, Eros, and the word "unarmed"—"he went into a chamber and unarmed himself."   Was it glorious chance that Antony's body-servant bore the name Eros, name also of the god of Love?—For what is the theme of our play but human ambition, imperial greatness, cast away for love, slain in the end for love and by love.   "*All for Love: or The World Well Lost*"—Dryden, though he wrote a much inferior play on this very theme and model, packed the secret into his title .   We have come—Antony has come—to the very moment of realising all: yes, all: for he believes Cleopatra to be dead, as all else is broken. The battle has been for love: it is lost; and now Love (Eros) shall strip and slay him.   I suppose it is in the last degree unlikely that Shakespeare ever read the *Pervigilium Veneris*, the first printed edition of which appeared in Paris in 1577.   He has the gift by this time —notably in *Antony and Cleopatra* he has the gift—of charging his words with overtones and undertones so that they mean, or we feel them to mean, far more than they actually say. Still there, in the *Pervigilium* stands the line—

Totus est inermis idem quando nudus est Amor.
Love naked, love unarmed, is armed complete.
—Totus est inermis idem quando nudus est—Eros.

"Eros," "unarmed"—Shakespeare catches these two notes together, adds a third of his own, and strikes the magnificent chord. The Eunuch Mardian has delivered his false news.

Antony.   Dead, then?
Mardian.   Dead.
Antony.   Unarm, Eros; the long day's task is done,
And we must sleep . . .
                    Off, pluck off:
                . . . Apace, Eros, apace!
No more a soldier. Bruised pieces, go:
You have been nobly borne. From me awhile.
                    [*Exit Eros.*
I will o'ertake thee, Cleopatra, and
Weep for my pardon. So it must be, for now
All length is torture: since the torch is out,
Lie down and stray no farther: now all labour
Mars what it does; yea, very force entangles
Itself with strength: seal then, and all is done.
Eros!—I come, my queen. Eros!—Stay for me:
Where souls do couch on flowers, we'll hand in
    hand,
And with our sprightly port make the ghosts
    gaze:
Dido and her Æneas shall want troops,
And all the haunt be ours. Come, Eros, Eros!

              Re-enter Eros.

Eros.   What would my lord?

Antony.   Since Cleopatra died
I have lived in such dishonour that the gods
Detest my baseness. I, that with my sword
Quarter'd the world and o'er green Neptune's
     back
With ships made cities, condemn myself to lack
The courage of a woman; less noble mind
Than she which by her death our Cæsar tells
"I am conqueror of myself." Thou art sworn,
     Eros,
That when the exigent should come—which now
Is come indeed—when I should see behind me
The inevitable prosecution of
Disgrace and horror, that, on my command,
Thou then wouldst kill me: do't; the time is
     come:
Thou strikest not me, 'tis Cæsar thou defeat'st.
Put colour in thy cheek.

Eros.   The gods withhold me!
Shall I do that which all the Parthian darts,
Though enemy, lost aim and could not?

Antony.   Eros,
Wouldst thou be window'd in great Rome, and
     see
Thy master thus with pleach'd arms, bending
     down
His corrigiable neck, his face subdued
To penetrative shame, whilst the wheel'd seat
Of fortunate Cæsar, drawn before him, branded
His baseness that ensued?

Eros.   I would not see't.

Antony.   Come, then: for with a wound I must be cured. . . .

Enough: but here you have it—the amazing process
in operation under your eyes. Is that not reason enough
for rejoicing that the Board has changed an O into an

E and made *Antony and Cleopatra* at length one of its prescribed Plays?

V

But I have a stronger reason.

I do most ardently desire this play to be reckoned— as it has never been reckoned yet, but I am sure it deserves to be—among the very greatest, and in some ways the most wonderful, of Shakespeare's triumphs. I want it to stand at length—in your estimation at any rate—as a compeer of *Hamlet, Macbeth, Lear, Othello*: no less.

"Wonderful" is at any rate the word; and Coleridge gives it to me. "The highest praise," he says, "or rather form of praise," of this play

—which I can offer in my own mind, is the doubt which the perusal always occasions in me, whether the *Antony and Cleopatra* is not, in all exhibitions of a giant power in its strength and vigour of maturity, a formidable rival of *Macbeth, Lear, Hamlet* and *Othello*. *Feliciter audax* is the motto for its style comparatively with that of Shakespeare's other works, even as it is the general motto of all his works compared with those of other poets. Be it remembered, too, that this happy valiancy of style is but the representative and result of all the material excellencies so expressed.

He goes on—

Of all Shakespeare's historical plays, *Antony and Cleopatra* is by far the most wonderful. There is not one in which he has followed history so minutely, and yet there are few in which he impresses the notion of angelic strength so much;—perhaps none in which he impresses it more strongly. This is greatly owing to the manner in which the fiery force is sustained throughout, and to the numerous momentary flashes of nature counteracting the historic abstraction. As a wonderful specimen of the way in which Shakespeare lives up to the very end of this play, read the last part of the concluding scene. And if you would feel the judgment as well as the genius of Shakespeare in your heart's core, compare this astonishing drama with Dryden's *All for Love*.

Now, when Coleridge wrote, Dryden's *All for Love* had been acted at least ten times to *Antony and Cleopatra's* once. And so we may forgive him that, groping toward the truth by instinct, he hesitates and just misses to declare it. "The highest praise . . . which I can offer in my own mind, is the doubt which the perusal always occasions in me." "Of all Shakespeare's *historical* plays, *Antony and Cleopatra* is by far the most wonderful." Upon that he pauses. After admitting that the audacity of its style distinguishes it above Shakespeare's other works even as that audacity is Shakespeare's general distinction above other poets, he trails off to admit the "numerous momentary flashes of nature counteracting the historic abstraction." What he means by "historic abstraction" heaven knows. History is not abstract, but particular; as Aristotle long ago pointed out. It narrates what Alcibiades did or suffered. Coleridge is talking cotton-wool. Hazlitt shows himself no less cautious—

This is a very noble play. Though not in the first class of Shakespeare's productions, it stands next to them, and is, we think, the finest of his *historical* plays. . . .

He goes on: "What he has added to the actual story, is on a par with it," but promptly admits that which really means everything—

His genius was, as it were [why "as it were"?], a match

for history as well as nature, and could grapple at will with
either. The play is full of that pervading comprehensive
power by which the poet could always make himself master
of time and circumstances—

and, with that, Hazlitt too, having like them that dwelt
in Zebulon and the land of Naphtah seen a glimmer,
wanders off to remark, "The character of Cleopatra is a
master-piece. What an extreme contrast it affords to
Imogen!" O yes—and as the Victorian lady in the
stalls observed to her companion when Sir Herbert
Tree presented this very play, "How different, my dear,
from the home life of *our* beloved Queen!"

And then comes along Gervinus, solemnly between
his little finger and his enormous useful thumb measur-
ing out the play against history and condemning it.
"The crowd of matter," murmurs Gervinus, checking
it, "creates a crowd of ideas." Vengeance on a crowd
of ideas!

"A wanton multiplicity of incidents and personages
pass before our eyes; political and warlike occurrences
run parallel with the most intimate affairs of domestic
life and of the affections": and, as if all this were not
sufficiently shocking, "the interest is fettered to the
passion of a single pair, and yet the scene of it is the
wide world from Parthia to Cape Misenum."

But if you are setting out to show how the passion
between one man and one woman can crack the pillars
of a wide world and bring down the roof in ruin (which
is precisely what this play does), surely the grander
the sense of that world's extent you can induce upon
your audience's mind, the grander your effect! Surely
for dramatic purpose Shakespeare could have extended
Parthia to China and Cape Misenum to Peru, and with
advantage, if those remoter regions had happened just

then to be discovered and included in the Roman Empire.

VI

In a previous lecture, speaking to you of Aristotle's dictum that the tragic hero in drama should preferably be a person of high worldly estate, I suggested that the chief reason for this was a very simple one, and indeed none other than Newton's Law of Gravitation—the higher the eminence from which a man falls the harder he hits the ground—and our imagination. I believe this to be true and yet not all the truth: for as Dr. Bradley says, quoting the end of Chaucer's *Monk's Tale*:

> An-hangèd was Cresus, the proudè kyng:
> His roial tronè myghte hym nat availle.
> Tragédie is noon other maner thyng.

The pangs of despised love and the anguish of remorse, we say, are the same in a peasant and a prince; yet, not to insist that they cannot be so when the prince is really a prince, the story of the prince, the triumvit, or the general, has a great-ness and dignity of its own. His fate effects the welfare of a whole nation or empire; and when he falls suddenly from the height of earthly greatness to the dust, his fall produces a sense of contrast, of the powerlessness of man, and of the omnipotence—perhaps the caprice—of Fortune or Fate, which no tale of private life can possibly rival.

We must not press this too far, or in every play. For, as Sir Walter Raleigh points out, in *Hamlet* (for example) the issue of the events upon the State of Den-mark scarcely concerns us. "The State of Denmark," says he, "is not regarded at all, except as a topical and picturesque interest. The tragedy is a tragedy of pri-vate life, made conspicuous by the royal station of the chief actors in it." Yes: but in all *historical* drama, may be, and in *Antony and Cleopatra* most certainly, most eminently, the sense of reacting far-reaching issues *is* a necessary part of our concern. We are not sympathetic merely to the extent of having our emotions swayed by Cleopatra and Antony in turn. We are the world, the stake this pair are dicing away. We watch not only for their catastrophe but for ours, involved in it. Philo gives the thematic phrase in the twelfth and thirteenth lines of the first scene of the first act:

> The triple pillar of the world transform'd
> Into a strumpet's fool.

—Every word important, and "world" not the least important, since, if and when the pillar cracks, the roof of a world must fall. I put it to you that anyone insensitive to this dominant, struck by Shakespeare so early in the play and insistent to the end through all that crowding of great affairs which so afflicts the good Gervinus, must miss, roughly speaking, some two-thirds of its meaning. For Gervinus, "by these too numerous and discordant interruptions that psychical continuity is destroyed which is necessary to the development of such a remarkable connection of the innermost affections as that between Antony and Cleopatra."

Pro-digious!

VII

But indeed the theme itself is overpoweringly too much for our poor commentator, as it has ever been too strong for all but the elect. For it is of Love: not the pretty amorous ritual played, on a time, by troubadours and courtiers; not the delicate sighing languishment which the Elizabethans called Fancy; not the business

as understood by eighteenth century sentimentalists: but
Love the invincible destroyer—"Ερως ανίκατε μάχαν
—destroying the world for itself—itself, too, at the last:
Love voluptuous, savage, perfidious, true to itself
though rooted in dishonour, extreme, wild, divine,
merciless as a panther on its prey. With this Love,
wayward, untameable, Shakespeare here dares to traffic
and with the end of it—the latest dream "on the cold
hill side"—

> I saw pale kings and princes too,
>   Pale warriors, death-pale were they all;
> Who cry'd—"La belle Dame sans merci
>   Hath thee in thrall!"

Yet—why do I seek farther than Shakespeare's own
writ?—

> Yon sometime famous princes, like thyself,
> Drawn by report, adventurous by desire,
> Tell thee, with speechless tongues and semblance pale,
> That without covering, save yon field of stars,
> Here they stand martyrs, slain in Cupid's wars;
> And with dead cheeks advise thee to desist
> For going on death's net. . . .

Though he have never read Sappho, how ignorant is
he of this world's history, he who knows not that at any
moment a woman may turn—nay, has turned—the
whole of it upside down by turning a man inside out:
as Herodotus, "father of history," starts—as the Book
of Genesis itself starts—each with a woman at the
bottom of the whole mischief!

What matters her name? Eve, or Helen of Troy, or
La Belle Dame Sans Merci, or Cleopatra? She is our
common mother, and she is that which makes Troilus

turn incredulous to Diomed and gasp, "Think, we had mothers." And it is she who warns—

If thou love me, take heed of loving me!

—as it is she who hears—

Thou art the grave where buried love doth live,
Hung with the trophies of my lovers gone.

She is the Universal in the particular. She is the woman who cried on the wall of Troy, "Yonder goeth one son of Atreus, wide-ruling Agamemnon, goodly king and mighty spearsman: and he was husband's brother to me, —bitch that I am." Saying this, she yet wears

. . . the face that launched a thousand ships
And burnt the topless towers of Ilium.

She is "royal Egypt"; and withal

but e'en a woman, and commanded
By such poor passion as the maid that milks
And does the meanest chares. . . .

She is the woman Pater saw in the depths of La Gioconda's smile. "She is older than the rocks among which she sits; like the vampire she has been dead many times, and learned the secrets of the grave; and has been a diver in deep seas, and keeps their fallen day about her; and trafficked for strange webs with Eastern merchants . .,. and all this has been to her but as the sound of lyres and flutes. . . ." Yes, and "her feet go down to death; her steps take hold on hell; her ways are moveable that thou can'st not know them." Comely she is as Jerusalem, terrible as an army with banners. She is Eve, she is Rahab, she is Helen; but

most of all she is Cleopatra, "my serpent of old Nile";
for if a serpent betrayed the first woman, into this one
he has insinuated himself, and works, and dies in the
end of his own bite.

> *Charmian.*   O eastern star!
> *Cleopatra.*   Peace, peace!
> Dost thou not see my baby at my breast,
> That sucks the nurse asleep?

VIII

Let me here interpose a word which, though it will
at first seem to you a mere *obiter dictum* and irrelevant,
has some bearing on our subject.

They have now done away with compulsory Greek at
Oxford, as well as here: and I have no great objection
to that; because my own instinct abhors every kind of
compulsion, but specially any compulsion practised on
the human mind.   If we cannot induce young Englishmen to want to know Greek for its own sake, for the
ineffable beauty of its literature and the inestimable
worth of its content: if we have taught it so stupidly,
fenced about its wells and streams, its green walks and
whispering recesses, with deserts of grammar and fron-
tiers of syntax so arid that few any longer desire to learn
Greek, pant to learn Greek;—why then we have been,
in this as in other things, fools in our generation, and
Greek is too good for us.   Nor have I, keeping a sense
of humour amid the strokes and discouragements of
life, any serious quarrel with those who, voting down
compulsory Greek in the name of "liberty," use the very
moment as an occasion, and this liberty as a cloak, to
substitute another form of compulsion more to their
mind. Almost always this happens. The Pilgrim

Fathers braved the Atlantic in the name of Religious
Liberty; and promptly planted, on the other side, a
religious tyranny of their own, at least as harsh, at least
as cruel, as the one they had left at home, and by
several degrees uglier.

People say that, since our universities have ceased to
make Greek compulsory, the study of Greek will die
out of the land. I do not myself believe this. But,
say that it is so. Then I warn my countrymen—and
will cite two great examples for proof—that gracious as
the old Greek spirit is, and, apt to be despised because
it comes jingling no money in its pocket, using no art
but intellectual persuasion, they had wiselier, if only
for their skins' sake, keep it a friend than exile or cage it.
For, embodying the free spirit of man, it is bound to
break out sooner or later, to re-invade: and this guest,
so genial when we entreat it kindly, is—like its most
representative god, Phœbus Apollo—a deadly archer
when it breaks prison and the great bow-string starts
to twang:

ὡς ἔφατ' εὐχόμενος, τοῦ δ' ἔκλυε Φοῖβος 'Απόλλων,
βῆ δὲ κατ' Οὐλύμποιο καρήνων χωόμενος κῆρ...

So spake he in prayer, and Phœbus Apollo heard him, and
came down from the peaks of Olympus wroth at heart,
bearing on his shoulders his bow and covered quiver. And
the arrows rattled upon his shoulder in his wrath, as the god
moved: and he descended like to night. Then he sat him
aloof from the ships and let an arrow fly; and the silver bow
clanged, and the sound was terror. First he shot down
the mules, and the dogs as they ran: then he turned and,
aiming his barb on men, he smote; and the pyres of the dead
burned continually in multitudes.

You may think this a fancy: but I warn you, it is no

fancy. Twice the imprisoned spirit has broken loose upon Europe. The first time, over half of Europe, it slew an enthroned religion; the second time it slew an idea of monarchy. Its first access made, through the Renascence, a Reformation: its second made the French Revolution. And it made the French Revolution very largely (as any one who cares may assure himself by reading the memoirs of that time) by a simple translation of a Greek book—Plutarch's *Lives*. Now Plutarch is not, as we estimate ancient authors, one of the first rank. A late Greek, you may call him, an ancient

> musical at close of day:

an easy garrulous tale-teller. That but weights the warning. If Plutarch, being such a man, could sway as he did the men who made the French Revolution, what will happen to our Church and State in the days when a Plato comes along to probe and test the foundations of both with his Socratic irony? Were this the last word I ever spoke, in my short time here, I would bid any lover of compulsory "Natural Science"—our new tyranny—to beware that day.

IX

Paulo minora canamus. Amyot translated Plutarch in his free way, and North translated Plutarch out of Amyot, and Shakespeare read North and (there is no doubt of it) was fascinated by this translation at a double remove. "About the year 1600," says Mr. Frank Harris truly, "Shakespeare seems to have steeped himself in Plutarch. For the next five or six years, whenever he thinks of suicide, the Roman way of looking at it occurs to him." This is equally true of Macbeth's

> Why should I play the Roman fool, and die
> On mine own sword?

of Laertes'—

> I am more an antique Roman than a Dane

of Antony's—

> The miserable change now at my end
> Lament nor sorrow at, but please your thoughts
> In feeding them with those my former fortunes
> Wherein I lived, the greatest prince o' the world,
> The noblest, and do now not basely die,
> Not cowardly put off my helmet to
> My countryman, a Roman by a Roman
> Valiantly vanquish'd.

Lastly, of Cleopatra's echo:

> Good sirs, take heart:
> We'll bury him; and then, what's brave, what's noble,
> Let's do it after the high Roman fashion,
> And make death proud to take us.

And I would have you note by the way, and even though it lead us off our track for a moment, that the future fate of the world—whether the West should conquer the East, or the East the West—did actually and historically hang on the embraces of Cleopatra and Antony, as delicately as it had once hung balanced on the issues of Marathon. I do not urge that we are, any of us, the better off because the cold priggish mind of Octavius prevailed over the splendid whoredoms of Egypt: though I think it probable. But it was—for the second time—a great crisis between Europe and Asia; and again, in the second bout, as in the first, Europe

won. And I do not say—as I hardly believe—that
Shakespeare realised the full weight of the argument
that rested on his "triple pillar of the world," or that he
realised what a stupendous roof came down with its
fall. I only note here that Shakespeare, with superla-
tive skill, sets all this fate of a world rocking in the em-
brace of one man and one woman, both fatally loving:
and I note that this idea of the high Roman fashion
steadily, in Cleopatra's own thought, conquers her
whose magnificent wantonness has challenged Rome
and the West. Her victory in death is her defeat.
She dies *as a Roman*: the more a Roman because death
will deliver her, sensitive, from the eyes of Rome which
her own eyes have never seen.   But she has imagination
to see, to shudder from the very streets of it, and their
populace, and the spectacle of her naked self dragged
through this capital.

Cleopatra.   Now, Iras, what think'st thou?
            Thou, an Egyptian puppet, shalt be shown
            In Rome, as well as I: mechanic slaves
            With greasy aprons, rules and hammers, shall
            Uplift us to the view: in their thick breaths,
            Rank of gross diet, shall we be enclouded
            And forced to drink their vapours.
Iras.   The gods forbid!
Cleopatra. Nay, 'tis most certain, Iras: saucy lictors
            Will catch at us like strumpets, and scald rhymers
            Ballad us out o' tune: the quick comedians
            Extemporally will stage us and present
            Our Alexandrian revels; Antony
            Shall be brought drunken forth, and I shall see
            Some squeaking Cleopatra boy my greatness
            I' the posture of a whore.
Iras.   O the good gods!
Cleo.   Nay, that's certain.

Iras.   I'll never see 't.

But that is what *had* to be seen. And the East—that is, Cleopatra—has, above its turbulent passions, very clear eyes.

X

It sees, and shudders from, the cold calculating politics of the West, to which it has to succumb. The calm policy of Octavia's self-sacrifice lies outside its understanding as outside its morals. To marry—to give yourself to a man so coldly, on a sense of honour, for any State! Octavia is, be it acknowledged, after her own lights an extremely noble woman: but are hers the true lights, after all?

Let us get back to Plutarch. He, good fellow, simply tells the story. That is his gift: he gives it to us, and there is an end. Cleopatra's beauty, says he, was not so passing, as unmatchable of other women. That is no explanation. Indeed it would seem by every report collected that Cleopatra was by no means an absolutely lovely woman—that is to say, a woman absolutely lovely when, or if, seen (as the phrase is), "in repose": and perhaps one may dare to say, not cynically, that a certain sort of woman may often look her best in a certain kind of repose. As Antony puts it, of his wife Fulvia, in this very play—

She's good, being gone.

But even Plutarch makes us feel that, somehow, Cleopatra was miraculously winning. Here we come face to face with Shakespeare's main difficulty, which (as I pointed out a fortnight ago) he deliberately in the very first speech and before the play is two minutes' old, thrusts upon us—

Look, where they come:
Take but good note, and you shall see in him
The triple pillar of the world transform'd
Into a strumpet's fool.

Now I would have you note that Shakespeare, when he
has a dramatic miracle to work, never—I think I am
accurate in saying *never*—hides the difficulty from himself or from us.   Audiences, here in Cambridge, are
fleeting as water: only the Professor goes on, like the
River Duddon—

Still glides the Stream, and shall for ever glide;
The Form remains, the Function never dies:
    While [*you*], the brave, the mighty, and the wise,
[You] Men, who in [your] morn of youth defied
The elements, must vanish;—be it so!
    Enough, if—

Well, enough if it give me an excuse for repeating, on
this matter of Shakespeare's habitual honesty as a con-
juror, some few words from a previous Lecture, on
Macbeth.   Of Macbeth as a tragic hero I said:

Shakespeare makes this man, a sworn soldier, murder
Duncan, his liege-lord.
    He makes this man, a host, murder Duncan, a guest with-
in his gates.
    He makes this man, strong and hale, murder Duncan, old,
weak, asleep and defenceless.
    He makes this man a murderer, not as Brutus was, but
merely for his own advancement.
    He makes this man murder Duncan, who had steadily
advanced him, who had recently promoted him, who had
never been aught but trustful, who (that no detail of
reproach might be wanting) had that very night, as he retired, courteously bethought him and sent the gift of a dia-
mond to his hostess.

To sum up (I said): in place of extenuating Macbeth's guilt as disclosed in the chronicle, Shakespeare doubles it, redoubles it, plunges it deep as hell, and then—tucks up his sleeves.

So with this play. Philo's words, which I quoted, are spoken in no rhetorical extravagance, but as the sad verdict of a man of the world, a soldier, a friend who, without sentimentality, loves Antony passing well. And we feel it to be the just verdict: the *punctum indifferens* or standard of the normal man which Shakespeare is ever careful to set in his tragedies. What Horatio is to the feverish cerebration of *Hamlet*, Philo is in less than a dozen words to the passionate excess of this play. What Rome reports in scandalous gossip he sorrowfully confirms: and when he has spoken it, we know that it is so. How then, of such a pair, shall Shakespeare make a tragedy of high seriousness? how can he compel us to follow either of such a pair—nay, but he will have us follow both—sympathetically? How can he bring them both to end so nobly that, all contempt forgotten, even our pity is purged into a sense of human majesty? How from the orts and ravages of this sensual banquet shall he dismiss us with ''an awed surmise'' that man is, after all, master of circumstance and far greater than he knows?

XI

Shakespeare had Plutarch: and Plutarch has the story: but with Shakespeare the story is never the secret. He will take, in his own large indolent way, any man's story and make it his property; nor does he care how the facts may seem to damn hero or heroine, so only that he have the handling of their motives. Many excellent persons profess themselves shocked by the scene where, close on the end, Cleopatra plays the cheat, handing Cæsar a false schedule of her wealth, and is detected in the lie. Here is the narrative in Plutarch—

Then she suddenly altered her speech, and prayed him [Cæsar] to pardon her, as though she were affrayed to die and desirous to live.

At length, she gave him a brief and memorial of all the ready money and treasure she had. But by chance there stood Seleucus by, one of her treasurers, who to seem a good servant, came straight to Cæsar, to disprove Cleopatra, that she had not sent in all, but kept many things back of purpose. Cleopatra was in such a rage with him that she flew upon him, and took him by the hair of the head, and boxed him well-favouredly.

Shakespeare found this in Plutarch and used it, because it is truth; not mere truth of fact, but truth of that universal quality which (as Aristotle noted) makes Poetry a more philosophical thing than History. Cleopatra did not tell that falsehood by chance. She told it naturally, because she was courtesan in grain: born a liar and born also royal Egypt, she cannot sentimentalise one half of her character away at the end, to catch our tears. We must accept her, without paltering, for the naked, conscientiousless, absolute, royal she-animal that she is. Cover the courtesan in mistaken truth, and by so much you hide out of sight the secret of her majesty—with her no secret at all, for she is regnant, rather, by virtue of being shameless.

XII

With such a woman our excellent Plutarch can make no weather at all. "Now her beauty," he reports, "was not so passing, as unmatchable of other women, nor yet such, as upon present view did enamour men with her;

but so sweet was her company and conversation, that a man could not possibly but be taken. And besides her beauty, the good grace she had to talk and discourse, her courteous nature that tempered her words and deeds, was a spur that pricked to the quick. Furthermore, besides all these, her voice and words were marvellous pleasant: for her tongue was an instrument of music to divers sports and pastimes, the which she easily turned to any language that pleased her," etc. All of which is all very well, but we feel (do we not?) that Plutarch might continue in this strain for twenty years without explaining Cleopatra or her charm to us. It is all description, and of a being we know by instinct to be indescribable.

Shakespeare can get plenty of description out of Plutarch to help the impression of Cleopatra's magnificent luxury. I quoted in my last lecture the famous description of her barge upon Cydnus. But all that is *description:* of externals, accessories; helpful but quite undramatic. Getting nearer to the woman, he can make an observer tell us, and truly, that

> Age cannot wither her, nor custom stale
> Her infinite variety: other women cloy
> The appetites they feed, but she makes hungry
> Where most she satisfies.

And that (mark you) is superbly said: we turn back to it as to a last word. But, still, it is somebody's description. It is not the flashing, the revealing, word, that can only, in a drama, be spoken by the person, spoken here by Cleopatra herself.

"Plutarch," it has been said, "states the fact simply, and lets be: his genius lies in telling a story, in recording a jest or a speech, in drawing the *outside* of things: the subtile dialogue which reveals character is beyond his simple art. Hence we hear of the golden galley with oars of silver and purple sails, the flutes and howboys and all her magnificent circumstance: her charm is not made credible. But what Plutarch leaves us to take on faith, Shakespeare gives us to behold. Again the witch lives. . . ."

Ay, and in the very words she first utters. Grand doting was never more subtly played with—

Cleopatra. If it be love indeed, tell me how much.
Antony. There's beggary in the love that can be reckon'd.
Cleopatra. I'll set a bourn how far to be beloved.
Antony. Then must thou needs find out new heaven, new earth.
            Enter an Attendant.
Attendant. News, my good lord, from Rome.
Antony.   Grates me: the sum.
Cleopatra. Nay, hear them, Antony:
            Fulvia perchance is angry; or, who knows
            If the scarce-bearded Cæsar have not sent
            His powerful mandate to you, "Do this, or this;
            Take in that kingdom, and enfranchise that;
            Perform't, or else we damn thee."
Antony.   How, my love?
Cleopatra. Perchance! nay, and most like:
            You must not stay here longer, your dismission
            Is come from Cæsar; therefore hear it, Antony.
            Where's Fulvia's process?   Cæsar's I would say?
              both?
            Call in the messengers.   As I am Egypt's queen,
            Thou blushest, Antony, and that blood of thine
            Is Cæsar's homager: else so thy cheek pays
              shame
            When shrill-tongued Fulvia scolds. The
              messengers!

Antony. Let Rome in Tiber melt, and the wide arch
Of the ranged empire fall! Here is my space.
Kingdoms are clay: our dungy earth alike
Feeds beast as man: the nobleness of life
Is to do thus; when such a mutual pair
And such a twain can do't.

There you have the lists set, and the play not 40 lines gone! Into those 40 lines is already compressed the issue as the world sees it, critical but well-wishing, through the eyes of Philo: the issue as Antony sees it—

Here is my space.
Kingdoms are clay . . .

and the hints of half-a-dozen coils through which, en tangled in jealousies, Cleopatra's mind is working.

XIII

I shall say nothing of the minor characters of the play save this—that the true normal, or *punctum indifferens* —which you always find somewhere in any tragedy of Shakespeare's—is to be sought, not in Octavius, but in some spectator such as Philo or even the loose-moralled Fnobarbus. Cæsar Octavius represents rather the cool enemy, blameless, priggish, who, as this world is ordered, inevitably overthrows Armida's palace—but is none the more lovable for the feat. His character has already been given us, ineffaceably, in a single line of *Julius Cæsar.* He and Antòny dispute which is to command the right, and which the left, of the army before Philippi. "Why," demands Antony, "why do you cross me in this exigent?" To which Octavius responds with that serene stupidity only granted to a young egoist that he may prevail—

I do not cross you: but I will do so.

The whole point of Octavius—and of Octavia (upon whom Gervinus, recognising the abstract German housewife in a wilderness of Latins, expends so many tears)—is that they are ministers of fate precisely because incapable of understanding what it is all *about*. Precisely because he has not the ghost of a notion of anyone's being such a fool as to lose the world for love, we see this politician predestined to win. Nor—the beauty of it!—will he ever divine the sting in Cleopatra's word to the asp, as she applies it to her breast—

> O, couldst thou speak,
> That I might hear thee call great Cæsar ass
> Unpolicied!

It is not only, of course, by direct representation of Cleopatra in her gusts of passion—now real, now simulated—that Shakespeare weaves the spell. The talk exchanged among Iras, Charmian, Alexas and the Soothsayer is as deft and witty an introduction to Venusberg as ever playwright could invent: and, after that, "Let Rome in Tiber melt!" "Melt Egypt into Nile!"

XIV

Gervinus writes out a long laboured estimate of Antony's character. It is all idle; because, the lists being those of passion, all we want is, of Antony that he should be generous and lusty and great; all we want of Cleopatra is tnat she shall be subtle and lustful and great: both lustful, both unmistakably great. With all his detailed portraiture of "my serpent of old Nile" Shakespeare triumphs in this play, the closer you examine it, by a very sublime simplicity: he triumphs by making this pair royal *because* elemental; *because* they obey impulses greater even than Rome, though it stretch from Parthia to Cape Misenum. I do not deny that Shakespeare has spent pains in making Mark Antony lovable to us, so that Dryden and every playwright who makes him a soft voluptuary must necessarily fail. But truly this is a woman's play, in which the man has to be noble in order that the woman may win a high triumph and perish in it. I would even call it the paradox of *Antony and Cleopatra* that it at once is the most wayward of Shakespeare's tragedies, dependent from scene to scene on the will of a wanton, and withal one of the most heavily charged with fate and the expectancy of fate. Who can forget the hushed talk of the guards and the low rumbling of earth underfoot that preludes the arming of Antony, when Cleopatra misarrays him?

Antony.   Eros! mine armour, Eros!
Cleopatra.   Sleep a little.
Antony.   No, my chuck. Eros, come; mine armour, Eros!
            Enter Eros *with armour.*
        Come, good fellow, put mine iron on:
        If fortune be not ours to-day, it is
        Because we brave her: come.
Cleopatra.   Nay, I'll help too.
        What's this for?
Antony.   Ah, let be, let be! thou art
        The armourer of my heart: false, false; this,
        this. . . .

and if any object that the supernatural prelude to this is out of place in tragedy, I am content to answer him with a word from an early page of Plutarch. "There be some," says Plutarch, "who think these things to be but fables and tales devised of pleasure. But methinks, for all that, they are not to be rejected or discredited, if we will consider Fortune's strange effects upon times, and of the greatness also of the Roman empire; which had never achieved to her present possessed power and authority if the gods had not from the beginning been workers of the same, and if there had not also been some strange cause and wonderful foundation."

But I marvel in this play most of all, and whenever I read it, at the incomparable life-likeness of Cleopatra, which follows her through every bewildering trick and turn, caprice or gust of passion, equally when she queens it, or fools it, modulates her voice to true or to false passion, or beats her servants and curses like a drab—and she can do all within any given two minutes. It is not lime-lantern that follows Cleopatra about the stage: she carries everywhere with her the light—her own light —of a convincing if almost blinding realism. I am not, as you know, overfond of those critics who read Mary Fitton, or some other "dark lady" into everything Shakespeare wrote: but I must make them the handsome admission that if Shakespeare did not take some actual particular woman for his Cleopatra, I am clean at a loss to imagine how he created this wonder.

It surprises me—to take up a small point—that the most insistent of these critics, Mr. Frank Harris, should boggle, all of a sudden, over Cleopatra's

Here's sport indeed!

when she and her women are drawing Antony aloft. This, says Mr. Harris,

Seems to me a terrible fault, an inexcusable lapse of taste. I should like to think it a misprint, or a misreading; but it is unfortunately like Shakespeare in a certain mood, possible to him, here as elsewhere.

Yes, yes, Mr. Harris! It is shockingly bad taste. But it seems to me mighty fine hysteria.

XV

Let me read the whole passage, not to controvert Mr. Harris, but as leading up to a word upon which I shall conclude because it seems to me the *last* word upon this play.

Enter, below, Antony, *borne by the* Guard.

Cleopatra.   O sun,
    Burn the great sphere thou movest in! darkling
        stand
    The varying shore o' the world. O Antony,
    Antony, Antony! Help, Charmian, help, Iras,
        help;
    Help, friends below; let's draw him hither.
Antony.   Peace!
    Not Cæsar's valour hath o'erthrown Antony,
    But Antony's hath triumph'd on itself.
Cleopatra. So it should be, that none but Antony
    Should conquer Antony; but woe 'tis so!
Antony. I am dying, Egypt, dying; only
    I here importune death awhile, until
    Of many thousand kisses the poor last
    I lay upon thy lips.
Cleopatra.   I dare not, dear,
    Dear my lord, pardon, I dare not,
    Lest I be taken: not the imperious show
    Of the full-fortuned Cæsar ever shall
    Be brooch'd with me; if knife, drugs, serpents,
        have
    Edge, sting, or operation, I am safe:
    Your wife Octavia, with her modest eyes
    And still conclusion, shall acquire no honour
    Demuring upon me. But come, come, Antony,

Help me, my women,—we must draw thee up;
Assist, good friends.

Antony.   O, quick, or I am gone.

Cleopatra. Here's sport indeed! How heavy weighs my
      lord!
Our strength is all gone into heaviness;
That makes the weight. Had I great Juno's
      power,
The strong-wing'd Mercury should fetch thee up
And set thee by Jove's side. Yet come a little—
Wishers were ever fools—O, come, come, come;
          [*They heave Antony aloft to Cleopatra.*
And welcome, welcome! die where thou hast
      lived:
Quicken with kissing: had my lips that power,
Thus would I wear them out.

All.   A heavy sight!

Antony. I am dying, Egypt, dying:
Give me some wine, and let me speak a little.

Cleopatra. No, let me speak, and let me rail so high,
That the false housewife Fortune break her
      wheel,
Provoked by my offence.

Antony.   One word, sweet queen:
Of Cæsar seek your honour, with your safety.
    O!

Cleopatra. They do not go together.

Antony.   Gentle, hear me:
None about Cæsar trust but Proculeius.

Cleopatra. My resolution and my hands I'll trust;
None about Cæsar.

Antony. The miserable change now at my end
Lament nor sorrow at, but please your thoughts
In feeding them with those my former fortunes
Wherein I lived, the greatest prince o' the world,
The noblest, and do now not basely die,
Not cowardly put off my helmet to

My countryman, a Roman by a Roman
Valiantly vanquish'd. Now my spirit is going;
I can no more.

Cleopatra.   Noblest of men, woo't die?
Hast thou no care of me? shall I abide
In this dull world, which in thy absence is
No better than a sty? O, see, my women,

                    [*Antony dies.*

The crown o' the earth doth melt. My lord!
O, wither'd is the garland of the war,
The soldier's pole is fall'n: young boys and girls
Are level now with men; the odds is gone,
And there is nothing left remarkable
Beneath the visiting moon.   [*Faints*

Charmian.   O, quietness, lady!

Iras.   She's dead too, our sovereign.

Charmian.   Lady!

Iras.   Madam!

Charmian. O madam, madam, madam!

Iras.   Royal Egypt,
Empress!

Charmian.   Peace, peace, Iras!

Cleopatra. No more, but e'en a woman, and commanded
By such poor passion as the maid that milks
And does the meanest chares. It were for me
To throw my sceptre at the injurious gods,
To tell them that this world did equal theirs
Till they had stol'n our jewel. All's but naught;
Patience is sottish, and impatience does
Become a dog that's mad: then is it sin
To rush into the secret house of death,
Ere death dare come to us? How do you,
    women?
What, what! good cheer! Why, how now,
    Charmian!
My noble girls! Ah, women, women, look,
Our lamp is spent, it's out! Good sirs, take heart:

> We'll bury him; and then, what's brave, what's
> noble,
> Let's do it after the high Roman fashion,
> And make death proud to take us.

After that will you refuse to consent with me that the ,last word upon this play should be of its greatness? All these people, whatever of righteousness they lack, are ,great. They have the very aura of greatness.

And they are great, of course, not in their dealing with affairs, with the destinies of Rome or of Egypt— for it is by their neglect or misprision or mishandling of these that they come to misfortune and allow meaner men, calculators, to rise by their downfall: but great as the gods are great, high-heartedly, carelessly. Note how finely, when the whole stake has been thrown and lost, they sit down to their last earthly banquet. They seem in their passion to stand remote above circumstance. They are indifferent to consistency. Says Enobarbus, when Antony will leave for Rome—

> Under a compelling occasion let women die: it were pity
> to cast them away for nothing; though, between them and a
> great cause, they should be esteemed nothing.   Cleopatra,
> catching but the least noise of this, dies instantly; I have
> seen her die twenty times upon far poorer moment. . . .

Yet she plays as largely with real death. She

> hath pursued conclusions infinite
> Of easy ways to die.

—and the way she finally chooses is most regal. Like the gods too, these people are exempt of shame: as absolutely above it as Zeus, father of gods and men, who could be ridiculous enough in his amours and yet, when

all is said, remains a very grand gentleman. They are
heroic souls in this disorderly house of Alexandria—
even to pretty mischievous Charmian. Hear her, as she
closes Cleopatra's eyes and stands up herself, as the
Guard bursts in, to take the stroke. Hear her and mark
her last word—

Charmian.	So, fare thee well.
	Now boast thee, death, in thy possession lies
	A lass unparallel'd. Downy windows, close;
	And golden Phœbus never be beheld
	Of eyes again so royal! Your crown's awry;
	I'll mend it, and then play.
	Enter the Guard, *rushing in.*
First Guard.	Where is the queen?
Charmian.	Speak softly, wake her not.
First Guard.	Cæsar hath sent—
Charmian.	Too slow a messenger.
	[*Applies an asp.*
	O, come apace, dispatch: I partly feel thee.
First Guard.	Approach, ho! All's not well: Cæsar's be-
	guiled.
Second Guard.	There's Dolabella sent from Cæsar; call him.
First Guard.	What work is here! Charmian, is this well
	done?
Charmian.	It is well done, and fitting for a princess
	Descended of so many royal kings.
	Ah, soldier! [*Dies*

A GOSSIP ON CHAUCER (I)

L ET me begin with a few lines from Browning's
little poem, *How it Strikes a Contemporary*

I only knew one poet in my life:
And this, or something like it, was his way.

You saw go up and down Valladolid,
A man of mark, to know next time you saw.
His very serviceable suit of black
Was courtly once and conscientious still,
And many might have worn it, though none did:
The cloak, that somewhat shone and showed the threads,
Had purpose, and the ruff, significance . . .
You'd come upon his scrutinizing hat
Making a peaked shade blacker than itself
Against the single window spared some house . . .
Or else surprise the ferrel of his stick
Trying the mortar's temper 'tween the chinks
Of some new shop a-building, French and fine.
He stood and watched the cobbler at his trade,
The man who slices lemons into drink,
The coffee roaster's brazier, and the boys
That volunteer to help him turn its winch.
He glanced o'er books on stalls with half an eye,
And fly-leaf ballads on the vendor's string,
And broad-edge bold-print posters by the wall.
He took such cognizance of men and things,
If any beat a horse, you felt he saw;
If any cursed a woman, he took note;

Yet stared at nobody,—*you* stared at him,
And found, less to your pleasure than surprise,
He seemed to know you and expect as much. . . .

I

Through Aldgate Street, London, on any day between
1374 and 1385 there passed, to and from his work, a
stoutish man soberly clad, with a forked beard, a whim-
sical elvish face, and eyes which, while bent on the
cobbles, somewhat noted everybody and everything
that passed. "Thou lookest," he wrote of himself, "as
thou woldest fynd an hare, for evere upon the ground I
se thee stare." The shyest of men to accost! Noting
his fellows in this subdolent way, he exchanges greet-
ings with few. His daily work takes him down to the
riverside and the wharves, for he is a Comptroller of the
Customs and Subsidy of wools, skins and tanned hides
in the Port of London: where, all day long, for the
usual fees, he has to examine bills of lading and draw up
the rolls of receipts with his own hand, always at desk
or moving among the merchandise. That downcast eye
is vigilant here, too. One John Kent, having tried to
smuggle some wool to Dordrecht, finds the whole con-
signment seized and sold by auction, and Geoffrey
Chaucer—for that is the Comptroller's name—pockets
seventy-one pounds four shillings and sixpence as his
share of John Kent's fine.

At nightfall ledgers are closed; and this man, with
the same quick step as he came, and in a like abstraction,
threads his way back to Aldgate, where his lodgings are
over the gateway itself, on the city wall, and where
lighting his lamp or candle, he is lost in quite other
books, not ledgers: until, as he reads or writes, in a
dream, Jove's eagle stands over his shoulder and ad-

monishes that Jove has pity of this wandered service in scholarship. "And for this cause," says Jove's eagle—

And for this cause he hath me sent
To thee: now herkne, by thy trouthe!
Certeyn, he hath of theë routhe,
That thou so longë trewély
Hast servèd so ententifly
His blindë nevew Cupido,
And fair Venus goddesse also,
Withoutë guerdoun ever yit,
And nevertheles hast set thy wit—
Although that in thy hede ful lyte is—
To makë bokës, songës, dytees,
In ryme, or ellès in cadence,
As thou best canst, in reverence
Of Love, and of his servants eke,
That have his servise soght, and seke;
And peynest thee to preyse his art,
Although thou haddest never part;
Wherfor, al-so God me blesse,
Jovës halt hit greët humblesse
And vertu eek, that thou wolt make
A-night ful ofte thyn heed to ake,
In thy studië so thou wrytest,
And evermo of love endytest. . . .
　　　Wherfor, as I seyde, y-wis,
Jupiter considereth this,
And also, beau sir, other thinges;
That is, that thou hast no tydinges
Of Love's folk, if they be glade,
Ne of noght ellès that God made;
And noght only fro fer contree
That ther no tyding comth to thee,
But of thy verray neyghébores,
That dwellen almost at thy dores,
Thou herest neither that ne this;

For whan thy labour doon al is,
And hast y-maad thy rekeninges,
In stede of reste and newè thinges,
Thou gost hoom to thy hous anoon;
And, also domb as any stoon,
Thou sittest at another boke,
Til fully daswèd is thy loke,
And livest thus as an hermyte,
—Although thyn abstinence is lyte.

No: it was no "total abstinence" man who wrote *The Canterbury Tales!* As a matter of historical fact, in 1374, on the 23rd April—the day which was to be Shakespeare's birthday—the king granted Chaucer a pitcher of wine daily, to be received in the Port of London from His Majesty's butler.

II

Now what is the history of this man? What is he studying? Of what is he writing? What are the visions he sees in his chamber above the gate in that narrow circle of lamplight, after the porter below has shot the bolts, and in the archway of Aldgate the rumble of the city's traffic has fallen suddenly to silence for the night?

Geoffrey Chaucer was born—the exact date is disputed—in 1340 or a little earlier; in Thames Street, London, begotten of John Chaucer, citizen and vintner, upon his lawful wife Agnes, kinswoman and heiress of the city moneyer, Hamo de Compton. These data are significant. The man was born pat on the edge of the hour when England *found herself;* when a hundred different currents in Court, Church, Parliament; in law, language, learning, art, commerce, rural and domestic economy; drew together with accelerating pace, as by suction, and almost suddenly coalesced in one great tide of consciously national life. He is born in the capital city, "leve London," which is the vortex, the heart, the pumping-engine (so to speak) of this new lusty blood. He is born on the very bank of the royal river which symbolises this miracle. He is born *pur sang* of the merchant class, which had done more than any other to effect the miracle.

As for London, or that part of it which crowded about his first home, all vestiges of it disappeared, of course, long ago, in the Great Fire. But if we consult Stow's *Survey* with its map, we shall see that the child's window almost overhung the river: still in those days, and for centuries, "silver Thames" renowned for swans;

> Where many a ship doth rest with toppe-royall:

that it looked up-stream on the right to Great London Bridge with its houses and tall chapel; down-stream to the Tower; and full across to the fair open country of Surrey, backing or visible between waterside houses, outskirts of Southwark—a suburb sparse enough just opposite the lad's window, but huddling thickly to the right, as it neared the bridge-end, and congregated in travellers' inns and stables around the great church of St. Mary Overies—St. Mary-over-the-Water. The streets in which the boy grew up rattled with business, teemed with folk: porters, wharfingers, tradesmen, apprentices, sailors ashore, scriveners, taverners and their clients, clergy of all orders, rich merchants with their wives "full royall to behold." The upper storeys, wood or wood-and-plaster, bulged out over colonnades of traffic, almost overhung the wharves. His own kins-folk lived and had their occupation in or about Vintry Ward: and the trick of the wine-trade did not escape this

observant child or miss to be reported by him later in
the *Pardoner's Tale.*

> Now kepe yow fro the whyte [wine] and fro the rede,
> And namely fro the whytė wyn of Lepe,
> That is to selle in Fish-strete, or in Chepe.
> This wyn of Spaynė crepeth subtilly
> In othere wynės, growing fastė by,
> Of which ther ryseth swich fumositee,
> That whan a man hath dronken draughtės three,
> And weneth that he be at hoom in Chepe,
> He is in Spayne, right at the toune of Lepe,
> Nat at the Rochel, ne at Burdeux toun;
> And thannė wol he seye, "*Sampsoun,*[hic!] *Sampsoun.*"

[In other words, if you leave a cask of good claret too
close alongside a cask of cheap fuddling Cadiz stuff,
the contents are—or were in those days—liable to get
mysteriously mixed.]

John Chaucer, the father, had some connexion with
Court, possibly as victualler; and in 1338 accompanied
the King to the Continent. Very likely the mother had
influence too. At any rate we find young Geoffrey, at
the age of sixteen, a page in the household of the
Duchess of Clarence. In 1359 he joined the invading
army which Edward III led into France, and was there
taken prisoner. In March of the following year he
regained his liberty, the King paying sixteen pounds
towards his ransom. In 1367 he was granted a pension
of twenty marks for life as valet of the King's household.
In 1368 his patron, Lionel, Duke of Clarence, died,
and Chaucer appears to have been transferred to the
service of John of Gaunt. The young man was already
writing verse, and in 1369 lamented the recent death of
John of Gaunt's wife, Blanche, in a poem entitled *The
Deth of Blaunche the Duchesse.* In 1370 and 1372 he

travelled on diplomatic missions abroad, the second taking him to Genoa, Pisa, Florence. It is important to note that he remained in Italy for nearly eleven months. Apparently he did his diplomatic work to the royal satisfaction; for in 1374 he received that grant of a daily pitcher of wine of which we have spoken; on June 8 was appointed to his Comptrollership of wools, etc.; and less than a week later received a life pension of ten pounds "for the good service rendered by him *and his wife Philippa* to the said Duke, to his consort, and to his mother the Queen." This is the first distinct mention of Chaucer's wife: and some have pleased themselves with the fancy that his marriage was yet another stroke of luck in this lucky year; in which moreover (in May) we find him taking the lease of the house over the city gate. But a Philippa Chaucer is mentioned as one of the Ladies of the Chamber to Queen Philippa in 1366 and subsequently, and this may well be the poet's wife. In 1366 Chaucer would be twenty-six or so.[1]

III

But what was this man writing, or practising to write, on those evenings over the gateway? Well, it is certain (1) that he had been versifying, translating, freely rendering, for years past; (2) that his early models—as one might expect from his first campaigns and detention in

[1] Back in 1357, or thereabouts, when Chaucer was receiving, as page to the Duchess, "an entire suit of clothes, consisting of paltock (or short cloak), a pair of red breeches, and shoes," there is found in the same household account-book frequent mention of one Philippa Pan—"Pan" being conjectured as short for "Panetaria," mistress of the pantry. "Speculations suggest themselves," says Dr. E. A. Bond, "that the Countess's (she was Countess of Ulster as well as Duchess) attendant Philippa may have been Chaucer's future wife." "It is quite possible," says Skeat; "it is even probable."

France—were French models; that he had already made, for instance, what has come down to us of his translation of *The Romaunt of the Rose*, had written some *Ballades*, and possibly some stories of French origin (that of Constance, for example) which he kept by him and in later years furbished up to be included in the *Canterbury Tales*.

But from the time of his return from Italy he is seen to be intent on other and greater models. He had lived in Florence, where the great memory of Dante was but of yesterday, not yet overtaken by temporary eclipse: and he, Chaucer, had far too much of the artist in him to miss seeing that *The Divine Comedy*—though not to his temperament—in mere mastery soared miles above *The Romaunt of the Rose* and yet miles further above the ordinary romances. We do not know if he met Boccaccio, or travelled to Padua for the honour of being presented to Petrarch. But he certainly knew the work of both. He boldly takes *Troilus* from the one, the story of Griselda from the other, to name no other conveyings: and while we have no positive evidence that he was acquainted with the *Decameron* the whole framework of *The Canterbury Tales* is *aut Decamerone aut nullus*.

What, then, was this man trying to do with this inspiration, these models?

He was trying to copy the models; to express the inspiration, to make all that had seized on him tractable in the fresh but untutored language that men have come to talk in his own country—a merry country, but, lacking a literature, lacking so many tales to lift and gladden the heart—merry tales, tender tales, even sorrowful tales: but all *amusing*. Of such Italy, as he had found, was full.

For rendering the *fabliaux* into English Chaucer's

genius had scarcely a limitation. On the other hand, for catching the lyrical gust of the thirteenth century he had but a small talent, while for handling the majestic themes, the solemn verse, of Dante he had neither language at hand nor power to invent it. His whole temperament, too, debarred him.

IV

We must acknowledge these limitations in our "Father of English Poetry." Chaucer is, to begin with, not a truly lyrical poet. For lyric he can compare neither with the Scotsmen, Henryson and Dunbar, who followed adoring, nor with his unknown predecessors who wrote the song of *Alisoun* and *Blou Northern Wynd*, nor with any of a score of troubadours and trouvères from whom they derived, nor again with many a humble carol-maker or ballad-maker of his times. Take, for example, this lovely specimen written (we dare say) in his lifetime by some innominate author:

> Jesu, swetė sonė dere!
> On porful bed list thou here,
>   And that me greueth sore;
> For thi cradel is ase a bere,
> Oxe and asse beth thi fere:
>   Weepe ich mai tharfore.
>
> Jesu, swetė, beo noth wroth,
> Thou ich nabbė clout ne cloth
>   The on for to folde,
> The on to foldė ne to wrappe,
> For ich nabbė clout ne lappe;
> Bote ley thou thi fet to my pappe,
>   And wite the from the colde.

Or take a stanza from Dunbar's *Of The Nativity Of Christ*—

Syng, hevin imperiall, most of hicht!
  Regions of air mak armony!
All fishe in flud and foull of flicht,
  Be myrthfull and mak melody!
  All *Gloria in Excelsis* cry!
Hevin, erd, se, man, bird and best,
  He that is crownit aboue the sky
Pro nobis Puer natus est—

Or take a verse or two from the age-old ballad wherein
the ghost of Clerk Saunders comes to May Margaret's
window and claims her troth.

"Are ye sleeping, Marg'ret?" he says,
  "Or are ye waking presentlie?
Give me my faith and troth again,
  I wot, true love, I gied to thee" . . .

"Thy faith and troth thou sallna get,
  And our true love sall never twin,
Until ye tell what comes o' women,
  I wot, who die in strong traivelling."

"Their beds are made in the heavens high,
  Down at the foot of our good Lord's knee,
Well set about wi' gillyflowers;
  I wot, sweet company for to see.

"O cocks are crowing on merry middle-earth,
  I wot the wild fowls are boding day;
The psalms of heaven will soon be sung,
  And I, ere now, will be miss'd away."

Then she has taken a crystal wand,
  And she has stroken her troth thereon,
She has given it him out at the shot-window,
  Wi' mony a sad sigh and heavy groan

"I thank ye, Marg'ret; I thank ye, Marg'ret;
　And ay I thank ye heartilie;
Gin ever the dead come for the quick,
　Be sure, Marg'ret, I'll come for thee."

It's hosen and shoon, and gown alone,
　She climb'd the wall, and follow'd him,
Until she came to the green forèst,
　And there she lost the sight o' him.

"Is there ony room at your head, Saunders?
　Is there ony room at your feet?
Or ony room at your side, Saunders,
　Where fain, fain, I wad sleep?" . . .

Then up and crew the red, red cock,
　And up and crew the gray:
"'Tis time, 'tis time, my dear Marg'ret,
　That you were going away.

"And fair Marg'ret, and rare Marg'ret,
　And Marg'ret o' veritie,
Gin e'er ye love another man,
　Ne'er love him as ye did me."

(Forgive me for having been decoyed, by the beauty of
it, into quoting at such length.) Great as he is, Chaucer
had command on none of these exquisite notes. When
Chaucer writes a lyric, it has merit, but a merit nowise
comparable.

Flee fro the prees, and dwelle with sothfastnesse,
　Suffyce unto thy good, though hit be smal. . . .

Is not *that*, rather, his note? Or—

To you, my purse, and to non other wight
　Compleyne I, for ye be my lady dere! . . .

or,

Sin I fro Love escapèd am so fat. . . .

or,

Alone walking, in thought pleyning,
And sore sighing, all desolate
Me remembring of my living
My deth wishing bothe erly and late. . . .

To be fair, we must allow that Chaucer, as an improvisatore, can break into something like lyrical ecstasy when a story catches hold of him and he is, like a true artist, feeling with the hearts of his characters. Constance's farewell to her children will occur to you as an example; but I will rather quote you here Troilus' outbreak of agony as he stretches his hands to the shut windows of the palace containing his lost love.

Than seyde he thus, "O paleys desolat,
O hous, of houses whylom best y-hight,
O paleys empty and disconsolat,

O thou lanterne, of which queynt is the light,
O paleys, whylom day, that now art night,
Wel oughtestow to falle, and I to dye,
Sin she is went that wont was us to gye!

O paleys, whylom croune of houses alle,
Enluminèd with sonne of allè blisse!
O ring, fro which the ruby is out-falle,
O cause of wo, that cause hast been of lisse!
Yet, sin I may no bet, fayn wolde I kisse
Thy coldè dores, dorste I for this route;
And fare-wel shryne, of which the seynt is oute!"

Nor am I saying for a moment that Chaucer is the worse artist for keeping the lyrical element well down in his narrative: and I am the less likely to hold this because

I strongly hold that in our day the lyric exercises over poetry a sway which has grown disproportionate if not tyrannical. But I do say that Chaucer's lyrical gift lifts him but a very little way to being the excellent poet that his contemporaries saluted as "Master," and we, these five hundred years and more later, salute as one of the very great. I will go further and say that in practice he was careless of the lyric. The songs of the Provençals were dead stuff to him, did not interest him. The trouvères and the long-winded romancers that followed—though more dead to us—lay nearer to him, and he was really concerned with these, to convert and improve them.

V

A far heavier handicap, and one that *a priori* would almost disqualify for even second-class award any poet who ran such long courses as Chaucer habitually entered for [and, I may add, almost habitually broke down in before reaching his goal], is his innocence of deep thought, high seriousness; of that intensity which the Greeks called σπουδαιότης.

I hinted to you in a previous lecture that, while Langland cannot begin to vie as a poet with Chaucer, in that he has no comparable gift of using language or making a poem, Chaucer was never troubled by that penetrating depth of vision by which, in his awkward way, Langland reached to see in a mere plowman—a bowed and tortured minister of the fields—the image of Christ crucified.

Yet Chaucer, in the frank gallantry of genius, dares to take his ease in Sion (a perfectly well-bred ease) with a poet a thousand miles removed above our poor Langland —to consort with the great Dante himself—to convey and embody page after page of Dante almost word for word into his own writings; and, to our amazement the result is not ludicrous! Upon my word, when one comes to consider, it looks like the combined impudence and imprudence of a man who should steal a blast-furnace to help ripen his cucumbers.

But on this point, and on the spiritual difference between the two men, let me quote some words of James Russell Lowell, because they are not likely to be bettered in our time.

Before Chaucer, modern Europe had given birth to one great poet, Dante: and contemporary with him was one supremely elegant one, Petrarch. Dante died only seven years before Chaucer was born. . . . Both were of mixed race, Dante certainly, Chaucer presumably so. Dante seems to have inherited on the Teutonic side the strong moral sense, the almost nervous irritability of conscience, and the tendency to mysticism which made him the first of Christian poets—first in point of time and first in point of greatness. From the other side [the Italian] he seems to have received almost in overplus a feeling of order and proportion, sometimes well-nigh hardening into mathematical precision and formalism. . . . Chaucer, on the other hand, drew from the South a certain airiness of sentiment and expression, a felicity of phrase, and an elegance of turn hitherto unprecedented and hardly yet matched in our literature, but all the while kept firm hold of his native soundness of understanding, and that genial humour which seems to be the proper element of worldly wisdom. With Dante, life represented the passage of the soul from a state of nature to a state of grace. . . . With Chaucer, life is a pilgrimage, but only that his eye may be delighted with the varieties of costume and character. There are good morals to be found in Chaucer, but they are always incidental. With Dante the main question is the saving of the soul, with Chaucer it is the conduct of life. The distance between them is almost that between holiness and prudence. Dante applies himself to the realities and Chaucer to the scenery of life, and the former is consequently the more universal poet, as the latter is the more truly national one. Dante represents the justice of God, and Chaucer his loving-kindness. If there is anything that may properly be called satire in the one, it is like a blast of the Divine wrath, before which the wretches cower and tremble, which rends away their cloaks of hypocrisy and their masks of worldly propriety, and leaves them shivering in the cruel nakedness of their shame. The satire of the other is genial with the broad sunshine of humour, into which the victims walk forth with a delightful unconcern, laying aside of themselves the disguises that seem to make them uncomfortably warm, till they have made a thorough betrayal of themselves so unconsciously that we almost pity while we laugh.

If I may add to this, I should say that Chaucer, who stood at the parting of the ways; and probably—from all we know of his life at court and abroad—talked French as easily as he talked English, and is, by the compilers of handbooks, preached at you for the most typically English of English authors—is actually the most thoroughly French. I, at any rate, know of no English author so near in spirit to Molière, nor of one who so constantly brings life under the great ruling spirit of France—*sagesse*. What does the French mother say to her child from morning till night?— "Angélique, sois tu sage, donc!" What does the English mother say?—"Jane, be good!" I shall have a word to say concerning this *sagesse* of Chaucer's, and in defence of it, when we come to discuss *The Canterbury Tales*, which best illustrate it. For the present I am content to note that Chaucer was not only incapable of expressing—he was incapable of feeling—the high intense intellectual emotion you will find (say) in Words-

worth's *Lines . . . above Tintern Abbey;* but that he
was incapable even of surmising

> that blessèd mood
> In which the burthen of the mystery,
> In which the heavy and the weary weight
> Of all this unintelligible world,
> Is lightened—

simply because he has never felt the burthen; and to ask
you to note, remembering Dante, remembering Virgil
and his *Sunt lachrymæ rerum et mentem mortalia tangunt,*
that what separates Chaucer from Wordsworth is not a
mere juniority of four hundred years, but a native difference of mind and temperament.

VI

Well, again, what was this man in the gatehouse
trying to do?

He was trying to render the *fabliaux* of France and
Italy into English: I think, just that and no more. I
cannot discover that he was greatly concerned, as an
artist, with improving them, or improved them otherwise than unconsciously. Tact was his guide in that.
His oft-quoted line

> The lyf so short, the craft so long to lerne —

refers to the Art of Love, *Ars Amatoria,* not to literary
composition.

No: he was trying to popularise these tales in English,
then rapidly becoming the habitual speech of his countrymen from the labourer up to the King and his court.

What he *did* was another matter. As genius so often
proves greater than it knows, what he did was a far
greater thing. Let me repeat a short passage from

Newman which I quoted here to an earlier generation in a lecture *On the Art of Writing.*

When a language has been cultivated in any particular department of thought, and so far as it has been generally perfected, an existing want has been supplied, and there is no need for further workmen. In its earlier times, while it is yet unformed, to write in it at all is almost a work of genius. It is like crossing a country before roads are made communicating between place and place. The authors of that age deserve to be Classics both because of what they do and because they can do it.

Now Chaucer, of course, did not *create* English. It takes a mort of men to create a speech. What he did, besides writing poetry, was this:—as Lowell truly and excellently says, he "found his native tongue a dialect and left it a language."

VII

And this naturally brings me to the practical point on which very briefly I shall conclude today. How are *we* to read Chaucer, whether to ourselves or aloud? How are we to pronounce his language, whether aloud or alone with our lips muted? How are we to scan him?

Well, my advice may be heretical; but in sum it amounts to this: that, since Chaucer wrote to give pleasure, we should read him in the way (and by any one of us it is soon learnt) that brings the most pleasure to our ear. When teachers of phonetics tell me that Chaucer wrote in a dialect, they leave me cold. When Skeat assures me that "the dialect of Chaucer does not materially differ from that which has become the standard literary language; that is to say, it mainly represents the East-Midland, as spoken in London (I presume by the educated) and by the students of Oxford and Cambridge," I am temperately grateful: for I should have pronounced him, or tried to pronounce him, in that way anyhow. I seem to owe, not only that pleasure to myself, but that compliment to the man who, more than any other, made educated English.

Dialect changes. If you will consult *Pickwick* you may convince yourselves that less than a hundred years ago Cockneys did not drop their "*h*'s" as they do now, but they regularly transposed *v* and *w*, as they don't now. (For "very well" Sam Weller said "werry vell.") "Educated" pronunciation changes. Our grandfathers and grandmothers dropped the "*h*" in "hospital," called "lilacs" "laylocks," and pronounced "obliged" as "obleeged." Less than a hundred years ago, many a Yorkshire country gentleman dropped his "*h*'s" as a matter of course. The rudest descendant of the Pilgrim Fathers would not do this. Once you start treating the well of English undefiled as a "dialect," what prevents your reading the *Prologue* in London or East-Midland dialect thus?

> A good woife was ther of besoidè Bawth
> But she was somdel deef and that was scanthe
> Of cloth-maiking she haddè swich an haurnt
> She pawsèd hem of Wypers and of Gaurnt.

And I am the more emboldened to distrust those gentlemen who lay down elaborate rules whereby we must pronounce Chaucer when I pass on to their elaborate rules for scanning him—rules which convey nothing to me save the information that their inventors have the wrong shape of ear for poetry.

Anyone can, at the expense of a very small initial trouble, learn to scan Chaucer without an effort. It is not in the nature of Chaucer to be difficult.

The main trouble, of course, lies with the muted or feminine "*e*," terminating a word. Well, the French have that; so why not—mindful that the French have been, for a century, by far the most thoughtful masters of the technique of verse—why not follow their rule?

With them their feminine "*e*," which was always sounded (though softly, lightly) until the sixteenth century or even later, and is still sounded by Southern French provincials, has faded out of the pronunciation of good speakers, and is replaced by a careful pause, accounting for it in the rhythm. You can, if you will, obeying Skeat, read

> Whan dthat Aprill-a with his shoures soot-a, etc.

and, if it like your ear, so be it. For me, I prefer to rely on the pause, and believe that half the prosodists living would be relieved of half their difficulties, along with half the excuse for their existence, if they could only learn to value pause in their scansion above accent and "short" or "long" syllables. I counsel you, at any rate, to read Chaucer with a free ear, using your own habitual speech; and he will come to you easily, naturally— while ever modulated by a slight well-bred medieval intonation that makes him all the more winning. He will come more than half-way to meet you: for, good fellow! he wants to please you, all the time.

A GOSSIP ON CHAUCER (II)

I

WE have left Chaucer, for some while, just where and how he would have asked us to leave him—for as long as we liked: married and domiciled, pensioned by the Court, while still in public employ; now and again trusted on foreign missions; but, in ordinary, checking by day the shipments of hides and fleeces in his custom-house by London Dock, at nightfall returning to sup and sit late by the lamp in his chamber over the archway of Aldgate. We have examined what he is trying to do in these studious hours. Since his Italian travels, attracted from his early French models, he has been possessed with an ambition to turn those Italian tales, which are the joy of Europe, into English, in a form of verse that will sing to his countrymen; to weight them moreover with moral wisdom borrowed from the great Italians and the Classics, or, rather, so much of the Classics as through the Italians he had delightedly gleaned. To compass this meant making English verse adaptable to it.

There was no question with him, you understand, of inventing the stories themselves, or the passages of moral philosophy that recommended them. To his French contemporary, Eustace Deschamps, he was just "le grand translateur." As Lowell says—

If the works of the great poets teach anything, it is to hold mere invention somewhat cheap. It is not the finding of a thing, but the making something out of it after it is found, that is of consequence. Accordingly, Chaucer, like Shakespeare, invented almost nothing. Whenever he found anything directed to Geoffrey Chaucer, he took it and made the most of it. It was not the subject treated, but himself, that was the new thing.

We may add a wise "aside" of Dryden's—the moral is not obsolete today—"The Genius of our Countrymen, in general being rather to improve an Invention, than to invent themselves."

But, again you understand, the subject, or the story, still meant everything to him; *His* being the new thing, meant nothing to him. His contemporaries and followers hailed him for it, and rapturously. But I find small evidence in his own writing that he cared for his fame, or even that he was vividly aware of it. His aim, I repeat, was to popularise these Continental tales, this European philosophy, in England. To do this he had to invent the *means:* and in this way, and for this purpose, he, more than any man, invented English Verse. Less consciously than Dante had sought "the Illustrious Vulgar"—the Italian speech for educated Italians—but quite as practically, Chaucer was shaping an Illustrious Vernacular: less consciously than Dante and Dante's followers, yet by no means unconsciously or without deliberation.

Do not think that in those evenings of his, over the gatehouse, he was entirely occupied with these tales. This curious man has an "educational bent," which, among our later poets, only Milton can match. He translates Boëthius; a highly significant enterprise: for still (as in King Alfred's time, five hundred years before)

Boëthius is the bible of European culture, the standard work that no gentleman's library should be without: and just as Alfred, laying the foundation of Anglo-Saxon prose, translates Boëthius or causes him to be translated, so in turn Chaucer must retranslate it, that this new English which is coming to be spoken may attain rank as a literary language. Ten years or so later he compiles a Treatise on the Astrolabe for his son's instruction.

Litel Lowis my sone, I have perceived wel by certeyne evidences thyn abilite to lerne sciencez touchinge noumbres and proporciouns; and as wel considere I thy bisy preyere in special to lerne the Tretis of the Astrolabie. . . .This tretis, divided in fyve parties, wole I shewe thee under ful lighte rewles and naked wordes in English; for Latin ne canstow yit but smal, my lyte sone. But natheles, suffyse to thee thise trewe conclusiouns in English, as wel as suffyseth to thise noble clerkes Grekes thise same conclusiouns in Greek, and to Arabiens in Arabik, and to Jewes in Ebrew, and to the Latin folk in Latin.

—which, if you remember, is pretty much what Don Quixote said to Sancho Panza on a certain occasion:

The great Homer wrote not in Latin, for he was a Greek; and Virgil wrote not in Greek, because he was a Latin. In brief, all the ancient poets wrote in the tongue which they sucked in with their mother's milk, nor did they go forth to seek for strange ones to express the greatness of their conceptions: and, this being so, it should be a reason for the fashion to extend to all nations.

But, to return to Chaucer and to "litel Lowis":

And, Lowis, yif so be that I shewe thee in my lighte English as trewe conclusiouns touching this matere, and nought

only as trewe but as many and subtil conclusiouns as ben
shewed in Latin in any commune tretis of the Astrolabie,
con me the more thank; and preye God save the King, that
is lord of this langage, and alle that him feyth bereth and
obeyeth, everech in his degree, the more and the lasse.

So, you see, he already claims English as "the King's
English."

II

We constantly find this "educational bent" even in
Chaucer's verse. In the *House of Fame*, for example,
under a hooded eye, Jove's eagle talks for all the world
like a scientific professor—or at least like a lecturer in
phonetics—and would proceed from phonetics to astronomy but that the listener has had enough of it.
"Wilt thou," asks the eagle in the manner of Mr.
Barlow:

> "Wilt thou lere of sterrès aught?"
> "Nay, certeinly," quod I, "right naught—"

in unfaltering accent, and the scandalised bird can only
reply that it is a pity, because the lesson would have
been full of intellectual improvement.

And again when we say that in his verse at this time
Chaucer, acclimatising Italian stories and something of
Italian thought in English, was breaking away from
the French manner, we must talk, and think, warily.
It is of course extremely convenient for memorising
handbooks to divide him into three periods, sharp and
neat.—"Period i, French: Minor Poems, Romaunt of
the Rose, etc.; Period ii, Italian: from his first Italian
journey to 1380 or therabouts—Monk's Tale, Parson's
Tale, Clerk's Tale, Man of Law's Tale . . . Troilus;

Period iii, English: Legend of Good Women, bulk of Canterbury Tales," and so on. I say that this may be convenient, and I allow that it follows an actual trend. But actually, if you want to know truly how poets and artists behave, they do not slice themselves down into periods for the convenience of the schoolmaster. Their progress towards realising themselves in their work is no more constant, can no more be measured by chain and tape or set out in terms of mileage, than yours or mine towards moral or spiritual perfection. Let me illustrate this by the career of a poet who lived four hundred and fifty years after Chaucer and affected his contemporaries more widely and for the while about as deeply.

Byron "commenced poet" as a conservative in form, if not a reactionary. He took, for his first masters, Pope —Pope of *The Dunciad*, too—and Crabbe: and so far as he had a conscious theory about his art, it continued reactionary to the end: which means that his developed practice and his obstinately stationary theory end in reducing one another to nonsense. In effect Byron turned to be the most passionate rebel of his age. As a critic has said, "There is more of the spirit of the French Revolution in *Don Juan* than in all the works of the author's contemporaries: but his criticism is that of Boileau, and when deliberate is generally absurd. He never recognised the meaning of the artistic movement of his age." He wrote of Pope, "Neither time, nor distance, nor grief, nor age can ever diminish my veneration for him who is the great moral poet of all times, of all climes, of all feelings, and of all stages of existence. . . . Your whole generation are not worth a canto of the *Dunciad*, or anything that is his." Now this was the generation of Coleridge, Wordsworth, Scott, Shelley,

Keats—and Byron himself. Byron himself, the while, was writing poetry which, if it meant anything, gave his own criticism the lie.

I see no reason to doubt that Byron's theory and his practice, though incompatible, were both—and equally—honest. Macaulay's judgment that "personal taste led him to the [eighteenth century], his thirst of praise to the [nineteenth]," is trope rather than truth. More of charity lies in the plain alternative that he would have chosen to obey his theory, but his fiery instinct would not suffer it. In truth, as the critic I have quoted goes on to say, "he had little affinity, moral or artistic, with the spirit of our so-called Augustans, and his determination to admire them was itself rebellious."

Well, given a man in that mind, what *naturally* happens? Such a man feels forward; he feels back. He writes late under the lamp, red-hot, by impulse; he goes shivering to bed; he wakes, and in the light of morning abhors what he has written. He falls back on theory and its discipline, writes carefully, and fails to "bring it off." Cold theory approves, but life has given place to inanition. He *feels* this: he thinks of his readers, and knows that *they* certainly will feel it.

Put shortly, the man is trying to do many things at once, and is doing one thing well, another ill; is advancing, is harking back; is subject to moods; nay, for a bet, today will as likely write in one fashion as in another. Examine cantos 1 and 2 of *Childe Harold*, then pass to the tales Byron interposed between them and canto 3—*The Giaour, The Bride of Abydos, The Corsair, Lara*—and you see him harking back to Crabbe almost pathetically. So you get, in *The Corsair* for example, such lines as—

Unlike the heroes of each ancient race,
Demons in act, but Gods at least in face,
In Conrad's form seems little to admire. . . .

which is right Crabbe. And not only is this hard to
reconcile with the freedom he had already achieved in
Childe Harold. It is irreconcilable with the freedom he
achieves quite frequently in these very poems. You
know how he wrote them; at night and so to speak on
his dressing-table, as he—vain composer and spoilt child
of society—jaded or excited—unlaced himself after ball
and rout. Knowing that the stories were written thus
(for he tells us so), we can trace through them his moods,
now of dejection and recall to theory, anon of rebellion
and daring. And in the end—at the very end—what
does he come to? Why back to the prose he had been
writing all the time in his letters! The best wit in *Don
Juan*, with rhyme to help it, gets just as far as the
habitual wit of his letters.

III

Now let us refer this illustration back to Chaucer, and
all we have to deduct is that Chaucer was a more
equable man (though a man of moods), living a more
equable life. But against this we have to throw far
more into the scales.

(1) To begin with—and this must weigh enormously
in the comparison—Byron was using or adapting a
poetical language made to his hand: Chaucer had to
invent his vehicle as he went along; and for this triumph
alone men venerated him in the seventeenth and
eighteenth centuries, even while they adjudged him
"rude," "uncouth," "Gothic," "scarce readable."
He has been so far familiarised to us that an ordinary

student in these times (I think this may be taken for granted) reads him with less labour than did Dryden or even Gray. Yes, I really do not think you or I need make so much of his "difficulty," or need find it so formidable, as did these two great men, who have left the hindrance on record. But there the fact is: that Chaucer had almost incessantly (with the aid, may be, of his contemporary, John Gower) to make his vehicle as he went; and when you think of him as escaping from that style to this, you must reckon the mere human weariness of such an effort, after the mere schoolwork had been so difficult.

(2) Secondly—I pursue the comparison—Byron, darling and scandal of the town, could hear how he was succeeding almost as soon as he had written. There was Society, eager for his "latest"; there were the news-papers—at farthest, the Quarterlies. But this quiet man in the gatehouse lacked all the apparatus—I will not say of advertisement—but of self-criticism, of "re-collection." One of the great simple facts to bear in mind is that he wrote in an age before printed books. Conceive yourselves writing such a poem as *Troilus* in an age before printed books, and waiting, after you had written in faith, to discover what men thought of it, to be rewarded, confirmed.

It is just there, Gentlemen, that when I think of Chaucer, I worship the man—for vulgarising, those reams and reams of verse, all meant for popularising, and all done on faith! For what, when it was written, were the means to popularise it, to spread it?

In a previous lecture, Gentlemen, on "The Commerce of Thought," I tried to indicate to you some of the subtle ways in which learning spread through Europe in those times when books were not; how the fame of

Abelard, travelling along the roads, would draw crowds to Paris; how, spirit attracting spirit as matter attracts matter, Europe—in those days before printing, long before such things as newspapers, railways, telegraphs, telephones, wireless, etc.—was a vast sounding board, so that a poem, or a heresy would run from Northumbria to the delta of the Danube before you could overtake it.

I shall say more of this by and by. For the moment I impress on you that in the fourteenth century an experimenter, such as Chaucer was, would have to wait for the approval or the criticism of his fellows; and that the interval for self-distrust, maybe for dejection—an interval which every conscientious author knows, to his pain—being for Chaucer so far prolonged, he had far more temptation than any modern poet to halt, to hesitate, to try back after trying forward. This thought alone should mitigate our wonder when we find him in 1386—well at the close of his so-called Italian period and just on the eve of *The Canterbury Tales*—writing a thing so purely French in style and inspiration as the Prologue to *The Legend of Good Women*.

IV

There is another reason. Some of us, as, growing older, we exchange old gods for new, suffer from a disposition to turn and smash and trample on our abandoned idols. I don't know why this should be; why, for instance, many men today, to whom in their youth Tennyson was a joy, seem unable to speak of Tennyson save with an almost savage derision. I confess that *In Memoriam* no longer fulfils my soul's deepest cravings, that the *Idylls* now read as very much of their age and very little for all time; that in short (and to use a phrase of Burke's) I no longer bait my horses at that good old inn. But I never pass its sign without a lift of the hat for remembered days of young delight and entertainment, for magic casements opening on the road to Camelot, on Tigris and silken sails and "Bagdad's shrine of fretted gold," on the Isle of Lotus—

> There is sweet music here that softer falls
> Than petals from blown roses on the grass,
> Or night-dews on still waters between walls
> Of shadowy granite, in a gleaming pass . . .

On St. Agnes' Eve and the snowed convent roof, on the streets "dumb with snow" through which Sir Galahad rode,

> The tempest crackles on the leads,
>   And, ringing, springs from brand and mail;
> But o'er the dark a glory spreads,
>   And gilds the driving hail. . . .

on Maud's garden, on nightingales warbling without, on yonder mountain height, and an awful rose of dawn: and I know to the end that Tennyson is a mighty poet.

But you also know that instinct for iconoclasm: and you surely know that, if the reading public be liable to it, still more liable is the careful craftsman upon discovery or upon conviction that he has been wasting his time on false models—

> The lyf so short, the craft so long to lerne.

Well, Chaucer never felt it. He turned, to be sure, from French to Italian themes. But for him this involved no revulsion of feeling against his old love. "Why, indeed, should it?" he would have asked in his debonair way.

And indeed, as his literary education had been French, French he remained, while treating of Italian themes, while working on English prosody. Traditional English verse—alliterative verse—had no attraction for him; even so little (as Professor Ker points out) had the typical Italian metres. In one short passage only he imitates the *terza rima* of Dante; he translates a sonnet of Petrarch's but not in the Petrarchan form; he reads and paraphrases poem after poem, written in the Italian octave stanza, but he never uses that stanza:

Chaucer, though he went far beyond such poetry as that of his French masters and of his own *Complaint to Pity*, never turned against it. He escaped out of the allegorical garden of the Rose, but with no resentment or ingratitude. He never depreciates the old school. He must have criticised it—to find it unsatisfying is to criticise it, implicitly at any rate; but he never uses a word of blame or a sentence of parody.

He *does* parody the English ballad-stanza, you remember, in the burlesque of *Sir Thopas*.

V

Let me bring all this to a particular test. Your handbooks will tell you that *The Man of Lawes Tale* was a comparatively early work of Chaucer's; that it had lain some while by him before he took it, furbished it up, and thrust it into the body of *The Canterbury Tales:* and so far your handbooks are right. But they go on to say that this must be so, because Chaucer took the tale of Custance from the Anglo-Norman Chronicle of Nicholas Trivet, an English Dominican who died some time after 1334, which tale Gower also used in his *Confessio Amantis;* wherefore it *must* date from Chaucer's "French period"; in which they are quite wrong. They reach a right conclusion by demonstrably false reasoning. Chaucer *at any time in his life* was capable of paraphrasing Trivet. Our real assurance that *The Man of Lawes Tale* is an early work refurbished rests on two grounds: (1) upon a comparison of Chaucer's narrative with Trivet's, (2) upon a sense—it needs not be more than elementary—of the difference between Chaucer's earlier and his later manner. Using these two, you find that the problem works out with a simplicity almost ludicrous. For, to begin with, the insertions made in the strict narrative almost invariably fall into complete stanzas or blocks of stanzas; secondly, they never advance the narrative, but are either the poet's reflections on it or invented speeches put into the mouths of the characters at this or that crisis of the tale; and thirdly, they are, as poetry, so far superior to the level run of the story that no reader, once on the track, can mistake them for anything but additions. You are reading (let us say) the flat narrative of how the king's messenger bears a false letter commanding that Custance and her child are to be put on board ship and cast adrift: you are reading that

> This messager or morwe, whan he wook,
> Unto the castel halt the nextĕ wey
> And to the constable he the lettre took. . . .

when of a sudden you bring up against *this*, of Custance on the sea-strand.

> Hir litel child lay weping in hir arm
> And kneling, pitously to him she seyde,
> "Pees, litle sone, I wol do thee non harm."
> With that hir kerchief of hir heed she breyde,

And over his litel yĕn she it leyde;
And in hir arm she lulleth it ful faste,
And in-to heven hir yĕn up she caste.

"Moder," quod she, "and maydė bright, Marye,
Sooth is that thurgh wommannės eggėment
Mankind was lorn and damnèd ay to dye,
For which thy child was on a croys y-rent;
Thy blisful yĕn sawe al his torment;
Than is ther no comparisoun bitwene
Thy wo and any woman may sustene.

Thou sawe thy child y-slayn bifor thyn yĕn,
And yet now liveth my litel child, parfay!
Now, lady bright, to whom alle woful cryen,
Thou glorie of wommanhede, thou fairė may,
Thou haven of refut, brightė sterre of day,
Rewe on my child, that of thy gentillesse
Rewest on every rewful in distresse!

O litel child, allas! what is thy gilt,
That never wroughtest sinne as yet, pardee?
Why wil thyn hardē fader han thee spilt?
O mercy, derė constable!" quod she;
"As lat my litel child dwelle heer with thee;
And if thou darst not saven him, for blame,
So kis him onès in his fadres name!"

VI

This that I have been quoting to you is Chaucer at
his best, the Chaucer who had found himself. It has
sometimes occurred to me to wonder, when people talk
of Chaucer's being so racily English, if England be not
(in spite of Puritans) the jolly land she is because our
literature has kept her so constant to this good fellow's
tradition—that the jolliness is actually Chaucer's aura
inherited.

He probably started to write *The Canterbury Tales* in the year 1386 or thereabouts. In the previous year he had a stroke of luck, the king allowing him a deputy to do most of his work as Comptroller at the Wool Quay. In 1386 he was elected a Knight of the Shire for Kent, and sat in Parliament. The next year he lost his wife. He had just given up his lodge over Aldgate and gone to a new house—it seems, near Greenwich. Also he had, about the same time, lost his appointment as Comptroller. Altogether—and although the *Tales* by no means reflect it—he must have been a sad man in this while, and in 1385 there is evidence that he was also impoverished. But in 1389 he received the fairly lucrative post of Clerk of the King's Works at the palace of Westminster; and also served, next year, on a Commission to repair the banks of the Thames between Greenwich and Woolwich. Towards the end it is pretty clear that fortune had definitively turned her face aside from him, and that he lacked employment. He died, poor, on October 25, 1400; and they buried him in Westminster Abbey. As you know, he left *The Canterbury Tales* unfinished.

VII

I shall not indulge in any panegyric upon *The Canterbury Tales*. It consists rather with the purpose of these lectures to send you straight to good things which so straightly commend themselves. Two men—Dryden in his *Preface to the Fables*, and James Russell Lowell in *My Study Windows*—have written superlatively well about them. Read those two essays, and for enjoying Chaucer—which is, or ought to be, the real business—you will need no third guide.

Hear Dryden:

In the first place, as he is the father of English poetry, so I

hold him in the same degree of veneration as the Grecians
held Homer or the Romans Virgil. He is a perpetual
fountain of good sense; learn'd in all sciences; and, therefore, speaks properly on all subjects. As he knew what to
say, so he knows also when to leave off; a continence which is
practised by few writers, and scarcely by any of the ancients
excepting Virgil and Horace. . . . Chaucer followed Nature
everywhere, but was never so bold to go beyond her; and
there is a great difference of being *poeta* and *nimis poeta*, if
we may believe Catullus, as much as betwixt a modest
behaviour and affectation. . . .

Some of his persons are vicious, and some virtuous; some
are unlearn'd or (as Chaucer calls them) lewd, and some are
learn'd. Even the ribaldry of the low characters is different: the Reeve, the Miller, and the Cook, are several men,
and distinguished from each other as much as the mincing
Lady-Prioress and the broad-speaking, gap-toothed Wife of
Bath. But enough of this. . . . 'Tis sufficient to say, according to the proverb, that *here is God's plenty*. We have our
forefathers and great-grand-dames all before us, as they
were in Chaucer's days: their general characters are still
remaining in mankind, and even in England, though they
are called by other names than those of Monks, and Friars,
and Canons, and Lady-Abbesses, and Nuns: for mankind
is ever the same . . . though everything is altered.

That is well and justly said. Let me add this to it, that
since Dryden's time, as before it, England has never
had a story-teller comparable with Chaucer in his power
of visualising all sorts and conditions of men and putting
them on canvas for us in half-a-dozen strokes: no, not
even Dickens is quite his match, for Dickens was unsure,
seldom or never right, often preposterously wrong,
when it came to delineating an English lady or an
English gentleman. And this further let me add. When
you open upon that procession in the immortal Prologue
(to which Dryden mainly refers)—that "Gorgeous

Gallery of Gallant Inventions"—bethink you that
Chaucer came to it through Allegory, of all approaches!
Compare it with the shadowy, stationary, featureless
crowd in *Piers Plowman*, and the difference between
literary tact and tactlessness stands revealed. Afterwards go on to admire the artfulness, the story-telling
technique—Defoe was to recapture something of it—
with which Chaucer is ever dropping in some little
detail: as the late Alma Tadema used to say, when he
painted a fly on one of his marble pillars, "to make it
look so it was really happen." He has seen a poor
wretch going to execution, and at once you see, too, the
very lines on his face; he tells you in a casual way that
women sleep more lightly than men; the Friar comes
into the room and looking around for a snug seat, drives
away the cat. The cat knows the warmest corner. The
Friar knows that the cat knows, and Chaucer knows
that the Friar knows. And he just tells it as if idly,
casually, but with that disinterestedness which (as
Lowell well observes) made the Greeks masters in art.
Do you know Longfellow's sonnet of him?

> An old man in a lodge within a park;
> The chamber walls depicted all around
> With portraitures of huntsmen, hawk, and hound
> And the hurt deer. He listeneth to the lark
> Whose song comes with the sunshine through the dark
> Of painted glass in leaden lattice bound;
> He listeneth and he laugheth at the sound,
> Then writeth in a book like any clerk.

> He is the poet of the dawn, who wrote
> The Canterbury Tales, and his old age
> Made beautiful with song; and as I read
> I hear the crowing cock, I hear the note
> Of lark and linnet, and from every page
> Rise odours of ploughed field or flowery mead.

Matthew Arnold, noting this mundane cheerfulness,
and not looking very far beyond or beneath it, tells us
"And yet Chaucer is not one of the great classics," in
that his poetry lacks the σπουδαιότης, the high and
excellent seriousness, which Aristotle assigns as one of
the grand virtues of poetry. It would be cruel to
Arnold's memory to suspect him of the British fault of
mistrusting for serious whatever happens to be illumi-
nated by humour. But I do suspect him of having over-
looked *Troilus*, one of the most nobly serious poems in
our language. See Pandarus with the hero, as he

> Took up a light and found his countenance
> As for to look upon an old romance. . . .

Is that not "serious?" I quoted to you, the other day,
the lament of Troilus before Criseyde's deserted house.
Hear the conclusion:

> O yongè fresshè folkès, he or she,
> In which that love up groweth with your age,
> Repeyreth hoom from worldly vanitee,
> And of your herte up-casteth the visage
> To thilkè God that after his image
> Yow made, and thinketh al nis but a fayre
> This world, that passeth sone as flourès fayre.

> And loveth Him, the which that right for love
> Upon a cros, our soulès for to beye,
> First starf, and roos, and sit in hevene above;
> For he nil falsen no wight, dar I seye,
> That wol his herte al hoolly on him leye.
> And sin He best to love is, and most meke,
> What nedeth feynèd lovès for to seke? . . .

> Thou Oon, and Two, and Three, eterne on-lyve,
> That regnest ay in Three and Two and Oon,
> Uncircumscript, and al mayst circumscryve,

Us from visible and invisible foon
Defende; and to thy mercy, everychoon,
So make us, Iesus, for thy gracè, digne,
For love of mayde and moder thyn benigne!   Amen.

Is *that* not serious? I will tell you, moreover, of a subject on which Chaucer is never less than tenderly, exquisitely, serious; it is when he pities children and commends them, as he always does, to Our Lady in Heaven. Recall Custance's prayer that I read to you just now, and turn to the Prioresses Tale, adapted from the tale of little Hugh of Lincoln—

As I have seyd, thurgh-out the Jewerye
This litel child, as he cam to and fro,
Ful merily than wolde he singe, and crye

O *Alma redemptoris* ever-mo,
The swetnes hath his hertè percèd so
Of Cristes moder, that, to hir to preye,
He can nat stinte of singing by the weye. . . .

"O martir, souded to virginitee,
Now maystou singen, folwing ever in oon
The whytè lamb celestial," quod she, . . .

But in face of that, even Arnold as good as takes back his words.

VIII

A note in conclusion:
I have spoken of the mere practical difficulty a poet must have found in those days, when printed books were none, to get a hearing. But in a previous lecture I tried to astonish you with evidence of the immense, insatiable, intellectual curiosity of the Middle Ages; to convince you that you never know, or at least—as Emerson said of Brahma—

> They know not well the subtle ways
> I keep, and pass, and turn again.

And in other lectures, this term and last, I have hammered on the text that *all spirit is mutually attractive even as all matter is mutually attractive.*

In 1378, when Chaucer was setting out on his second Italian journey, he procured letters of general attorney, allowing John Gower and Richard Forrester to act for him during his absence from England. Now John Gower was Gower the poet, of whose friendly help and criticism Chaucer (as I have hinted) almost certainly availed himself. It is enough to say here that they were both working at the same time on the same models; that Gower translated or converted the very stories used by Chaucer for *The Wyf of Bathes Tale, The Phisiciens Tale, The Maunciples Tale;* that each obeyed his own genius without servility to the other; and yet that both were workers together for a common cause—the invention of a new kind of English poetry which should be of the vernacular, racy, *and* of the great European tradition in style and theme. I do not forget, of course, there were lyrical twitterings before the dawn; or that sundry innominate poets were writing in Chaucer's lifetime—the author of *Pearl*, for one—for another, the author of that famous exquisite little Carol—

> I sing of a maiden
>   That is makèles,
> King of all kinges
>   To her sone sche ches . . .
>
> He cam also stille
>   To his moderès bour,
> As dew in Aprille
>   That falleth on the flour . . .

Moder and maiden
  Was never non but sche;
Well may swich a lady
  Godės moder be.

In that we have a something which Chaucer, for all his grace and gifts, could not compass. Yet it remains true that with Chaucer, and not before Chaucer, the sun is up and the large long day of English poetry begins.

By the men of his age his death was felt as the quenching of its most radiant star. From their unnumbered if not innumerous laments I select the following famous lines by Hoccleve.

Allas! my worthy maister honorable,
  This londės verray tresour and richesse!
Dethe by thy dethe hath harm irreparable
  Unto us done: hir vengeable duresse
  Despoilėd hath this lond of the swetnesse
    Of rethoryk: for unto Tullius
    Was never man so lyk amongės us.

Also who was heyr in philosofye
  To Aristotle in our tunge but thou?
The steppės of Virgile in poesye
  Thou folwedest eke, men wotė wel ynow,
  That combre-worldė that my maister slow—
    Wolde I slayn were!—Dethe was to hastyf
    To renne on thee and reve thee of thy lyf. . . .

She might han tarried hir vengeance a whyle
  Til some man hadde egal to thee be;
Nay, let be that! she wel knew that this yle
  May never man forth bringė lyk to thee,
  And her officė needės do mote she:
    God bade hir so, I truste as for the beste;
    O maister, maister, God thy soulė reste!

And this veneration endured—kept bright by the practice of Scotland—until in time Spenser followed, who lies beside Chaucer now in Westminster Abbey. Spenser, attempting, in the second and third cantos of Book Four of *The Faerie Queene*, a conclusion of *The Squieres Tale* begs pardon for his pillage of

> Dan Chaucer, well of English undefyled,
> On Fames eternall beadroll worthie to be fyled. . . .
> Then pardon, O most sacred happie spirit,
>   That I thy labours lost may thus revive,
> And steale from thee the meede of thy due merit,
>   That none durst ever whilest thou wast alive,
>   And being dead in vaine yet many strive:
> Ne dare I like, but through infusion sweete
>   Of thine owne spirit, which doth in me survive,
>   I follow here the footing of thy feete,
> That with thy meaning so I may the rather meete.

AFTER CHAUCER

I

IT has been, I believe, more than once remarked—
but I am thinking of a passage in Dr. Courthope's
History of English Poetry, where he puts the remark,
most appositely, almost in the forefront of his first
volume—that to us modern men the medieval mind is
far stranger than the mind of an ancient Greek or an
ancient Roman; that as men of the world we should
feel much more at home if we found ourselves of a sudden listening to the talkers in Plato's *Symposium*, or
with our arm in Horace's on the Sacred Way, than if
we were as abruptly transported to a seat at Arthur's
Round Table, or even at the high table of Jocelyn de-
scribed in Carlyle's *Past and Present*. Our contribu-
tion to the talk with Socrates would doubtless be very
small talk indeed; smaller even than that of his inter-
locutors as evoked by Plato. But we should understand the allusions, or most of them; the matter would
be interesting; and, as it infected us, we might even
catch some of the Socratic fire. By our library lamp,
at any rate, we do hold easy communion with these
souls so long departed, and recognise the truth of Cory's
beautiful *Invocation*:

O dear divine Comatas, I would that thou and I
Beneath this broken sunlight this leisure day might lie;

Where trees from distant forests, whose names were strange
 to thee,
Should bend their amorous branches within thy reach to be,
And flowers thine Hellas knew not, which art hath made
 more fair,
Should shed their shining petals upon thy fragrant hair.

Then thou shouldest calmly listen with ever-changing looks
To songs of younger minstrels and plots of modern books,
And wonder at the daring of poets later born,
Whose thoughts are unto thy thoughts as noon-tide is to
 morn;
And little shouldst thou grudge them their greater strength
 of soul,
Thy partners in the torch-race, though nearer to the goal.

. . . Or in thy cedarn prison thou waitest for the bee:
Ah, leave that simple honey, and take thy food from me.
My sun is stooping westward.   Entrancèd dreamer, haste;
There's fruitage in my garden, that I would have thee taste.
Now lift the lid a moment; now, Dorian shepherd, speak:
Two minds shall flow together, the English and the Greek.

I do not think we could rely upon any such communion of spirit with any ghost out of the Middle
Ages—unless perchance, it were Chaucer's.   We should
not feel any such familiar ease at a medieval board.
We should only be horribly shy of "putting our foot in
it"; an oppression of wonder at what on earth everyone
was driving at.   Without subscribing to the theorist
who roundly accounted for the Middle Ages—as somebody will hereafter account for 1914–1917—by positing
that everyone in Europe was mad just then, I confess
to a shiver of uncanniness when brought in contact
with the sort of mind that was ready to divide Christen-
dom over the date of Easter and die in the last ditch for
a fashion of the tonsure.

Dr. Courthope has his own conclusion on this:

Finally, the fact that we ourselves find more in common with the life of the Greeks and Romans than with the life of Europe in the Middle Ages, means that, in the city states of antiquity, as in our own times, civil standards of thought prevailed while in the medieval period the predominant cast of thought was feudal and ecclesiastical.

II

This is a part of the explanation, no doubt; though, I believe, not the whole. I may be deserting the disease for a symptom: but let me draw your attention to one point on which the men of the Middle Ages most curiously differed from us. I shall not be bold enough to speak of their painting, though in painting their contented acceptance of a limited range of religious subjects, endlessly repeated and improved, might support the theory. I admit the rapture and even the frolic of architecture in which these men let themselves go. But when it comes to any art that touched the human voice, chanted or spoken or written, by all our slight tradition of their music and on all the super-abundant evidence of their prose and verse, they had a liking, even a passion for *monotony*.

It would perhaps be fairer to put it that our age has conceived a horror of monotony which they never felt. For monotony has lasted well down in our literature, and without consciousness of offence. *The Faerie Queene*, for all its beauty, is monotonous; so, for all its interruptions is Sidney's *Arcadia;* so, in mass, are the Sermons of the Golden Age of the Pulpit; so is almost any English novel down to Scott. By monotony I mean monotony: not length, nor tedium, nor dullness. We, reading in more vivacious days, from crowded

shelves, by better light, may find the one or two authors
of whom I am to speak tedious and dull. But I suggest that the true explanation lies in our quite modern
abhorrence of the monotonous. Let me read you a few
lines from Gower, and let me in fairness choose Gower
at about his best, in the tale of Constance, and pit him,
telling the very same tale as Chaucer, against the lines
I quoted from Chaucer the other day. This was
Chaucer, as you may remember—

> Hir litel child lay weping in hir arm,
> And kneling, pitously to him she seyde,
> "Pees, litel sone, I wol do thee non harm."
> With that hir kerchief of hir heed she breyde,
> And over his litel yën she it leyde;
> And in hir arm she lulleth it ful faste,
> And in-to heven hir yën up she caste. . . .

—whereupon follows that lovely invocation:

> "Moder," quod she, "and maydè bright, Marye. . . ."

Now listen to Gower.

> Upon the See thei have hire broght,
> Bot sche the causè wistè noght,
> And thus upon the flod thei wone,
> This ladi with hire yongè Sone:
> And thanne hire handès to the hevene
> Sche strawhte, and with a mildè stevene
> Knelende upon hire barè kne
> Sche seide, "O hihè magestè,
> Which sest the point of every trowthe,
> Tak of thi wofull womman rowthe,
> And of this child that I schal kepe."
> And with that word sche gan to wepe,
> Swounende as ded, and ther sche lay;
> Bot he which allè thingès may

Conforteth hire, and atè laste
Sche loketh and hire yhen caste
Upon hire child and seide this:
"Of me no maner charge it is
What sorwe I soffre, bot of thee
Me thenkth it is a gret pitè,
For if I stervè thou schalt dèie:
So mot I nedès be that weie
For Moderhed and for tendresse
With al myn holè besinesse
Ordeignè me for thilke office
As sche which schal be thi Norrice."
Thus was sche strengthèd forto stonde;
And tho sche tok hire child in honde
And yaf it sowke, and evere among
Sche wepte, and otherwhilè song
To rockè with hire child aslepe.

Now what shall we say of this passage?—which I
have chosen because it exhibits Gower at about his
best, and also because it strikingly holds up Gower and
Chaucer in competition, dealing with the same story
of Constance, at the same moment of that story; while
we have preserved for us the actual common original,
Nicholas Trivet's *Anglo-Norman Chronicle*, upon which
both writers worked.

Well, to begin with, we must allow that Chaucer and
Gower see the scene with a quite different degree of
vivacity.   Gower happens to be good here: he is, here
and otherwhere, a sincere man all the way he goes.
But at one point, he is not *seeing* at all—

And with that word sche gan to wepe,
Swounende as ded. . . .

We all know that a woman may swoon, as she may
weep; but no woman—not even Constance, poor soul
—can do both together.

If we had not Chaucer, Gower would (I submit) be good, and even very good. He is, to be sure, here and elsewhere and everywhere, monotonous. But I protest that Lowell's complaint overshoots the mark.

Gower [says Lowell] has positively raised tediousness to the precision of science, he has made dulness an heirloom for the students of our literary history. As you slip to and fro on the frozen levels of his verse, which give no foothold to the mind, your nervous ear awaits the inevitable recurrence of his rhyme, etc.

This derision, from which I subtract nothing by cutting it short, simply tells me that Lowell missed to understand one of the main charms which men of the Middle Ages accepted, and even asked, of Poetry. In the days of these men, before the era of printing, a book was a book, to be read and re-read, as collectors gloat over a treasure. If you open any of their favourite allegories or romances of Alexander, or Arthur, or the Grail, it simply stares at you out of the page that they enjoyed monotony for its own sake. I cannot, for my part, perceive that Chaucer himself had any grounded theoretical objection to it: he practised monotony often enough, until in the end his vivid genius saved him and us. Consider *Romaunt of the Rose*. Guillaume de Lorris began it, in the year 1200 or thereabouts, wrote 4070 lines, and died, leaving it incomplete. Jean de Meung took it up some forty years later, and added 18,004 lines: so that the poem finally extended to 22,074 lines; and this, for at least a century and a half, is the most popular book—the "best seller," so to speak—in Europe! It was about one hundred years old when Chaucer began to translate it.

What can we make of that, unless we recognise that a poet—or even a chronicler or prose-romancer—of the thirteenth or fourteenth century wrote in monotone and at inordinate length, to supply a felt want? But I bring you later evidence. Our own day has known no more single-hearted poet than William Morris; certainly not one more incapable of "faking" an honest feeling which held possession of him; certainly not one who drew breath either deeper or more even with the spirit of these men who made Medieval England. I, at any rate, know nobody born in these later years who can touch him at this point of understanding. Now Morris had within him the most amazing capacity of broken lyrical utterance. Take his *Summer Dawn*—"Pray but one prayer for me"—and linger on each delicate interrupted cadence; take any stanza from *Love is Enough*:

Ye know not how void is your hope and your living:
  Depart with your helping, lest yet ye undo me!
Ye know not that at nightfall she draweth near to me,
There is soft speech between us and words of forgiving,
  Till in dead of the midnight her kisses thrill through me.
  Pass by me, and hearken, and waken me not.

You find this master of this lovely broken speech falling, when he tells the tales of *The Earthly Paradise*, into length and monotone just as easily as a child falls asleep: because simply as a child he is obeying the right instinct.

Now I know that enjoyment of this monotony is hard to recapture. But it can be recaptured; and in reading Gower, the recapturing needs not be hard. For the *Confessio Amantis* is, after all, not one long-winded poem, but a collection of tales. Take one up, and when you have done with it—or even when you have had enough of it—lay the book down.

III

At any rate we have to remember that Gower was not a follower of Chaucer, but a contemporary, a friend, and a fellow-worker. They were both intent to do their best on an enormous adventure; to catch up for England the lee-way, of far more than a hundred years, by which she had fallen behind the rest of Europe in native literature and, save at the Universities, in culture.

Skeat has a theory that the two poets quarrelled; and that the hypothetical quarrel arose in this hypothetical way. Chaucer about 1380 wrote his first draft of *The Man of Lawes Tale* and lent it to Gower; Gower cribbed it for the *Confessio Amantis*; and then were recriminations. All this actually rests on no more evidence than that Gower, having made Venus in his first edition of the *Confessio* say,

> And gret wel Chaucer whan ye mete,
> As mi disciple and mi poete:

cut out the allusion in his second edition, and that Chaucer in his Prologue to that tale, later, used some sharp words which *may* be made to apply to Gower: and it all seems to me the sort of guesswork which Dr. Skeat was ever stern to condemn in others. Preferring, anyhow, to dwell on great men's proved understandings rather than on their suspected misunderstandings, I will repeat to you the three stanzas of the conclusion of *Troilus and Criseyde* which I quoted the other day, and insert one I then omitted; in which, as in a coffin of crystal, the name of Gower rests embalmed.

> O yongè fresshè folkès, he or she,
> In which that love up groweth with your age,

Repeyreth hoom from worldly vanitee,
And of your herte up-casteth the visage
To thilkė God that after his image
Yow made, and thinketh al nis but a fayre
This world, that passeth sone as flourės fayre.

And loveth Him, the which that right for love
Upon a cros, our soulės for to beye,
First starf, and roos, and sit in hevene above;
For he nil falsen no wight, dar I seye,
That wol his herte al hoolly on him leye.
And sin He best to love is, and most meke,
What nedeth feynėd lovės for to seke? . . .

O moral Gower, this book I directe
To thee, and to the philosophical Strode,
To vouchen sauf, ther need is, to corecte,
Of your benignitees and zelės gode.
And to that sothfast Crist, that starf on roae,
With all myn herte of mercy ever I preye;
And to the Lord right thus I speke and seye:

Thou Oon, and Two, and Three, eterne on-lyve,
That regnest ay in Three and Two and Oon,
Uncircumscript, and al mayst circumscryve,
Us from visible and invisible foon
Defende; and to thy mercy, everychoon,
So make us, Iesus, for thy gracė, digne,
For love of mayde and moder thyn benigne!

Amen.

IV

The making of good English Poetry was but one of
Gower's aims. Of the man we know little. He came
of good family; he *may* have been educated at Oxford;
he dwelt for a while in London; then retired to live
the life of a country squire in Kent. In his old age (he
died in 1408) blindness overtook him. He lies in the

Church of the Priory of St. Mary Overes—now called
St. Saviour's—Southwark, and under a fine tomb; his
figure recumbent upon it under a canopy. On the wall,
within the canopy, were once painted three figures, of
Charity, Mercy, Pity; but these are now obliterated.
So, too, are the scrolls of ivy once intertwined with the
three roses yet crowning him. Gone too is the inscription granting 1500 days' pardon to all who prayed for
the poet's soul—say a day out of Purgatory for any two
spent on the *Confessio Amantis*. There, with his coat-
armour he lies, in straight-buttoned gown, his hair
curling down on his shoulders, his head resting on three
books—*The Speculum Meditantis* (a French poem, lost);
the *Vox Clamantis*, a Latin poem in seven books on Wat
Tyler's rebellion; and the *Confessio Amantis*—his English Poem, of about 30,000 octosyllabic lines. What
head would not deserve—what head, whether deserving
it or not, would not sleep on such a pillow?

For us, Gentlemen, the *Confessio Amantis* is all that
matters of this: and although it extend to 30,000 lines,
and although we, in our day, have lost the love of
monotony, it happens to consist of a series of short
stories, of which you can easily read one, or even two,
at a time. I repeat my counsel to you to read him in
that way. I can almost promise you a surprise. You
will find the moral old man not only tolerable, but even
a bit wickeder and more amusing than fame makes him
out.

V

When we come to Chaucer's successors in England
—to Lydgate, Hoccleve, Stephen Hawes and the rest
—there is a different tale to tell.

John Lydgate (1370?–1450?) really is a dull dog.

He was a monk of Bury St. Edmunds, admitted to the Abbey at the age of fifteen, previous to which he asks us to believe that he was something of a young daredevil. The Abbey cured him of that, at any rate, and concurrently gave him so feeble a knowledge of the world that he could not write anon, in praise of St. Anne:

> He that intendeth in his herte to seke
>   To love the daughter of any womman fre,
> He must, of gentilles, love the moder eke
>   In honest wyse, by fygure as ye may see. . . .

Though jests against mothers-in-law may be cheap, this as a counsel of perfection, or even as a protest seems to go a thought too far. Bale asserts, but without evidence, that Lydgate studied at both the English Universities. At one time he "opened a school for the sons of noblemen," and (I quote from the *Dictionary of National Biography*) "through the reign of Henry IV (1399-1413) he spent much time in London, apparently seeking from men of rank recognition for his poetic efforts." He made the acquaintance of Chaucer, and appears to have submitted his poems to the great man. He avows himself a poetic child of Chaucer: a confession which may or may not have annoyed the alleged parent. *The Canterbury Tales* having been left incomplete, he represents himself as having fallen in with the Pilgrims at Canterbury, where the host, Harry Bailey, invites him to tell "a merry tale." Lydgate complies and recounts *The Siege of Thebes* in 4716 lines. The host had reckoned without his guest.

To John Lydgate I, for one, greatly prefer Thomas Occleve (or "Hoccleve": but since he was quite long enough in life, let us save what time we may by dropping the "*h*"). Thomas Occleve, then, who lived between 1370 and 1450—the dates are uncertain—was for twenty-four years a clerk in the Privy Seal Office and, by his own confession, in his poem *La Male Régle* (concerning his ill-regulated life) combined the earlier part of this tenure with the pursuits of a naughty youth about town. He frequented taverns: he went after pretty girls at St. Paul's—

> Venus femel lusty children deere—

and treated them to sweet wine and wafers, for which he says that he paid, but never went beyond kissing. I think, if you will compare Occleve's confession of wickedness with a ballade or two of François Villon (by a little his junior) you will tell yourselves that poor Occleve was not a very desperate sinner, and may even agree with Emerson that

> When half-gods go,
> The gods arrive.

But in a later poem—his *Complaint*—he tells us that he went out of his mind for some time; that sanity returned to him on a day of Hallowmass; but that his old friends have cut him and he finds himself forgotten. He tells also, very pathetically, how he looked anxiously in the glass to see if his face were not altered, and found himself, so to speak, "the same old fraud." It is a sorrowful story of an honest fellow gone wrong. He loved Chaucer, and his lines of lamentation for Chaucer are true poetry and sob out straight from a good man's heart.

Of a third poet, Stephen Hawes (who came later and died, or ceased, it is supposed in 1523), I can only report that I found his dulness abysmal. He wrote, among other things, *The Pastime of Pleasure,* or *The History of Graunde Amour and la Bel Pucel,* which opens with promise enough.   But the title goes on, *Conteining the Knowledge of the Seven Sciences* and *the Course of Man's Life in this Worlde.*   Wynkyn de Warde printed it in 1500.   It consists of about 6000 lines.   Towards the end it contains the really exquisite gem:

> O mortal folk you may behold and se
>> How I lie here, sometime a mighty knight:
> The end of joy and all prosperitee
>> Is death at last, thorow his course and might:
>> After the day there cometh the dark night,
>>> For though the daye be never so long,
>>> At last the bells ringeth to evensong.

It embeds this other pearl, yet nobler:

> For knighthoode is not in the feates of warre,
>> As for to fight in quarrell right or wronge,
> But in a cause which truth can not defarre;
>> He ought him selfe for to make sure and stronge,
>> Justice to keep mixt with mercy amonge;
>>> And no quarrell a knight ought to take,
>>> But for a truth, or for a woman's sake.

But you will search long in Hawes (I can testify) before you find a third peer of those two stanzas.   The main trouble with these poets is that, while Chaucer had an eye for life, an eye so vivacious and so vivifying that even in allegory his men and women, birds, beast, flowers, trees, take life as "things which you can touch and see," his followers have no eye save for Chaucer. For a century, then, the poets of England remain with their gaze fastened on the image of the singer they last heard, and at each generation their voice becomes

weaker, like an echo that repeats another echo. Lydgate imitates Chaucer, and Stephen Hawes imitates
Lydgate. "I try," says he,

> To followe the trace and all the perfytnes
> Of my maister Lydgate.

VI

Now these academic followers of Chaucer, admitting
everything in him but just the one thing in which his
genius lay, imitating him therefore at points on which
they might just as well have imitated Gower, occupy a
wholly disproportionate space in our text-books of
literary history: and, because they are dull, the fifteenth century, in which they practised and held the
ear of the Court, is steadily preached to you as a dull
period. It was nothing of the sort. It was, among the
Ballad-makers, fairly humming, teeming, welling with
song. As Mr. Alfred W. Pollard has well put it, in re-
editing a volume of the late Professor Arber's *English
Garner*:

> In the world of politics and statecraft a nation which has
> once begun to decline seldom, perhaps never, recovers itself.
> There are too many other dogs about for the bone which has
> once been relinquished to be resumed later on. . . . In
> the world of literature and thought the dogs are better bred,
> showing each other new hunting-grounds, and by example
> and precept often helping to restore a famished comrade to
> sleekness and vigour. Political conditions may not be
> gainsaid. A nation which has once lost its ideals cannot
> again produce a fresh, strong, and manly literature. But the
> possibilities of literature remain immense, and we cannot
> foretell in what country it may not revive and win fresh
> triumphs.

So while I do pretend to you that the fifteenth cen-

tury produced much of *great* poetry in England, I say
that it is mere blindness of criticism to preach that its
ideals were dead or sleeping, mere ignorance that re-
signs the tradition of Chaucer to the men of whom I
have been talking today.   I will not deny them some
credit for having prepared the way for Elizabethan
verse by getting rid of Chaucer's light and lissome, but
inevitably doomed, vowel-endings; or some sympathy
for the lumpishness which their efforts imposed on their
strains.   But you will not find the true course of English song in Lydgate, or in Occleve, or in Hawes.   The
true wells are running, but they are running under-
ground, among the country people, among the innominate minstrels who invented the ballad poetry of the
Scottish Border.   And when it bubbles into light it has,
along with that medieval taste which I, for one, find so
fascinating, a marvellous freshness, vivacity, sparkle.
Read a stanza of *The Nut-Browne Mayd:*

> Though it be sung of old and young
>   That I should be to blame,
> Theirs be the charge that speak so large
>   In hurting of my name:
> For I will prove that faithful love
>   It is devoid of shame;
> In your distress and heaviness
>   To part with you the same:
> For sure all tho that do not so
>   True lovers are they none:
> For in my mind, of all mankind
>   I love but you alone.

Mr. Pollard quotes the opening stanza of this immortal
ballad, and exclaims: "To say that English poetry was
dead when verse like this was being written is absurd.
It was not dead, but banished from Court."

VII

I have spoken of Ballads. Yet I am not thinking only
of Ballads or even of the Carols such as "He came al so
still," or *The Holy Well*, or *The Leaves of Life*—which
so haunt the imagination that hears and sees the old
singer chanting them through miry roads under the
frosty flying moon.

> All under the leaves and the leaves of life
> I met with virgins seven,
> And one of them was Mary mild
> Our Lord's mother of Heaven.
>
> "O what are you seeking, you seven fair maids,
> All under the leaves of life? . . .
>
> "We're seeking for no leaves, Thomas,
> But for a friend of thine:
> We're seeking for sweet Jesus Christ,
> To be our guide and thine."
>
> "Go down, go down to yonder town
> And sit in the gallery,
> And there you'll see sweet Jesus Christ
> Nail'd to a big yew-tree."

I say that I am not thinking only or even chiefly of
these. I am thinking chiefly of that Song of Songs which
is No man's and Everyman's, that poem divine in every
sense—*Quia Amore Langueo*. As usual in medieval
verse it opens with the singer wandering and coming on
a vision. Listen!

> In a valley of this restles mind
> I sought in mountain and in mead,
> Trusting a true love for to find.
> Upon an hill then took I heed;

A voice I heard (and near I yede)
In great dolour complaining tho:
See, dear soul, how my sides bleed
   Quia amore langueo.

Upon this hill I found a tree,
Under a tree a man sitting;
From head to foot wounded was he;
His hearte blood I saw bleeding:
A seemly man to be a king,
A gracious face to look unto.
I askèd why he had paining;
   [He said,] *Quia amore langueo.*

No Carol, no Ballad at its best, ever touches the aching poetry of *that.*

VIII

Yet one "academic" poem of this time, *The Flower and the Leaf*—anonymous, for long attributed to Chaucer himself—seems to me purely delightful. Its method is Chaucer's, its setting Chaucer's. Its sunshine is pervasive, a little less vivid than Chaucer's, but bland and gracious if with an almost lunar grace. Gracious, too, is the choice offered. "The flower that fadeth, the leaf that lasts"—

to whom do ye owe
Your service? and which will ye honour,
Tell me I pray, this year, the Leaf or Flour?

Here are four stanzas, of the Queen of the Flower and her train.

And at the last I cast myn eye asyde,
  And was ware of a lusty company
That came, roming out of the feld wyde,

Hond in hond, a knight and a lady:
The ladies alle in surcotes, that richly
    Purfylèd were with many a richè stoon:
    And every knight of greene ware mantles on,

Embroudered wel, so as the surcotes were,
    And everich had a chapelet on her hede;
Which did right wel upon the shyning here, [hair]
    Made of goodly flourès, whyte and rede.
    The knightès eke, that they in hond lede
        In sute of hem, ware chapelets everichon;
        And hem before went minstrels many on;

As harpès, pypès, lutès, and sautry,
    Al in greene; and on their hedès bare,
Of dyvers flourès mad ful craftily
    Al in sute, goodly chapelets they ware;
    And so, dauncing, into the mede they fare,
        In-mid the which they found a tuft, that was
        Al oversprad with flourès in compas:

Whereunto they enclynèd everichon
    With great reverence and that ful humblely:
And, at the lastè, there began anon
    A lady for to sing right womanly
    A bargaret in praising the daisy
        For, as me thought, among her notès swete
        She sayd, "*Si doucè est la Margarete!*"

But in England this sweet note of an earlier time
rarely lifts itself above the droning bourdon of the
moralists: and *The Flower and the Leaf* (as I have said)
is a stray unfathered child. If we would hear the
Chaucerian lay still pouring full and strong, we must
hie northward and across the Border where the poor
folk sing Ballads; to Scotland, where are not a few
genuine poets, and notably four: four authentic poets,
acknowledged poets, and yet imitators.

IX

The first is a King: James I of Scotland, born in July, 1394, was made prisoner at sea by the English in 1405, and remained nineteen years in captivity in various castles of this realm. During his imprisonment he wiled away the hours with music and poetry—especially with much fervent reading of Chaucer: and, as to any hero of Chaucer's, there came to him—poetically if not literally, "through his prison-bars"—the vision of a lady-love. But the vision was real, and her name Jane Beaufort, daughter of the Earl of Somerset and great-granddaughter of John of Gaunt. He loved her; she loved him; and in due time, ransomed at ruinous price and released, he married her in the church of St. Mary Overes (now St. Saviour's), Southwark, at the altar hard by the tomb of John Gower, and carried her away to Scotland; where thirteen years later he died, still like a hero of romance, in the Black Friars' monastery at Perth; where as the tale is told, the Queen's maiden, "Kate Barlass," thrust her arm through the bolt-sockets to bar out his murderers.

It is his love-story that he tells in *The King's Quhair* (quire, or book), and he must write it, he says, "because I have come so from Hell to Heaven." But either he has read his Chaucer to too good a purpose, or, being a king, he must not write too personally. At any rate those who seek *The King's Quhair* for palpitating personal details will find disappointment. The thing is right Chaucer in the seven-lined stanza which now, perhaps because a king had used it, has received the name of "Rime Royal"; right medieval in its setting— the sleepless night, the book, the vision half a dream, the May morning, and all the rest of it. Those who read it as a poem *of that sort* in the French-Chaucerian manner will find it a delight.

> Worschippe ye that loveris bene this May,
> For of your blisse the Kalenis are begounne.
> And sing with us, Away, Winter, away!
> Cum, Somer, cum, the suete sesoun and sonne!
> Awake for schame! that have your hevynnis wonne,
> And amorously lift up your hedis all:
> Thank Lufe that list you to his merci call!

X

Robert Henryson, the second Scot on our list, and the manliest, most original of them all, was a schoolmaster, of the Benedictine Abbey-school at Dunfermline, the precincts of which gave him the text for his poem—*The Abbey Walk:*

> Allone as I went up and doun
> In ane abbay wes fair to se,
> Thinking quhat consolatioun
> Wes best in to adversitie,
> On caise [by chance] I kest on syd myne e
> And saw this writin upoun a wall:
> *Of quhat estait, man, that thow be,*
> *Obey and thank thy God of all.*

He, too, is a sworn Chaucerian. He toasts his feet by the fire on a winter's night, takes "ane drink" to hearten him, and falls to reading, for still further comfort, Chaucer's *Troilus:*

> I mend the fyre and beikit me about,
> Than tuik ane drink my spreits to comfort,
> And armit me wel fra the cold thairout;
> To cutte the wynter nicht and mak it schort

> I tuik ane quair [book] and left all uther sport,
> Written be worthie Chaucer glorious,
> Of fayre Cresseide and worthie Troylus.

But having finished the tale, the good man, puzzled by Chaucer's letting the wanton Cressid off so lightly, is moved to take pen and add a canto, punishing the wretch, and yet with a fierce kind of pity. In *The Testament of Cresseyde*, she is first cast off by Diomede, for whom she had abandoned Troilus so heartlessly: she becomes a poor common drab and returns to her father Calchas, priest of Venus, but is ashamed to go "into the kirk." In a dream she hears herself condemned by Saturn to be smitten with disease and drag out her days in misery. She awakes, looks in her glass, and finds she is a leper. She creeps to the lazar-house, and lives and begs with the lepers. On a day Troilus rides past with his gallant company, and the lepers ask alms, Cresseid among them.

> Than upon him scho kest up baith her ene,
> And with ane blenk it come into his thocht
> That he sumtime hir face befoir had sene;
> But scho was in sic plye he knew hir nocht;

For that look, that hint, "of fair Cresseid, sum tyme his awin darling" he throws rich alms and passes on—

> And nevertheless not ane ane uther knew.

But while the other lepers wonder at the rich gift thrown to "yon lazarous," one of them tells that his friend is none other than Prince Troilus. Cressid, heartbroken, makes her lament and her testament, and dies: and from her corpse a leper takes and carries to Troilus the ring with the red ruby that he had given her aforetime: and Troilus cries from a bursting heart:

"I can no moir;
Scho was untrew, and wo is me thairfor!"

Sum said he maid ane tomb of merbell gray,
  And wrait hir name and superscriptioun,
And laid it on hir grave, quhair that scho lay,
  In goldin letteris, conteining this ressoun:
"Lo, fair ladyis, Cresseid of Troyis toun,
Sumtyme countit the flour of womanheid,
Under this stane, lait lipper, lyis deid."

—a noble, passionate poem, and (I dare to say) touched with the true fire of the masterpiece for which it was written as sequel.

But Henryson's individual genius breaks out through other doorways less romantically Chaucerian; notably, in his fables rehearsed from Æsop, whom with the right nonchalance of the Middle Ages he chose to make a Roman, and a "poet laureate" at that. These give him scope for that gift of painting in the Dutch manner (as we call it) which we noted just now in the opening of *Cresseid;* homely, racy, with just a hint of archness, in epithet or turn of phrase; that the Scots, may be, borrowed from their friends and allies, the French. Take these stanzas from his best-known tale, of the Town Mouse and the Country Mouse, or (as Henryson inverts it) *The . . . uponlandis mous and the burges mous:*

This rurall mouse in to the winter tyde
  Had hunger, cauld, and tholit gret distres.
The uther mous that in the burgh can byde
  Was gild brother and maid ane fre burgess;
Toll fre als, but custum mair or les,
  And fredome had to ga quhair ever scho list,
  Amang the cheis in ark, and meill in kist.

One day the Town Mouse has a fancy to pay a call on her sister:

> Furth mony wilsum wayis can scho walk,
>   Thraw moss and mure, thraw bankis, busk and breir,
> Scho ran cryand, quhill scho cum to ane balk:
> "Cum furth to me, my awin sister deir;
> Cry peip anis!" With that the mousse culd heir,
>   And knew hir voce, as kynnisman will do,
>   Be verray kynd; and furth scho come hir to.
> The hartlie Ioy, god! to if ye had sene,
>   Beis kyth quhen that thir twa sisteris met;
> And gret kyndnes was schawin thame betuene,
>   For quhillis thay leuch, and quhillis for joy thay gret,
>   Quhile kissit sweit, quhillis in armes plet;
> And thus thay fure, quhill soberit was thair mude,
> Syne fuet for fuet unto the chalmer yude.

Equal originality you will find in the very different styles of *Robene and Makyne* and of *The Bludy Serk*, a tale of man's redemption. *The Bludy Serk* is told in the ballad metre and in ballad narrative, but with a high earnestness to which but a few of the best ballads attain. Let me quote one that does so attain.

> *Lully, lulley! lully, lulley!*
> The faucon hath borne my make away!
>
> He bare him up, he bare him down,
> He bare him into an orchard brown.
>
> In that orchard there was an halle,
> That was hangèd with purple and pall.
>
> And in that hall there was a bed,
> It was hangèd with gold sa red.
>
> And in that bed there li'th a knight,
> His woundès bleeding day and night.

By that bede-sid kneeleth a may,
And she weepeth both night and day.

And at that bed's head standeth a stone,
Corpus Christi written thereon.

As for *Robene and Makyne*—arch and fresh and jolly as a small idyll by Theocritus—it is in all the anthologies and deserves to be: with the possible exception of Victor Hugo's *La Coccinelle,* the prettiest perfect thing ever written on the theme of "he that will not when he may."

XI

There are times when, by giving preference to Henryson, we seem to do grave injustice to the third Scots poet on our list—William Dunbar, wandering scholar, mendicant and minstrel. Or shall I say that there are moods: that these moods are provoked by the titles of "The Scottish Chaucer" and "The Scottish Skelton," given to him by his admirers and detractors? ["The Scottish Chaucer," "the German Milton," "the Australian Kipling," "Californian Burgundy," "the Cornish Riviera."] Of Dunbar the two epithets are about equally false; but together they hint this much of truth —that, for praise as for blame, critics find it extraordinarily difficult to keep their heads with him. He is an allegorist, of course, and not, to my thinking, a very good one: but he has, like Keats, when the story sticks and declines to move, a marvellous talent for splashing on colour to beguile your attention away from the misadventure, as a Spanish railway-guard, when the engine has broken down, will hold you spell-bound by the sonorous wealth of his vowel-sounds. For Dunbar is, above all things, a colourist: and when he really has a picture to paint, and can keep his palette under control, you are ready to swear that he is a very great poet indeed. Here, for an example, are two stanzas from a hymn *Of the Nativity of Christ.*

> *Rorate coeli desuper!*
>   Hevins, distil your balmy schouris!
> For now is risen the bricht day-star,
>   Fro the rose Mary, flour of flouris;
>
>   The cleir Sone, quhom no cloud devouris
> Surmounting Phebus in the Est,
>   Is cumin of his hevinly touris:
>   *Et nobis Puer natus est.*
>
> Archangellis, angellis, and dompnationis,
>   Tronis, potestatis and marteiris seir,
> And all ye hevinly operationis,
>   Ster, planet, firmament, and spheir,
>   Fire, erd, air, and water cleir,
> To Him give loving, most and lest,
>   That come in to so meik maneir;
>   *Et nobis Puer natus est.*

From another poem, though I have quoted it before from this desk, I shall quote again because it happens to be first favourite of mine. Returning Scotlandwards from his youthful wandering as mendicant-friar in Picardy, Dunbar stands upon London Bridge and—well, there was no Westminster Bridge in those days, so you must build it, and set Wordsworth upon it, and strike the balance for yourselves. This is Dunbar's invocation.

> London, thou art of townès *A per se:*
>   Sovereign of cities, seemliest in sight,
> Of high renoun, riches and royaltie;
>   Of lordis, barons and many a goodly knight

Of most delectable lusty ladies bright:
Of famous prelatis in habitis clericall:
Of merchantis full of substaunce and of **myght**:
London, thou art the flour of Cities all. . . .

Above all ryvers thy Ryver hath renowne,
  Whose beryall stremys, pleasaunt and preclare,
Under thy lusty wallys renneth down,
    Where many a swan doth swymme with wyngis feir;
    Where many a barge doth sail and row with are;
Where many a ship doth rest with top royall.
    O, towne of townes! patrone and not compare,
London, thou art the flour of Cities all.

Upon thy lusty Brigge of pylers white
  Been merchantis full royal to behold,
Upon thy stretis go'th many a semely Knyght
    In velvet gownès and in cheynes of gold.
    By Julyus Cesar thy Tour founded of old
May be the hous of Mars victoryall,
    Whose artillary with tonge may not be **told;**
London, thou art the flour of Cities all.

Strong be thy wallis that about thee standis;
  Wise is the people that within thee dwellis;
Fresh be thy ryver with his lusty strandis;
    Blith be thy chirchis, wele souning be thy bellis;
    Rich be thy merchauntis in substance that excellis;
Fair be their wives, right lovesum, white and small:
    Clere be thy virgyns, lusty under kellis: (hoods)
London, thou art the flour of Cities all.

I observe that a writer in *The Cambridge History of English Literature* remarks upon this, "the poem is, with all its conventionality of phrase, of considerable historical interest" (which of course is not a conventional phrase!). To me it makes a crowded but distinct and moving and very brilliant picture. But now let us turn and, in a stanza from his ambitious poem, *The Golden Targe*, watch our colourist at work upon a landscape he does not quite realise; and, to be fair to him, I will choose one which in the main is very beautiful:

> For mirth of May, wyth skippis and wyth hoppis
> The birds sang upon the tender croppis,
>   With curious notis, as Venus chapell clerkis:
> The rosis reid, now spreding of thair knoppis,
> Wer powderit brycht with hevinly beriall droppis,
> Throu bemes rede, lemying as ruby sparkis;
> The skyes rang for schoutyng of the larkis,
> The purple hevyn oure-scailit in silver sloppis
> Ouregilt the treis, branchis, leivis and barkis.

There is poetry here, scattered or "sloppit"; but you note how he ends by over-daubing it? Nay, he does not end there: he goes on,

> The cristall air, the sapheir firmament,
> The ruby skyès of the reid Orient
> Kest beryall bemes on emerant bowis grene. . . .

We are in Aladdin's cave. I think you will find that much of Dunbar's colouring is cheap, garish; that it will not, to live with it, hold better than a lamp to Chaucer's clean daylight.

And now I must pass to that part of his work—and it is no small part—in which Dunbar shows as merely odious. Chaucer no doubt is coarse when he chooses, but nobody not a fool will deny that Chaucer's coarseness is healthy; that he had a clean mind. And Rabelais is coarse of purpose, even gluttonously coarse, yet you cannot say that Rabelais had a dirty mind. It had too wide a pavement, swept to the corners with open laughter. I will even say—and hope it will not cost me my chair—that it belongs to my notion of a total man that he can open his lungs to the broadest human jest and laugh his soul clean of it: that indeed I distrust any fellow who cannot. But Dunbar has a dirty mind—a mind far dirtier (as I feel it to be) than Skelton's, whom Pope quite unfairly labelled "beastly": and Dunbar introduced into Scottish poetry that particular smatch of smuttiness for which—persisting as it did in her poetry down to Ferguson and Burns and beyond—Scotland has found a particular name—*Sculduddery*. For obvious reasons I shall not illustrate this by quotation: but it is there.

Also, at this time of day, one is honestly bored with the many "flytings"—or scoldings: performances in which Dunbar and some rival poet (say Walter Kennedy) stood and ballyragged, each calling the other "every name but what he was christened," to make mirth before James IV and his Court. The best one can say of these efforts is that they exhibit Dunbar as truly Rabelaisian in his command of riotous argot.

> Bot fowll, jow-jowrdane-hedit jevillis,
> Cowkin-kenseis, and culrown kewellis;
> Stuffettis, strekouris, and staflische strummellis;
> Wyld haschbaldis, haggarbaldis, and hummellis. . . .

And so forth. In the words of Abraham Lincoln, "for people who like that sort of thing, that is the sort of thing they'll like."

XII

The fourth of our Scottish poets, Gavin (or Gawain) Douglas, a bishop, shall occupy us but a moment. His notable work is a translation of the *Æneid*, though it scarcely belongs to humanism. He wrote prologues of his own to Virgil's several books, and in these he let himself go. How far he let himself go may be gathered from a few lines of his preface to the eighth book.

Sum latit lattoun, but lay, lepis in laud lyte;
Sum penis furth a pan boddum to prent fals plakkis; . . .
Sum prig penny, sum pyk thank with privy promyt;
Sum garris with a ged staf to jag throw blak jakkis.
   Quhat fynzeit fayr, quhat flattry, and quhat fals talis!
      Quhat misery is now in land!
      How mony crakyt cunnand!
      For nowthir aiths, nor band
        Nor selis avalis.

As Professor Gregory Smith says, "This audacious break in the web of the *Æneid* may have served some purpose of rest or refreshment . . . but it is not the devising of a humanist." Three of the prologues describe the country (*his* country, Scotland) in May, in autumn, and in winter, and give a foretaste of that Scottish talent for descriptive writing which culminated (I suppose) more than two centuries later in Thomson's *Seasons*.

These then—James I, Henryson, Dunbar and Douglas—were the four wheels of Scotland's poetic chariot in the period we are considering; and if we want a fifth wheel, we may take the popular Sir David Lyndsay (born *circ.* 1490), author of the *Dreme*, the *Testament of the King's Papyngo*, *Ane Satyre of the Threi Estatis*, and *Monarchie*. But Scotland in the fifteenth century teemed with poets, or "makers"—Wyntoun, Blind Harry, and a score of others whose memory Dunbar, when himself sick and like to die, in his *Lament for the Makaris*, conjured to his bedside the ghosts of the many who had predeceased him.

[Death] has done petuously devour
The noble Chaucer, of makaris flour,
The Monk of Bury, and Gower, all three:
Timor Mortis conturbat me, etc.

XIII

This may conclude our survey: and in summary we may start by noting two technical points and setting them down to the credit of these professional Post-Chaucerians, English and Scottish. (i) If they invented little, they yet did, by discipline of verse-form and stanza, set a standard and keep poetry, in an age when the language was being broken up and remade, from slipping back into old uncouth metres and (ii) within those verse-forms they did contain the new rebel language, and tame it, and adapt it to do, in greater hands, greater work. We shall have reason to thank them hereafter, when we come to the nobly undulating stanzas of Spenser.

But, for actual poetry, the fatal trouble with these men lay in their inspiration, that its source was mainly retrospective; that they steadily looked back to Chaucer, using their talents upon his genius, as men conscious and over-conscious of a legacy. It is equally significant and pathetic that almost every one of them, however full he may have been for page upon page, touches real and often passionate eloquence the moment he bethinks him of Chaucer: *then* his voice and his ambling verse break together—

O maister, maister, God thy soulè rest!

But literature marches with life, and is behoven, like everything else—more than anything else may be—to be up and doing. These men, preoccupied with the dead, drew little or no inspiration from their own busy hour, let be from the future: and this is the stranger because the earliest of them lived while Europe struggled with the throes of a new birth—of thought, of discovery, of scholarship, of the arts, of literature, and, above all, of poetry; while the later, had they but lifted their eye from their writing-desks would have seen, not the twilight between two worlds,

> one dead,
> The other powerless to be born—

but the dawn itself. For Greece had crossed the Alps —*Ecco Græcia nostra transvolavit Alpes.*

We have no time today, at the end of our survey, to enquire why this was: why these professional poets of the fifteenth century were as dead men burying the dead. But I will conclude by suggesting a line of enquiry.

The fifteenth century saw the rise of our nation—largely through its cloth trade and export of wool—to the first rank of commercial importance.

The capitalist makes his appearance: with the use of borrowed capital. Now the Church, as we know, strictly forbade usury: but as a learned Italian professor, Benvenuto da Imola, had remarked in the preceding century in a commentary on Dante, "he who practiseth usury goeth to hell, and he who practiseth it not tendeth to destitution." There were means of evasion, however: and sometimes the investor was so eager that he paid the borrower for borrowing.

I think you will find the historians and economists in substantial agreement that, in spite of our wars, the fifteenth century saw England a nation not merely materially prosperous by comparison with others, but actually and abundantly and increasingly so prosperous with a prosperity spreading and working like yeast in all classes, as by very plethora to burst the old feudal framework of society. But this yeasty rise of the middle and moneyed classes broke up more than the feudal "system." It destroyed the great redeeming idea of it— Chivalry.

Now it is ill when a class discards a creed, even a threadbare one, having nothing wherewith to replace it. And the Church just then did not help, being itself far gone in spiritual decay and nearing its ruin in England. Men built Churches, to be sure, of the comfortable unimaginative Perpendicular, which, by imposing regularity upon the fervours of the true Gothic, smoothed out all its meaning: they filled the windows with stippled glass out of which the old glory of colour had faded; and they built these churches in such profusion that one shivers at times to hear earnest Christians talk of the frenetic "restoration" (or "restruction") of sacred edifices in our day as evidence of our Church's vitality.

It is a century, or a century and a half—say from the death of Chaucer to the time of the sordid *Paston Letters* —concerned very much with material things; with marrying and giving in marriage (for money), with building, with markets, with (as M. Jusserand notes) books of cookery, of etiquette, of the art of pushing one's way into better society—you are enjoined not to take always the "whole" of the best "morsel"; but not a time conspicuously concerned with the soul.

To one great idea it held, however, and with more than a commercial devotion—our pride of the sea.

Kepe than the see abought in specialle,
Whiche of England is the towne walle;
As thoughe England were lykened to a citè,
And the walle enviroun were the see.
Kepe than the see, that is the walle of England,
And than is England kepte by Goddes hande.
Libelle of Englysshe Policie.

This may not be good poetry, but it has the right ring. Of the two chief glories of our birth and state, Poetry and the pride of Sea-faring, the men of the age we have been considering maintained the second, at any rate, and passionately.

THE "VICTORIAN AGE"

I

ONCE upon a time—this seems an appropriate opening for a talk about the Victorian Age— once upon a time a benevolent grandfather took me for a treat into a small round building which then stood upon Plymouth Hoe and advertised itself as a Camera Obscura. Perhaps I should explain to you that a Camera Obscura is, or was, a temple of alleged entertainment; and that the apparatus consisted of a darkened chamber lit only through a lens in the roof and having, beneath the lens a circular white table on which you gazed and saw a portion of the landscape outside, with the people and things moving upon it. A simple scientific toy!—but in those days we were easily entertained. You, who belong to a more critical generation, may incline to ask why anyone should pay twopence for admission to a panorama which he could view more distinctly for nothing by the simple process of staying outside.

Well, no doubt that hits on the secret why, with the growth of analytical reason, Cameras Obscura have had their day. But you would be on stronger ground, though quite wrong, if you argued that the appeal of realism is permanent (witness Madame Tussaud's) while that of romance must be transient, since it rests on energy, movement, phenomena in themselves and by nature fleeting. For I assure you that the moving throng upon the table made a vision far more romantic than had been the actual view of the actual promenaders outside. The heavy door of the chamber shut out their chatter and exchange of "good-days." These people within a few feet of us pursuing the zest of life like gnats in a miz-maze! In silence on that white table they met and gesticulated, lifted their hats or bowed; or they came to the edge of it——

Unconscious of their doom the little victims played—they came to the edge of it and so dropped off, like the people in the Vision of Mirza—dropped off and departed this life into nothingness; the pea-jacketted gentleman with the single eyeglass and the Piccadilly whiskers, the little lady who minced in elastic-sided Balmorals beneath a pagoda-shaped parasol, the non-commissioned officer in tight scarlet with a cane under his arm, either immediately following or immediately followed by the nursemaid wheeling a perambulator in shape like a Roman Chariot reversed. Sergeant, nursemaid, perambulator—all went over the table's edge, and were lost.

II

That queer, somewhat romantic, almost uncanny sensation of the Camera Obscura recurred the other evening, when, preparing to write these pages for you, I shut my eyes and let pass in review a procession of figures, men and women "of importance in their day," who crossed our country's stage while yet Victoria was Queen: Gladstone, aquiline of eye; Disraeli with a face like a mask—but whether painted for tragedy or for comedy none could guess, and he wouldn't tell; Lord Salisbury, huge of bulk, floundering up Piccadilly like

a whale with a wake of respectful curiosity astern—for
he carried an unconscious sea-shouldering greatness;
Tennyson, by no means unconscious of greatness;
Browning, hiding his under a glad confident guise of
middle-class prosperity; Swinburne, like nothing on
earth; modest Darwin; Huxley and Tyndall, no pair less
similar; Rossetti, William Morris, Millais—Millais hand-
somest of men; George Eliot, always suggestive somehow of a camel, with George Henry Lewes for driver;
Florence Nightingale; Gordon; Matthew Arnold and
Walter Pater; Carlyle with (to adapt his own phrase)
the east wind *and* the fire in his belly; Ruskin—to me a
bent figure in gown and velvet cap, moving Oxford with
eyes that, under bushy brows, seemed to look inward
on torture, rarely outward, but then always with inex-
pressible love.   Other Oxford figures are Dean Liddell
of the Lexicon, "in form and moving how express and
admirable!"   Jowett, round and cherubic: Mark Pattison and Robinson Ellis—great in desiccation.   So to
Cambridge to Monro, Thompson, J. E. B. Mayor and,
with Leslie Stephen, back to London to St. Paul's,
where you hear Church or Liddon preach; or, if you
prefer it, to Spurgeon's tabernacle or to the City Temple
to hear Dr. Parker; or to the Theatre and Irving—or
Nellie Farren—and thence back to the Savile, or the
Art's Club or the Garrick where you may sup perhaps
in company with Stevenson, Henley, Henry James; or
to Westminster where you may watch Parnell, Brad-
laugh, Randolph Churchill, playing their parts in the
tragi-comedy.   Of course, if you have a previous en-
gagement at Buckingham Palace, you will meet others
there diversely great; and your wife, if you have the luck
to possess one, will wear a bodice cut by Queen Victoria's
order to a lowness in the so-called neck to this day, or

up to a few weeks ago, shocking in a Tottenham Police Court.

"These for our greatest"—and behind them are Macaulay, Dickens, Thackeray, the Brontës, Newman, Mill, Clough, Kingsley, Martineau; while among them move Anthony Trollope and "Ouida," Froude, Freeman, Charles Reade, Wilkie Collins, Frith and Whistler, Burne Jones, Ford Madox Brown, with other strange ghosts—Kinglake, Burton of *The Arabian Nights*, Livingstone, James Thomson of *The City of Dreadful Night*, Laurence Oliphant, Coventry Patmore, Miss Braddon. I mix them at haphazard as they pass across the mind's eye's retina: but the Victorian stage was a crowded one anyhow.

III

And I grant you how much of a stage it all seems in review: how far removed even for those of us who can look back wistfully to the old theatre, the comfortable stalls! I seem to stand again gazing on that white table, and to see Disraeli with his eyeglass nearing the edge and tottering over to the tune of something from Gilbert and Sullivan. The Victorian Age is done; it is passing back into history even during this hour of yours which I occupy, who have seen numbers of these men and women and even been privileged to converse with some few of them; or rather, to listen and drink in admiration—of John Bright's exquisite voice softly repeating bad poetry by the fireplace of the Reform Club Smoking Room; of Meredith, at his own board, dragging spoons and forks towards him to illustrate over a bottle of Château Neuf du Pape, the disposition of Napoleon's force at Austerlitz.

They have all gone over the edge of the table, these
figures so commanding in their day; and the Victorian
Age, upon which some of you already shoot back the
light shafts of your ridicule, is a monument, closed as
definitely as any epoch in history can be closed.

For actually of course no epoch in history ever had
a definite beginning or a definite end. Even of the
Christian Era itself men were whispering surmises,

magnus ab integro sæclorum nascitur ordo

before and after it stole on them so quietly as it did: and
it yet may (I say it reverently and with conviction)with-
draw itself from an unworthy world "like a thief in the
night" with as soft a footfall as it came. Men and women
did not change their habits, opinions, natures, in 1837
or again in 1901, and what you laugh at as "Victorian"
includes a great deal that we laughed at as "Early Victorian" or, later, as "Mid-Victorian"; and your aversion
(say) for the Crystal Palace or Frith's *Derby Day*,
Tennyson's *Idylls of the King*, or, if you will, the novels
we poor fellows wrote in the 'nineties, is itself, and while
you feel it, passing and growing incorporate in the tragi-
comedy which the more it changes the more is the same
thing. Forgive me if in this, and quite in the Victorian
manner, I stress the obvious. I grant you the Victorian
Age is closed: definitely closed, if you will, by the late
War: that you can view it, with its many oddities and
certain glaring sins, yourselves shut off as I was in my
Camera Obscura. But I greatly desire to warn you
against the habit of viewing things so; of parcelling
theology, history, literature, what-not into periods,
and so excluding a sense of life's continuous variety,
energy, flow. These Victorians were your grandfathers
and fathers; they built this Lacedæmon which, after

some necessary pulling down, you will doubtless adorn; and lacking this sense of continuous energy you may even lose the great human mainspring of confident hope.

IV

But especially I would warn the cleverer of you against thinking in periods, to *despise* this, that, or the other. Yes, and even more specially against sneering at the Victorian Age: and this not only because to sneer at our fathers is ungracious if not ungrateful, and no good ever came of bad manners. Every free man ought to test his parents' opinions (I shall come to this by-and-by); but he should do so, I think, with tenderness, and a little compunction will do him no harm. Nor again shall I plead just here that to understand the Victorian Age actually concerns you more than to understand any other, since happily or unhappily you directly take over its work, to improve or to undo. I would rather begin by having you see for yourselves how cheap a trick is the sneer, and how easily played.

We have all been reading of late an extremely clever biographical study of the Queen who gave her name to that age—*Queen Victoria*, by Mr. Lytton Strachey. It is a briskly written book; artfully conceived and executed in the spirit of detraction; nicely adjusted to its hour; and cleverest of all in that it probes Victoria's weakest, most feminine, point—her adoration of her husband. Albert, the Prince Consort, was (be it granted) a figure at whom one could poke fun, and Mr Strachey, with his style, can contrive it so that Victoria's adoration appears extraordinarily funny.

As she watched her beloved Albert, after toiling with state documents and public functions, devoting every spare

moment of his time to domestic duties, to artistic appreciation, and to intellectual improvements; as she listened to
him cracking his jokes at the luncheon-table, or playing
Mendelssohn on the organ, or pointing out the merits of
Sir Edwin Landseer's pictures; as she followed him round
while he gave instructions about the breeding of cattle, or
decided that the Gainsboroughs must be hung higher up so
that the Winterhalters might be properly seen—she felt
perfectly certain that no other wife ever had such a husband. His mind was apparently capable of everything, and
she was hardly surprised to learn that he had made an
important discovery for the conversion of sewage into
agricultural manure . . . (p. 187).

The last vestige of the eighteenth century had disappeared; cynicism and subtlety were shrivelled into powder;
and duty, industry, morality, and domesticity triumphed
over them. Even the very chairs and tables had assumed,
with a singular responsiveness, the forms of prim solidity.
The Victorian Age was in full swing (p. 141).

Now that, let us agree, is very smart and amusing.
But observe that it tells little of Victoria save that she
was passionately in love with her husband—which in
itself is no bad thing in a wife, or at worst a venial error.
The book aims at showing up Albert the Good to ridicule, and transfers the ridicule, as by sleight of hand, to
the Age.

Well, let us agree again that Albert the Good was
a somewhat absurd figure and on top of that (if you
will, and as Mr. Strachey suggests) even a somewhat
dangerous one. He was a German, anyhow; and it is
the fashion nowadays to regard Germans as at once
absurd and dangerous, reconciling these notions in our
mind as best we may. Yet, after all, Queen Victoria
reigned for sixty-three-years-and-a-half, of which the
years of her married life made a bare third. What of her

forty years of Queenship in widowhood? What of the indomitable small lady in black to whom we—standing before you today as confessed Victorians acutely sensitive of our position, albeit born years and years after Prince Albert's demise—used in those later years to lift our silk hats as she drove down the cleared way of the Park with her scarlet outriders before and her Scots Gillies on the rumble behind her? A quaint outfit, to be sure; and a quaint figure if you will; yet, believe me, the sight of it lifted the heart along with the silk hat! She seemed the more diminutive for that her seat in the carriage was built low, purposely (legend said)—her life having been several times attempted or threatened, usually by lunatics. That may or may not be, but this is certain—that in April, 1900, in her eighty-first year, because Ireland had sent an extraordinarily large number of recruits to the South African War, she insisted on cancelling her usual trip to the Riviera and spending three weeks in Dublin, where, in spite of protest, she drove through the streets without armed escort, and the visit was a complete success. That was the Queen Victoria *we* knew.

Mr. Strachey notes the incident. But of course, to paint the Victorian Age as typically absurd to suit 1921's fashionable conception of it, he must go back almost forty years beyond that Dublin visit, and choose the Great Exhibition of 1851—Bless my soul, what hilarity we have all been getting out of it ever since! Why, thirty odd years ago even I, born some thirteen odd years after it, thought it amusing in a boyish book to laugh at the Great Exhibition of 1851! But time and practice and the birth of genius which time sooner or later brings about have together perfected the right funny way of writing about 1851, and the pigments for

painting the lily can all be found in Victoria's own innocent journals and Sir Theodore Martin's *Life of the
Prince Consort.* So this is how you set to work.

V

Of the sixty odd years of the reign, you choose the
eleventh or twelfth as its apex—yes, I am afraid you
must go back as far as that. You suggest that by 1849,
at latest, the Victorian Age is in full swing, and even
the domestic furniture "with a singular responsiveness"
playing up. Mr. Strachey proceeds:

Only one thing more was needed: material expression
must be given to the new ideals and the new forces, so that
they might stand revealed in visible glory before the eyes of
an astonished world. It was for Albert to supply this want.
He mused, and was inspired, the Great Exhibition came into
his head.

Two years of preparation pass, and then, on May 1st,
1851—which is seventy years ago, mark you—the
Queen opens the great show "amid scenes of dazzling
brilliancy and triumphal enthusiasm." Well again,
every great International Exhibition and World's Fair
or whatever you choose to call it—and there have been
some not negligeable—has had its origin in that day;
with hundreds of thousands of shows—agricultural,
floral, mechanical, pictorial and so on—which must
have given pleasure, in these seventy years, to some
hundreds of millions of people. It set going at the time,
no doubt, a deal of giddy talk about inaugurating an
Era of Universal Peace. But it was an idea.
One author's business, however, being to make folly

of it, he has plenty of material in our gracious lady's
own innocent record of the day. So he goes on:

Victoria herself was in a state of excitement which bor-
dered on delirium. She performed her duties in a trance
of joy, gratitude, and amazement, and, when it was all over,
her feelings poured themselves out in her journal in a tor-
rential flood. The day had been nothing but an endless
succession of glories—or rather one vast glory—one vast
radiation of Albert. Everything she had seen, everything
she had felt or heard, had been so beautiful, so wonderful
. . . the huge crowds, so well-behaved and loyal—flags
of all nations floating—the inside of the building so immense, with myriads of people and the sun shining through
the roof—a little state-room, where we left our shawls—
palm-trees and machinery—dear Albert—the place so big
that we could scarcely hear the organ—thankfulness to
God—a curious assemblage of political and distinguished
men—the March from "Athalie"—God bless my dearest
Albert, God bless my dearest country!—a glass fountain—
the Duke (of Wellington) and Lord Anglesey walking arm-
in-arm—a beautiful Amazon, in bronze, by Kiss—Mr.
Paxton (the architect), who might be justly proud, and rose
from being a common gardener's boy—Sir George Grey in
tears, and everybody astonished and delighted.

This trick of quoting in apposition is effective enough:
but not difficult; and in effect it does not make for
truth. "Go write your lively sketches," says Bishop
Blougram dismissing Gigadibs, the literary man. Some
of us who remember that old lady, diminutively seated
in her carriage for her day's driving after the long day
of duty inexorably pursued, would rather incline to dismiss him with a "Hang it all, Sir! If the 1st May, 1851,
was a day of ecstasy to her, she was a woman, a little
more than thirty, and she was in love, and it is long ago."

VI

For my part, and as one not wishing to parade his opinion, or even to disclose it until forced into protest, I think the Great Exhibition of 1851 must have been a mighty fine affair. Yes, and in more combative mood—not now—I could put up a spirited defence of Sir Joseph Paxton's Crystal Palace as a by-no-means unbeautiful building, which, as a design for an emergency—a big and entirely novel emergency—met it courageously and admirably fulfilled its purpose.

I will go further and maintain that as men, having made a discovery, set to work on it in honest earnest, inventing and adapting means to ends, they are pretty sure sooner or later to find their work taking on beauty or breeding, out of mistakes, new work which gradually takes on beauty. If we choose to think in periods and talk of "The Victorian Age," why then we must admit that the period, with its railways, steamships, machinery in general—its telegraphs, telephones and general harnessing of electricity to the service of man—its taming of wildernesses to grow human food—its discovery of the internal combustion engine prefacing not only revolution of traffic by land and water, but conquest of the very sky—was one of a scientific activity (we may even say, of a scientific explosiveness) which man had to meet in a hurry, often by the crudest makeshifts. These would be ugly enough as a rule, as unrealised ideas are ugly by nature. Brunel's monster steamship, *The Great Eastern*, was ugly enough: but you have seen Brunel's idea passing into shape in the great modern liners: and these again are full of imperfections: yet with a little imagination can you not foresee these in turn either passing into things of beauty, as a new fleet improves on their seaworthiness, or else passing out and giving place to an improving race of airships? If this seem fanciful, let me use a homelier illustration.

I dare say some of you have a certain affection for Paddington Station as a gate to the West. But I dare say also that it has occurred to few of you ever to think of Paddington Station as a thing in itself beautiful. If you ever thought of its glass roof—which, serving its purpose, and yours, never asked for your attention—you probably took it for granted as a thing admittedly ugly; and so, taking the Mid-Victorian gospel of art for granted, did I, year after year and several times a year; until one evening when, as Rudyard Kipling puts it,

Romance brought up the nine-fifteen

with a pilot-engine puffing smoke between the electric lights and the late sunlight filtering through the roof, the scales fell from my eyes and I saw Paddington Station for what it is, a thing of beauty or reaching to beauty. For the first time, having some minutes to spare, I played what the Americans call the "rubberneck," and in the twilight was dimly, but as never before, aware of that glass roof, surmising its span, its proportion and fitness for its purpose. Some weeks later —as these things happen—a very eminent engineer, a friend of mine, told me casually that he had lately spent some days on Brunel's roof over Paddington Station, testing it with a view to repairs, and that the farther he tested the skill of it, with its intricate ply of iron and glass against cold and heat, the more reverently he stood on that structure acknowledging its designer's genius. Well, that is a digression. I recur to my appeal to you not to think in periods.

We talk of the "Elizabethan Age" for example: and

of the Elizabethan Drama as a peculiar glory of that age: and of Shakespeare as its bright particular star. As a matter of history, Queen Elizabeth came to the throne in 1558, at the age of twenty-five, and had reigned some twenty-eight years before the youth Shakespeare ever came up to London to try his fortune. By 1595 or so he had learnt his art, and wrote a very charming play, *A Midsummer Night's Dream*, admittedly early and containing (in Act II, Scene 1) an allusion to Elizabeth as

> a fair vestal thronèd by the west

at whose heart Cupid had lately been aiming an arrow in vain. Now, if we reckon it out, at the time of this mischance of Cupid, Elizabeth's age was sixty-two. She died (after a reign of forty-five years) some eight short years on the other side of this virginal compliment, and *all* the very greatest plays—if (omitting possibly *Hamlet*) you count *Othello, Macbeth, Lear, Antony and Cleopatra, The Tempest*, as Shakespeare's greatest—belong to the reign of her successor, James I. That is what comes of thinking in periods.

VII

May I quote you a personal experience and a piece of personal observation? Shortly before coming up to Cambridge, some eight or nine years ago, I dedicated to my future pupils an anthology entitled *The Oxford Book of Victorian Verse*. As it turned out, I could hardly have chosen an unhappier name for a propitiatory offering. No: it was not the word "Oxford" that young Cambridge objected to: *that* would have been intelligible! It was the word "Victorian"—which in my innocence I had deemed good enough to ingratiate most people. For not only had University youth started the fashion, since widely spread, of scorning all things "Victorian"; in Cambridge it raged with something like virulence: and this, please observe, in 1913—a year and a half before the War: so that folks who nowadays account for the fashion by arguing that the earthquake of the War caused this cleavage between young and old are explaining a previous effect by a subsequent cause. (Another illustration of the peril of thinking in periods!) In 1913 these young men were not merely content—to use Plato's phrase—with laying hands on their father Parmenides. If Parmenides had been Victoria, and Victoria, so to speak, had not been a lady, they would have strangled him and thrown him out of the window. They were quite ingenuous about it, and so the especial *virus* was easily traced; to a book, a novel, *The Way of All Flesh*, by Samuel Butler, until then popularly (and yet not very popularly) known as the author of *Erewhon:* to a book which, published in 1903 after its author's death, hung fire for a few years before exploding, but was twice reprinted in 1910 and has been reprinted, I believe, in every subsequent year save one.

There were contributory causes, of course; and you may think it paradoxical of me to ascribe so much to a novel of which so large a number, even of educated people, know little or nothing. But fashions start in mysterious ways. (It was my privilege, years ago, to be acquainted with a tall and personable young man, who dressed himself with extreme care, but one morning, having mislaid his pearl tie-pin, and being in a hurry, stuck a gilt safety-pin into his cravat and so fared forth to his Club. Within a fortnight every really well-

dressed youth in Piccadilly wore a gold safety-pin in
his tie.)

I assure you there could be no doubt about it. The
view of these young men, your immediate forerunners,
took its focus and derived its sanction unmistakably,
confessedly, from Samuel Butler's *The Way of All Flesh*.
Now *The Way of All Flesh* is a work of indubitable, if
distorted, genius: and its publisher today adorns its
paper jacket with praises by men no less eminent than
Mr. Bernard Shaw and Mr. Arnold Bennett. It is admittedly and—as Butler's biographer, Mr. Festing
Jones, has been at pains to show—almost literally auto-
biographical: and it deals with the insensate warping
and bullying of a boy's life by a pair of sanctimonious
parents. For example, with the pitiless thrashing of
a child aged about five because, when commanded to
say the word "come," his infant mouth could achieve
nothing nearer than "tum," and persisted in saying
"tum" in spite of threats.

"Very well, Ernest," said his father, catching him angrily
by the shoulder. "I have done my best to save you, but if
you will have it so, you will," and he lugged the little wretch,
crying by anticipation, out of the room. A few minutes
more and we could hear screams coming from the dining-
room across the hall . . . and knew that poor Ernest was
being beaten.

"I have sent him up to bed," said Theobald [the *pater
familias*] as he returned to the drawing-room, "and now,
Christina, I think we will have the servants in to prayers,"
and he rang the bell for them, red-handed as he was. . . .

The man-servant William came and set the chairs for the
maids, and presently they filed in. First Christina's maid,
then the cook, then the housemaid, then William, and then
the coachman. I sat opposite them and watched their

faces as Theobald read a chapter from the Bible . . . more absolute vacancy I never saw upon the countenances of human beings.

Then follows a description of the ceremony, with some reflections aroused by it, which I have no time to read to you. Reading it to myself I found it delightfully satirical; but, for the life of me, I could find nothing peculiarly Victorian about it. The great Milton himself (in default of boys of his own) used to beat unmercifully the small nephews entrusted to his tutelage. And was there not a saying old as Solomon about "sparing the rod"? Probably Abraham, and certainly Sir Thomas More, held family prayers: as, for that matter, so did my own grandfather, though he never beat me in his life (my dear grandmother, if he had ever tried, would have told him about it): while my own parents, whatever their faults, had been kind. I daresay, if a man has been consistently ill-treated by his parents in childhood he has a right, later, to hold them up to public opprobrium. As to that I offer no opinion: it is a question of what a man feels to be permissible, which again works back in a circle to his upbringing. But to me the passage, so typically and recently Victorian to my young friends, seemed very far off, if not as old as the hills.

And then, enquiring further, I found that this story, published in 1903, after Butler's death, had been begun about 1872 (when I happened to be eight years of age) and finished in 1884 (when I was a callow undergraduate); and that it narrates the childish experiences of a man born a few years after my own father, and about two years before Victoria came to the throne.

And the typically "Victorian" father of this child was born in 1802, or thirty-five years before that event! And again that is what comes of thinking in periods!

Now I ask you to consider this. If, in the second year of the reign of Queen Victoria, one of her Judges of Assize, Lord Denman, at Launceston, sentenced a boy of thirteen to penal servitude for life for stealing three gallons of potatoes; and if by the close of the reign such a sentence had become not merely illegal but unthinkable—so that, at the least, it had changed places with the offence and, if anyone, then the Judge rather than the criminal should have gone to penal servitude for life—Who were—who can have been—the wizards that wrought this topsy-turvy on the national conscience?

Or if, as I read of the condition of the labouring poor in Disraeli's *Sybil* or in Cobbett's earlier *Rural Rides*, or of the labourers' revolt against that 6s. a week which Sir Spencer Walpole had called their "inevitable and hereditary lot," or of the consequent hangings and transportations at Winchester, or Lord Ellenborough's argument in the House of Lords against Romilly's Bill for abolishing the death penalty for any crime lighter than stealing five shillings in a shop—mere transportation, his Lordship argued, was regarded by these people, and justly regarded, as "a summer airing by an easy migration to a milder climate"—if, as I read, I rub my eyes, and, called away to deal with a child's case in a police-court, find in the index of Stone's *Justice's Manual* two overflowing columns of index under the word "Children," almost every entry a reference to some law of protection or of considerate and lenient treatment—Who, I ask, were—who *can* have been—the agents of this amazing change save these amazing—yes, amazing—Victorians?

And they were. Read Charles Dickens, or the early chapters of Carlyle's *Past and Present,* if you would understand how these Victorians reformed the old horrible "poor-house"; read Elizabeth Barrett Browning's *Cry of the Children* or Hood's *Song of the Shirt* if you would divine what they did against the factories and sweated labour; ponder on Charles Reade's *It is Never Too Late to Mend,* or that awful documented story, Marcus Clarke's *For the Term of His Natural Life,* if you would learn how they fought the old penal system: read Charles Kingsley's *Yeast,* read] Ruskin through a dozen works, or read the life of William Morris; and acknowledge how these men battled for mere humanity.

Do you deride their art?—their painting, for example? Why talk of Frith's *Derby Day* as if that were representative? Turner painted his *Fighting Téméraire* in 1840: Millais his *Autumn Leaves* and *Sir Isumbras at the Ford* in 1856–7: and at the close of the reign John Sargent was painting Ellen Terry as Lady Macbeth under these very eyes. Why chat of Frith's *Derby Day* and not reckon these? Why omit the whole pre-Raphaelite movement?—the painters: Dante Gabriel Rossetti, Holman Hunt, Ford Madox Brown—the poets: Rossetti and his wonderful sister, Swinburne, Meredith?

I come down to applied art: to mere furniture, if you will. Why insist on envisaging the Victorian Age as one of rep curtains and horsehair sofas? To be sure as a child I knelt and bowed my head at family prayers over a horsehair sofa. Of anything she purchased my grandmother always asked first "that it should wear well."

But my first recollection of a London Theatre is a first performance at the old Opéra Comique of Gilbert and Sullivan's *Patience*, already travestying the "Æsthetic Movement," which had already consigned rep curtains and horsehair sofas to limbo—how long ago!

—Which brings me down to mere comfort. Speaking of mere comfort I should guess that a man born in England in the year 1844 and passing out of it, at the Psalmist's allotted span, in the early part of 1914, probably enjoyed the most comfortably expanding time in the whole range of human history. He would be, in 1851, just old enough to be taken by his papa and mamma to the Great Exhibition and to wonder at it intelligently: he would catch the Crimean War fever, and hear of the Balaclava Charge, while scarcely yet too old to play with lead soldiers: and, as he grew to manhood and beyond, the 'Varsity Boat Race and the Derby would mark his year as sporting events; while long distance travelling, telegraphs, Cook's tickets, competed for his roving patronage, and hot baths, electric light and central heating welcomed his return. But these are low considerations. Let us lift our eyes to higher thoughts. At the beginning of Queen Victoria's reign the Universe had been contrived in six days of twenty-four hours each, and it was blasphemous to hold that any stream of tendency could but beat itself in vain upon that rock of witness.

Well, we have seen what we have seen: the Oxford Movement, the Unitarians, the Agnostics, the Positivists, the Muscular Christians, the Salvation Army; all working in apparent opposition, but all alive, honest, in earnest (if too confident), and therefore all in travail for our spiritual good: and not least honest among them those genuine doubters of which the mid-century was full. They were sad enough about it, at any rate—such men as Newman, Clough, Martineau, and in earnest for truth and love of their fellows.—

> Still nursing the unconquerable hope,
> Still clutching the inviolable shade.

VIII

The contention of Youth and Age is eternal. I dare say that when the very oldest of Egyptian papyri is untombed, it will be found signed in hieroglyphic "Old Memphian" and its contents a lament over the tendency of the youth of Memphis to wear soft collars and their casual irreverent way of sitting down on the hole of the asp: or else it will be a pamphlet by some young blood, hotly commanding his elders to put up a reasonable justification of their prolonged existence.

The contention of Youth and Age is eternal: yes, and salutary for the race. I sympathise with both parties. It is my own view that no young man or young woman can live beyond a certain time under a parental roof without grave risk either of pauperising the intellect by filial docility—of taking parental opinions on trust—or of forfeiting good manners in rebellion. The break should be decisive; yet affectionate, regretful, either side tender for the other's feelings. In the last sad words of Don Quixote, "Look not for young birds in last year's nests."

But I am not here to preach: and so will conclude by reading you two short poems (short extracts, rather) by two Victorians; one an old man who speaks as an ageing man in 1847; the other a young poet much in favour now. And I would ask you to listen, because they say simply or subtly something that I feel, and want you to feel without explanation.

The first is in dialect, by William Barnes, the Dorset-shire poet. It speaks to the young from the heart of the ageing: and it is called:

Evenen, an' Maidens Out at Door

Now the sheädes o' the elems do stratch mwore an' mwore,
Vrom the low-zinkèn zun in the west o' the sky;
An' the maïdens do stand out in clusters avore
The doors, vor to chatty an' zee vo'k goo by.

An' their cwombs be a-zet in their bunches o' heäir,
An' their currels do hang roun' their necks lily-white,
An' their cheäks they be rwosy, their shoulders be beäre,
Their looks they be merry, their limbs they be light.

An' the times have a-been—but they cant be noo mwore—
When I had my jaÿ under evenèn's dim sky;
When my Fanny did stan' out wi' others avore
Her door, vor to chatty an' zee vo'k goo by.

.   .   .   .

But when you be a-lost vrom the parish, zome mwore
Will come on in your pleäzen to bloom an' to die;
An' the zummer will always have maïdens avore
Their doors, vor to chatty an' zee vo'k goo by.

Vor daughters ha' mornèn when mothers ha' night,
An' there's beauty alive when the feäirest is dead;
As when woone sparklèn weäve do zink down vrom the
    light,
Another do come up an' catch it instead.

Zoo smile on, happy maïdens! but I shall noo mwore
Zee the maïd I do miss under evenèn's dim sky;
An' my heart is a-touch'd to zee you out avore
The doors, vor to chatty an' zee vo'k goo by.

Well, that, Gentlemen, is how we, your seniors, must

revert to the Victorian Age: as in a Camera Obscura
"seeing folks go by"; not without a sense of human
greatness, how it passes—of human reputation, how it
is superseded—of the inevitable shrinkage of personal
hopes, ambitions, friendships, all certain to be wiped off
by gentle process of time even had not war interrupted
and violently obliterated them; not (you will perhaps
tell yourselves) without a touch of Victorian sentiment
—which, no doubt, the most of you very properly despise.
Yet I confess that when some of you bring to me, for
sympathy, verse and essays outspoken in contempt of
your fathers' age, and I rally my sympathy, I have
reverted in memory more than once to an hour in a
college garden employed by me in sentimentally saving
a robin from a son bent on patricide—and, as you read
on confidently, murmur to myself these lines by my
second poet, quoted by me in a previous lecture:

> So when I see this robin now,
> Like a red apple on the bough,
> And question why he sings so strong,
> For love, or for the love of song;
> Or sings, maybe, for that sweet rill
> Whose silver tongue is never still—
>
> Ah, now there comes this thought unkind,
> Born of the knowledge in my mind:
> He sings in triumph that last night
> He killed his father in a fight;
> And now he'll take his mother's blood—
> The last strong rival for his food.

But that thought is ungenerous. Let us consent and
conclude upon a word of the Victorian time which at
any rate is generous and brave. It is Walt Whitman's.

I am the teacher of athletes,
He that by me spreads a wider breast than my own proves
the width of my own,
He most honours my style who learns under it to destroy
the teacher.

INDEX